Pra

The Sea Forager's Guide to

MW01006123

"Through wit, poetry, and anecdotes, Lombard makes the case that the sincerest stewards of wild sea creatures are often those who intend to have them for dinner." —Alastair Bland, NPR's *The Salt*

"Really, the book is for anyone who loves the ocean because you can open it to almost any passage and learn and laugh."

—Tara Duggan, *San Francisco Chronicle*

"An unusual tome: part guide to urban fishery, part poetic ramble, part collection of anecdotes, part recipe book, it advocates for an ethical, considered approach to fishing the waterways of the Northern California coast."

—Eillie Anzilotti, *CityLab*

"Lombard is a divinely inspired whack job—think Frank Zappa meets Aldo Leopold. If you have ever considered the idea of gathering something good to eat from the beach or surf...you need this book."

—Bill Heavey, editor-at-large, *Field & Stream*

"You are truly blessed to have found this marine tome."

—Todd Selby, author, *Edible Selby*

"Lombard is a master of the nearshore environment, knowledgeable (and hilarious). This is, simply put, the best book on this subject ever written."

—Hank Shaw, James Beard Award–winning author, *Hunt, Gather, Cook: Finding the Forgotten Feast*

"The definitive guide to foraging the Northern Californian coast. Kirk has created an ecosystem that allows us to be sustainable citizens and, more importantly, sustainable eaters."

—Andrew Zimmern, James Beard Award–winning television host, *Bizarre Foods with Andrew Zimmern*

THE Sea Forager's GUIDE TO THE NORTHERN CALIFORNIA COAST

Kirk Lombard
Illustrated by Leighton Kelly

Ḣ

Heyday, Berkeley, California

Heyday would like to thank the following supporters whose exceptional generosity made this book possible.

Candelaria Fund
The Dean Witter Foundation
The Nature Conservancy
TomKat Charitable Trust
Topher Delaney

© 2016 by Kirk Lombard
Illustrations © 2016 by Leighton Kelly

Library of Congress Cataloging-in-Publication Data

Names: Lombard, Kirk, author. | Kelly, Leighton, illustrator.
Title: The sea forager's guide to the Northern California coast / Kirk
    Lombard ; illustrated by Leighton Kelly.
Description: Berkeley, California : Heyday, 2016.
Identifiers: LCCN 2015049657 | ISBN 9781597143578 (pbk. : alk. paper)
Subjects: LCSH: Seafood gathering--California, Northern | Seafood
    gathering--California--Pacific Coast. | Cooking (Seafood)
Classification: LCC SH400 .L66 2016 | DDC 641.3/9--dc23
LC record available at https://lccn.loc.gov/2015049657

Cover Art and Design: Leighton Kelly
Interior Design/Typesetting: Ashley Ingram

Published by Heyday
P.O. Box 9145, Berkeley, California 94709
(510) 549-3564
heydaybooks.com

Printed in Canada by Marquis

10 9 8 7 6 5 4

For Peter K. Lombard, 1935–2015
The best dad there ever was

Contents

PREFACE
Toward an Intertidal Citizenry

Human beings have been part of the intertidal foodweb in California for an estimated seventeen thousand years. To say that the intertidal zone was, for most of this period, a sort of supermarket for Native peoples is not mere hyperbole. Archeological excavations of shell middens leave little doubt about what coastal tribes were eating—and where they were getting most of it. As much as it may be clichéd to point out that Native American cultures generally share a reverence for the natural world, I think it's still important to remind ourselves of this occasionally. If you are a mussel picker or an ab diver or a poke poler, you are having an effect on the coastal ecosystem. When you harvest your food from the wild, you become a member of a very complex foodweb. So the question arises … what sort of member do you want to be?

     a. A consumer

     b. A citizen

A consumer is the kind of person who takes abundance for granted. The kind who doesn't think he has any effect, who has no problem bending the rules. The kind of person who thinks:

> *So the crab is a half inch short, so what?*
>
> *Or, I use a crowbar to get my mussels because it's more difficult to do it by hand!*
>
> *Or, There's no size limit on rockfish, so I'm perfectly justified in taking these four-inch dinks home and making a stew out of them.*
>
> *Or, There's no reason to fill in the clam hole—it's perfectly legal not to.*

The citizen of the intertidal zone is a different species. She's educated about the coastal ecosystem and passionate about protecting it. She understands that she has an impact and she does everything she can to minimize that impact— part of which entails following the rules and part of which entails understanding their shortcomings.[1] Taking a four-inch fish may be legal, but, she asks herself, is it ethical? The reason we want to target mature fish is to ensure they've spawned once or twice before we kill them. The reason it's illegal to use a tool on a mussel bed is because it *should* be difficult to get mussels. Using a crowbar is destructive and makes it too easy.

Look around you. Are there fifty other people pulling mussels in your spot? Ten other people poke poling? Forty people armed with throw nets waiting for the smelt to spawn in a small cove? Does any of this bother you? The citizen of the intertidal zone has no problem looking for mussels and eels somewhere else. One of the problems we have in our area is that people key in on one particular site because it's easy and accessible—and then they fish it or pick it until it's dead. Meanwhile, there are untouched areas a few miles away that seldom if ever get foraged. The consumer is lazy. The citizen is not afraid to explore.

As the modern populace has grown distrustful of life "on the grid," the idea of harvesting our food from nature has become increasingly popular. Whether this is a passing fad or the beginning of a new trend toward wild foods, the resources will be far better off if we act as stewards of them rather than as takers and exploiters.

In short, let's just be aware that as fishers and foragers, we are part of the food chain—but as stewards and citizens of it, we are also something more.

CHECK OUT MY SWIM BLADDERS

In the back of this book you will find five appendices. But as these sections are essential to the reading of this book, it seemed that the term *appendix*—a vestigial organ of little biological importance, found in several species of higher primate (and opossums, wombats, and mole rats)—wouldn't really apply. So we are renaming them *swim bladders*.[2] Even if you are somewhat familiar with the tools and rigs for fishing and foraging the California coast, these four sections are fundamental to a useful reading of this book. They also happen to contain some of Leighton Kelly's most interesting drawings and diagrams. So, in other words, you're really missing out if you don't check out my swim bladders.

---

1 Like them or not, it's the regulations that make each recreational fishery sustainable.

2 The swim bladder, or air bladder, is an organ that regulates buoyancy in certain species of fish—so that they don't have to expend excess energy flapping fins and tails to stay down. It is hoped that this book's Swim Bladders will have a similar effect on readers, minimizing the effort it might otherwise take to comprehend the minutiae of fishing and foraging the California coast.

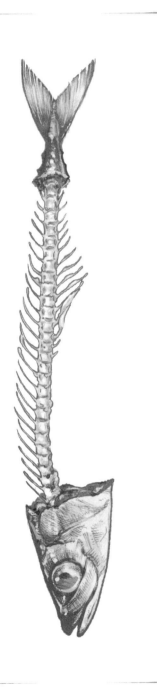

FORAGE FISH

Just a note on terminology: the term *forage fish*, normally synonymous with bait-fish, is used here to indicate that many of these species are better eaten than used merely for bait. For forage fish that are really best used as bait, see chapter 3.

They say the happiest people on earth reside in Denmark. Having traveled there several times, I must confirm that a happier, more sensible group of former coastal marauders would be hard to invent. One might ascribe the Danish public weal to several factors: (1) the brisk northern climes, (2) universal health care, (3) a relatively small and homogenous population. But I think there is one overlooked element in the formula for Danish happiness, and one that we here in the States neglect at our own peril: the immense nutritional, gastronomic, and ecological advantages of dining on small fish.[1]

The small fish of Danish preference, of course, is the Atlantic herring, *Clupea harengus*. And the preferred manner of preparing it is by pickling.[2] As absurd as it may seem, when one takes into account all the clean, crisp, life-affirming, oceanic flavors and nutrient loads in a little slab of herring meat, and the vast quantities of *sild* (pickled herring in Dansk) consumed in Denmark, it is not, I think, too much of a stretch to conclude that herring are at least partially responsible for the apparent happiness of the Danish people.[3]

---

1 The first two benefits will be discussed below, but as to the ecological benefits: many small schooling fishes have evolved to deal with the fact that virtually every piscivore on the planet (with the exception of mainstream American seafood consumers) wants to eat them. Hence, their populations tend to be fairly resistant to predation—resistant but not immune. The global tendency to turn sardines, anchovies, and menhaden into pellets to feed other, larger species of farmed fish is almost universally accepted as an unsustainable practice.

2 See "Pickled Herring à la Loren Wilson" in *Pacific Herring* below.

3 Many small schooling fishes are high in the omega-3 fatty acids that everyone is always raving about and, because most are relatively short lived and low on the food chain, they do not tend to bio-accumulate toxins the way large, long-lived, predatory fishes do.

Here in California we have been blessed with some of the most famously delicious small fishes on the planet, but curiously, the mainstream seafood-eating populace does not seem interested in any of them.[4] For the coastal forager, this is great news. Let the mainstream have its McFishwich (hake) sandwiches and its surimi (fake) crab rolls: it just means more smelt and sardines for us.

Many of California's populations of small schooling fishes are abundant, relatively close to shore, and (with patience, luck, and a few basics) eminently catchable. That doesn't mean you're going to slam the "nightfish" every time out, or find anchovies or sardines with 100 or even 90 (or even 80, 70, 60, or 50…) percent regularity. But if you understand a few basics, not only will your healthy protein intake increase drastically, but the occasional bass-plugging trip, or the hunt for that elusive shore-caught lingcod, will become a much more productive (not to mention fun) enterprise. And soon, you may find that the throw-net and the Sabiki rig are far more regular companions in the back of the truck than the pricey bait-caster and the tackle box loaded with expensive plugs.

SARDINE
Sardinops sagax

You can't really write about sardines without mentioning some history. Here it is in one page: on the West Coast, commercial sardine fishing began in earnest during WWI, and peaked from 1932 to 1944. The average spawning biomass of Pacific sardine during this period ranged from a staggering 3,881,000 tons in 1932 to a (still) robust 1,324,000 in 1944. Largely because of this fishery, Monterey became a thriving sardine hub, a bustling seaport where salty men armed with purse seines and lampara nets wrested a rugged living from the sea. The canneries hummed with activity, the streets roared with the sounds of industry. Business boomed (yep, right in the midst of the Depression) and through all this, the fishy effervescence

---

4 California ranks fourteenth in nationwide happiness polls.

of sardine wafted along the streets and byways … or as John Steinbeck so eloquently put it, "Cannery Row in Monterey in California is a poem, a stink, a grating noise, a quality of light, a tone, a habit, a nostalgia, a dream."

Then, in the late 1940s, the dream officially became a nightmare: the fishery crashed, the canneries went belly up, and the party ended. Traditionally, there have been two schools of thought on why this happened: the fishery manager's and the fisherman's. I'll let you decide which is which:

1. Greed/overfishing destroyed the stocks and they finally crashed in the 1940s.

2. Sardine populations fluctuate naturally, regardless of fishing pressure, and the late 1940s marked the natural end of an abundance period.

In hindsight, it seems likely that both got something right. The yearly takes (up to 1.4 billion pounds annually!) amounted to a lot of dead sardines. However, fish scales in core samples from the ocean floor have allowed biologists to track changes in sardine population dynamics over time and, according to the *California Living Marine Resources* report (2001), these core samples indicate that sardine "population declines and recoveries averaged about thirty-six and thirty years respectively."

So as it turns out, sardine populations likely would have declined in the late 1940s to some degree regardless of fishing pressure. Predictably, about forty years later, sardines showed signs of recovery. By the late nineties, the estimated spawning biomass of adult Pacific sardines off the West Coast was thought to be around 1.7 million tons. Not the 3.9 million tons of the 1932 estimate, but a significant improvement over the estimated 5,000-ton low in the 1970s. More recently, sardine stocks are showing signs of decline again. In fact, the National Oceanic and Atmospheric Administration, the federal agency entrusted with managing the sardine resource, closed the commercial sardine season to all but incidentally caught sardines in 2015. And just in case you thought we had learned something in the intervening seventy years, the old argument is back—mother nature versus overfishing—though most sensible people at this point admit that both factors likely contribute to periodic sardine declines.

All of this is immaterial to the recreational angler (that's you and me, unless you've got a purse seine boat docked somewhere). The comparatively infinitesimal number of sardines caught by people armed with ultralight rods and Sabiki rigs is unlikely to have any significant impact on sardine populations.

THE WHERE, WHEN, AND HOW

Though sardines have lived off the coast of California for thousands of years, they do not always show up locally in fishable numbers.[5] For instance, it can be a lot of work finding them inside San Francisco Bay. One year, you can't keep them off the hook; the next year, you can't find a sardine to save your Sabiki. By and large you will have a lot more success with sardines if you make the occasional trip to Santa Cruz or Monterey. If you live far from there, call the bait shops in Santa Cruz and Capitola and find out if the pier fishers are getting them before you get in the car. Sardines seem to like warmer waters, so the further south you go, the more likely you are to get into them. That said, there are summers in San Francisco when sardines can be caught from every pier between the Golden Gate Bridge and Candlestick Park.

Strangely, there seem to be resident sardine populations in several channels and estuaries inside the bay. Islais Creek, a small industrial canal at the south side of SF, is the most notable of these—which is somewhat ironic, given that in the 1950s more sardines were processed there than at any other spot on the planet. Dubbed "Shit Creek" by locals, Islais was once home to SF's "Butcher Town" and was used as a dumping ground for animal waste products. Now it sports a large sewer main, which has been known to leak raw sewage from time to time—hence the nickname. One wonders if there is some correlation between the raw sewage and the abundance of sardines at that location... *and one hopes there is not.*

In our area, sardines are a summer/fall fishery, though now and then you'll get sardines in the spring. As far as the tides go, everyone seems to have an opinion on this. Sardines can be caught at dead-low tide, high tide, and all the tides between. It's probably best to fish the two-hour window on either side of high water, but that might depend on the location. Several impassioned sardine aficionados swear to me that they get all their 'dines at or near the bottom of low tide.

Unfortunately, there is only one legal way to catch sardines recreationally: by hook and line. If you peruse the California sport fishing regulations (as of 2016), you will discover that sardines are not listed as one of the allowable species for throw-net wielders to take (which seems odd, since there's no bag limit on sardines). In truth, they swim at such high speeds it's nearly impossible to get a casting net on them in anything over six feet of water. So baitfish rigs (i.e.,

---

5 Of course, compared to anchovies, which are thought to have been here for at least a million years, sardines are recent arrivals in the California current. According to *California Living Marine Resources: A Status Report* (2001), "the tendency for tremendous variation in sardine biomass may be a characteristic of a species that has only recently occupied its habitat" (300).

Sabikis) are the way to go for sardines. A sardine can live up to sixteen years but most of those encountered by rod-and-reel fishermen are under twelve inches and eight years of age.

EAT THEM UP, YUM

Let's make something abundantly clear: a fresh, sparkling, grilled or stuffed and broiled sardine bears very little resemblance to the oil-slathered thing that the stock hobo picks from a can with grubby fingers, in the back of a boxcar, rattling across the wastes of dustbowl America in 1937. I have no data to

back this up, but I suspect that many people hear the word *sardine* and immediately think, *hobo food.* The association is no doubt due to the fact that canned sardines have long been a very cheap source of (healthy, ocean-based) protein. Even now, in 2016, a can of sardines at my local, overpriced, Somali-run corner store retails for only $1.89. (Come to think of it, it's quite possibly the cheapest item in the store. A bag of peanuts at this joint will run you $3.24 and a single package of toilet paper is a staggering $3.99.[6])

Frozen sardines and "fresh" sardines that have been sitting on the shelf in a fish market all week also contribute to the public's low opinion of this fish. In truth, nothing could be less inspiring than these bloody-eyed, thawed-frozen-and-rethawed sardines, with their scales rubbed off and their bellies blown out. If you've never caught your own sardines and eaten them the same day, but have only sampled quick-frozen sardines or the miserable fish market examples mentioned above, you can't be blamed for disliking them. There is no fish for which the difference between fresh and not fresh is more pronounced. And, as is the case with everything in this book, the best way to make sure sardines are truly fresh is to go out and catch them yourself.[7]

How to Debone or "Butterfly" a Small Fish

Note: Although it seems contrary to the very idea of harvesting wild food, you may want to leave your fish in the fridge for a day or two before attempting

---

6   And I thought all the Somali pirates were in the Indian Ocean.

7   You could buy them off a live-bait receiver or directly off one of the big seiners in Monterey, if you happen to be down there … but where's the fun in that?

this technique. When the fish are still in full rigor, the meat does not separate from the bone and you will likely end up with a bunch of mutilated carcasses.

Scale the fish (no scaling necessary for true smelts and mackerel).

Head and gut the fish (with anchovies you can pinch off the head at the gills and pull the guts out in a single move, but you still need to slit the belly open to de-bone them). Snip off the dorsal fins with cooking shears.

Holding the beheaded, de-finned, and gutted fish, place your thumb gently inside its body cavity, pressing softly on the spine. When the spine begins to separate from the meat, grab it near the front (where the head was) and lift it out in one shot.

PACIFIC HERRING
Clupea pallasii

THE WHERE, WHEN, AND HOW

Pacific herring live along the coast from Alaska to Central California, and are typically caught during their winter spawning runs by commercial fishermen using gill nets or by recreational anglers throwing Hawaiian casting nets from shore. Pacific herring can evidently live up to nineteen years, but it is rare to find any fish over nine years old in our area. California's main spawning locations are Crescent City Harbor, Humboldt Bay, Tomales Bay, and San Francisco Bay. Of the four, SF Bay is the mecca for herring hunters, both recreational and commercial.

In SF Bay, you are most likely to catch herring from shore in January and February, though spawning may occur from October to April in eelgrass beds and along rocky shorelines. The spawning range inside the bay is from San Quentin and Point Richmond in the north, to the west side of the San Mateo Bridge in the south. Famous herring locations include Point Richmond, San Quentin, Paradise Park, Tiburon, Sausalito, the Embarcadero, McCovey Cove, China Basin, Hunter's Point, Islais Creek, Candlestick Park, Coyote Point, and SFO. The challenge is figuring out exactly when and where the "silver darlins" intend to offer themselves up for slaughter. A pair of good binoculars or a bookmarked selection of all the webcams in SF Bay can help you find the diving birds, pelicans, sea lions, and seals that typically indicate a spawn, but you can't confirm anything until you go to the water and start throwing your net.[8]

As far as birds go, diving pelicans and big swarms of cormorants are the key. But large flocks of seagulls standing impatiently along rocky shoreline can often indicate a spawn in progress (or the aftermath of one). Gulls like to feed on the eggs left exposed as the tide goes out and will congregate in vast numbers whenever herring are spawning inshore.

As to the best tides … good luck finding a predictable pattern. Herring are caught at high tide, low tide, and all the tides between. Four years of reasonably good anecdotal data from my own tide logs show that inshore spawns often (but not always … in fact let's just say *sometimes*) start just prior to high water and may continue for a few hours or a few days, peaking during the outgo and slowing down around low water. Yes, if you're feeling impatient (read: desperate) you can paddle a kayak into deeper water to get them before or after they've moved inshore. But keep in mind that throwing a casting net from a seated position in a kayak requires above-average balance and coordination.

Contrary to popular belief, herring can be caught by Sabiki rig.[9] Every year you'll see a few lost souls doing this, but the primary recreational gear for herring is the Hawaiian casting net. If you're on a decent spawn, you should have no problem filling a five-gallon bucket in five to fifteen minutes with a four- to six-foot casting net. Unfortunately, there are always a few ne'er-do-wells out there with eight- to ten- foot nets, filling up garbage cans full of herring. These are not ideal citizens of the intertidal zone. In fact, I'm not sure what these folks are doing with their fish, but I doubt it's legal. A large net is unnecessary for this species. If you need a ten-foot net to fill half a bucket, you're fishing on the wrong day. Here's why you might want to consider a four- to six-foot net for herring (as opposed to a seven- to twelve-foot net):

> 1. Smaller nets are cheaper and you will be far less aggravated when you tear a hole in your net (as you will invariably do, since herring like to spawn on rocks) if you paid thirty-five dollars for it than you would be if you paid seventy-five dollars for it.

---

8   Or, cultivate a crew of trusted informants, preferably commercial captains, retirees, or independently wealthy herring aficionados—the only groups who have the time or incentive to follow the schools all winter.

9   Popular opinion holds that spawning fish are preoccupied with reproduction and therefore not interested in eating. Perhaps they are biting more from excitement than hunger, but herring will strike a bait rig while spawning. However, catching one herring at a time while everyone around you is pulling up ten pounds per throw of the ol' casting net can be, to say the least, a rather frustrating experience.

2. Catching herring is fun. If you want your fun to last ten seconds, use a big net. If you want it to last a while longer … use a smaller net.

3. Larger nets lead to wasted fish. Throw an eight-foot net into the middle of a spawning school of herring and you now have approximately sixty-five pounds (or one and a half five-gallon buckets) of herring to deal with—when all you really wanted was half a bucket, or less.

4. The kids you bring with you (and kids love this type of fishing more than anybody) will have a much easier time throwing a smaller net.

5. If you intend to throw a net from a kayak, which can be tricky, it's a lot easier with a smaller net.

Five Reasons (Despite Your Lack of Interest in Pickled Fish) Why You Might Want to Check Out a Herring Spawn

1. Because there are few natural events that occur inside an urban estuary that are as deeply awesome and life affirming as a herring spawn. We're talking thirty to sixty thousand seagulls (including, in 2014, a rare Iceland gull and a lesser slaty-backed!), plus harbor porpoises, sea lions, seals, pelicans dropping out of the sky, huge flocks of cormorants, surf scoters, and other diving birds. In fact …

2. … if you squint your eyes slightly and drown out the sound of the cars going by, and the gill net beaters on the herring boats, and the planes passing overhead, you can actually sort of imagine what the bay must have been like five hundred years ago.

3. Because we should honor the resilience of a creature that has been able to withstand all the abuse the human race has hurled in its path: oil spills, landfill, toxic waste, non-point pollution, extirpation of eelgrass beds, a roe fishery, a human-induced overpopulation of pinnipeds, et cetera.

4. Because if you don't celebrate the yearly return of this species, who will?

5. Because the kids will love throwing the net. And even if you have no intention of eating the catch, you'll have all your salmon, halibut, lingcod, and sturgeon bait for the year.

Eat Them Up, Yum

Foraging Roe When herring spawn in good numbers they usually carpet-bomb whole areas of shoreline with eggs. We're talking many thousands of pounds of spawn, clinging to intertidal rocks and algae, sometimes for miles.

For those folks who are merely in it for the roe, the bag limit on herring eggs is twenty-five pounds, kelp included—and yes, you need a recreational fishing license to gather roe. The eggs will be best if you can get them from a non-muddy area, and even better if they're clinging to a reasonably good eating seaweed like rockweed (*Fucus distichus*) or the invasive wakame

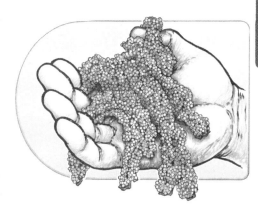

(*Undaria pinnatifida*), which grow (conveniently) in several places where herring spawn in SF Bay (see chapter 6). I personally find that herring roe is best when it's about an inch thick and still white-yellow. When it turns brownish and the individual eggs start to develop eyes, it's past its expiration date.

For many generations, Native American tribes of the West Coast have placed hemlock branches or edible seaweeds in areas where herring are likely to spawn. They then harvest branches and eggs together.[10] The traditional method of preparation is to blanch the roe by dipping it very briefly in boiling water and then to mix with candlefish grease. Since the latter is not readily available (given the virtual extirpation of candlefish in California), you might try bacon fat or butter. For me, blanched herring roe and a little soy sauce is all I need to be happy. Other folks brine the eggs and pickle them. But I find them quite salty on their own, and the usual pickling recipes seem to overwhelm the natural flavors.

Pickled Herring à la Loren Wilson

Far from your kitchen sink, scale and fillet your herring.[11] Yes, filleting your herring is a labor-intensive activity. One bucket will take between three and five hours of work—depending on your skill with the blade.

Cut the fillets into two-inch chunks. Brine these chunks overnight using this ratio: ½ cup brown sugar, ½ cup salt, 1 quart water. Make sure the fillets are covered by the brine solution and that you're using a plastic, glass, or stainless steel container (*not aluminum!*).

The next morning, pour out the brine and rinse the fillets thoroughly.

---

10 This is the same idea as the commercial HEOK (Herring Eggs on Kelp fishery) in SF Bay, where rafts festooned with *Macrocystis* kelp are strategically placed in areas where herring likely to spawn.

11 Nothing can clog a drain faster than herring scales—except maybe herring roe.

Prepare pickling liquid. These amounts are enough for about two quarts:

    4 cups water
    5 cups white vinegar (5%)
    3 tsp allspice
    4–5 bay leaves
    2 tsp fresh ginger, grated
    1 tsp mustard seeds
    2 tsp prepared horseradish
    3–4 tsp pickling spice
    ½–3 cups brown sugar (Loren uses 3 cups, I use ½ to 1)

Bring pickling liquid to a boil, then let it cool. Peel and slice 4–5 large red onions.

Pack your jars, alternating layers of fish and onions. Pour the cooled pickling liquid into the packed jars till all the layers are covered.

Put the jars in the refrigerator for two nights, then eat with pieces of buttered rye bread, a pilsner-style beer, and aquavit.[12] *Skol!*

Mike Chin's Smoked Herring

Our local Pacific herring do not have the high fat content of their larger Atlantic cousins and because of this, they can make for a challenging smoked meat. Of all the guys I've known who have attempted to create "kippers" out of California's herring, my old friend Mike Chin does the best job of it. Here's his recipe.

Brining To 1 quart of cold spring water (or the best water you've got), add about ½ cup of organic sea salt and 1 cup of brown sugar; stir until dissolved. Chill the brine in the refrigerator. Two quarts of this will be enough for 50 fish. When the brine is totally chilled (<40F), mix it and the fish together in a 1-gallon Ziploc bag or a large glass or plastic container. Do not shortcut the chilling; a warm brine will put you in the food-temperature danger zone (40F to 140F). Let the fish brine overnight (8–12 hours) in the refrigerator.

Pellicle Formation The pellicle is the dry, shiny film that forms over fish flesh when it's held in a cold, dry environment; it's supposed to aid in smoke penetration and to keep the fish from oozing white gunk as it is smoked (an aesthetic thing). Mike says he's not sure if it's necessary for whole fish with the skin on, but he does it anyway. Take the fish out of the brine, dry each one with a paper towel, then put them directly on wire racks in the fridge for a few hours.

---

12 Herring fillets pickled this way will keep for at least six weeks.

Smoking After pellicle formation, take the fish out of the refrigerator to let them come up to room temperature while you start prepping and warming up the smoker. On oiled smoker racks, place the herring on their sides. (Placing them belly down helps to drain liquids that might form, but the downside is that they tend to overcook a bit and stick.)

In most electric smokers, the heating element is controlled separately from the smoke generator. Your goal here is to keep up a steady "thin blue smoke" at low temperatures. Plan on 4–6 hours of total smoking time: an initial 2–3 hours of applewood smoke for flavor, then an additional 2–3 hours without applewood, just to cook the fish. The first two hours should be at about 140F and the remaining hours at about 170F.

The actual temperature settings aren't too critical, but the goal is to get the fish flesh up to 140F by the end of the smoking. Using a very small digital thermometer to probe the thick part of the biggest fish is the only way to be certain of the temperature of the fish flesh. Mike reports good results with a thermocouple probe about 1/16 inch in diameter.

The actual smoking time will vary, depending on the air temperature and humidity. A little less than 4 hours is okay, but much less will make your herring ooze. Mike says, "In my smoker, the fish turn a beautiful golden color when they're getting done."

When the fattest part of the fattest herring has reached 140–145F (and when, if you're lucky, the whole lot have turned golden), take the fish off the racks and let them cool a bit. Break one open, and the cooked fish should be luscious and oily. Like any hot-smoked (as opposed to cold-smoked) fish, it should either be eaten within a week or frozen.

The only problem is that the rib bones, which soften after sautéing or frying, will still be hard after smoking. Here are two methods that can reduce the bones, the first for before smoking and the second for after:

Deboning After brining, it's fairly easy to extract most of the backbone and the ribs. You'll still have a lot of the Y-bones, but they are generally soft enough to be eaten.

Pressure Cooking Wrap the finished smoked fish in aluminum foil, and place them in a pressure cooker with about an inch of water. Cook for about 45 minutes at 15 pounds of pressure. The rib bones (and often the backbone as well) will become soft enough to eat, though the flesh does tend to toughen a bit.

NICE GUY

There were five people fishing on Pier 7 when I arrived that morning. Five shivering, behooded desperados braving the wind and rain. To fish from a pier at 8 A.M. on a weekday morning, in the eye of a wild Pacific gale, one must be fairly obsessed. To fish for sand dabs in these conditions indicates a possible psychosis. Yet there they were: five seemingly normal, septuagenarian retirees going all out in their pursuit of the slimy, isopod-infested *Citharichthys sordidus*. I counted seven hooks on one line (four more than the legal three). The woman with the floppy rain hat and the light blue disposable surgical gloves had at least twelve. In addition to their rods, I counted three extra drop lines tied to the rails. The grumpy old Russian guy in the sweat-encrusted baseball cap, who, in warmer months, never fails to growl and spit at my feet as he sprints past me with his teeming buckets of jacksmelt, was fishing at least four rods (the legal limit is two). Yet despite all this, despite their disregard for Fish and Wildlife laws, their undeniable heartiness, diligence, correct assessment of the tides, fresh bait, multiple hooks, et cetera, they had a whopping total of two miniscule sand dabs and a half dozen herring to show for their efforts.

It is interesting to note that no matter how little English a person with a line in the water may know, he/she is almost always capable of one phrase: "No fish." On the pier this particular morning, I heard this universal profession of unhappiness uttered no less than five times—once for each angler. In each case, it was accompanied by a shake of the head, a shrug of the shoulders, and a deep and profound sigh—the subtext of which, in Cantonese (the dominant language on the downtown fishing piers), I imagine goes something like: *One can never know the mysterious ways of the ocean*. In Amer-English, this sentiment is best captured by that most overused yet somehow still poignant of all fishing clichés: *That's why they call it fishing, not catching*.

The wind blew. Someone yelled out. A baseball cap suddenly materialized at my feet. I grabbed it, handed it back to its owner, and noticed that a herring boat was moving up to the end of the pier. Usually when this happens, the pier fishers go berserk. But today everyone was smiling.

I looked down at the boat's deckhand. He looked up and waved. I waved back. He reached down and grabbed a large aluminum scooper that looked almost like a snow shovel.

At this, all the pier fishers suddenly gathered up their buckets and coolers and moved to the rail. They'd been through this drill before.

The deckhand filled his scooper with herring and catapulted them over his shoulder up onto the pier, which caused a general melee as everyone scrambled around filling up their buckets and calling out to one another. A few western gulls materialized, darting in and out. Somebody swore at them and shooed them away, but the gulls would not disperse. San Francisco seagulls are a force to be reckoned with. They're really more like the predatory skuas of the Antarctic seas than common western gulls. As the battle raged, the deckhand tied the boat to the end of the pier and started shoveling the herring in earnest. More seagulls dropped from the skies.

Showing that our species has, in fact, evolved an intellectual capacity superior to that of our most common ocean-going bird, one of the anglers tied his bucket to a rope and lowered it down to the boat. The deckhand filled it to the brim.

"Hey man," I said to the deckhand, "why are you giving away your fish?"

He squinted up at me, through the drizzle, and said, "I guess I'm a nice guy."

"I guess you are," I said.

"They been out here in the rain since 5:00 and we started feeling sorry for them. The fish are all males anyway."

One of the anglers stepped to the far rail of the pier and expressed his thanks in a sort of Cantonese/English patois. The deckhand smiled, put his hands together and bowed. The anglers laughed at this. They bowed back. The deckhand turned and said a few words to the captain. They both laughed, waved goodbye, and disappeared into the fog bank from which they had come.

An Early Christmas

'Twas six months before Christmas,
And on the state beach,
With seagulls a-swarming,
And whales in their breach.
I hopped from my pickup
And ran with great haste:
The surf smelt were spawning—
Not a second to waste !

Yes I hopped from my pickup
And ran to the shore,
With hopes that I'd fill
A bucket or more
With cucumberly surf smelt
To fry and to broil.
I slipped on my waders
And watched the surf roil !

And into that briny, tumultuous sea
I blind-tossed my throw-net
And pulled it to me.
Alas, it was brimming
and I was quite thrilled
Until I saw 'chovies
All hopelessly gilled !

The thrill of the catch
Was now quickly undone:
Each fish would have to be
Plucked, one by one.
From out of the net
I'd thrown in such haste,
An hour or more
I'd now have to waste.

Yes, an hour, or two
(or possibly three),
I sat on that beach
with my new Christmas tree,
Its needles and branches
composed of small fish,
As I set about pruning,
I made me one wish:

"Poseidon, please give me the wisdom," I
prayed,
"To never again blind-toss in the waves
To cultivate patience where fishing's concerned
And to put into practice this lesson I've learned:
When cast-netting surf smelt in the ebb and
the flow,
Make sure they're not 'chovies,
Then make the throw."

NORTHERN ANCHOVY
Engraulis mordax

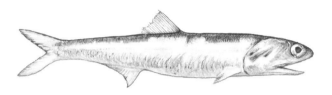

Yes, this really happened. It was at Montara State Beach about six years before the writing of this book. I was driving south on Highway 1 and saw what looked like a huge surf smelt spawn: seals and cormorants driving the fish toward shore, seagulls going berserk, whales and dolphins just past the breakers. Truth is, I realized it was anchovies, not smelt, when the net was in midflight, but even so, I didn't really consider what a royal pain in the anal fin it was going to be to pluck twenty pounds of gilled anchovies out of my throw-net. In any case, the hassle of getting them out of your net is something to consider when targeting anchovies. I've often noticed that even in shallow areas, where a throw-net would work to great effect, anchovy aficionados will stick by their trusty Sabiki rigs: evidently they've all experienced the miseries of anchovy Christmas tree-farming firsthand. But it seems to me the obvious solution would be to special order a ¼-inch mesh throw-net and catch them by the pound rather than by the ounce.[13] Or maybe I'm missing the point … maybe the relaxed, meditative aspect of catching anchovies one at a time (more like six at a time, really) is what the Sabiki crew is all about. In any case, anchovies are pretty much the smallest fish you are ever likely to catch, so there's not much excitement to reeling them in—only the excitement of slowly filling your bucket with delectable little fish.

THE WHERE, WHEN, AND HOW

Northern anchovies live to a ripe old age of seven years and evidently can reach lengths of ten inches. If you catch a ten-inch anchovy, take it to a taxidermist and get it mounted—it's a trophy fish.

In our area, anchovies tend to be caught in the summer. Like many other so-called forage fishes, their populations fluctuate by year and even by season.

---

13   Over-the-counter throw-nets in California are almost all ³/₈-inch mesh: the ¼-inch ones need to be special ordered. Remember that it's really difficult to catch fish with a throw-net in anything over ten feet of water. And that, despite the fact that ¼-inch nets are considerably heavier than the regular ones, they sink very slowly.

The best spot in San Francisco for anchovies is the Embarcadero shoreline between Piers 32 and 7. I have no idea why this is, but if you're desperate to catch your own anchovies, take your Sabikis, hop on BART, and head downtown.[14] Many of the old-timers who fish those piers bait their Sabikis with tiny pieces of shrimp. The author, however, finds this to be an aggravating and unnecessary extravagance. For anchovies, go with a small to medium Sabiki rig and fish the two-hour window on either side of high water. Other notable areas for anchovies: Monterey Wharf, Capitola Pier, Half Moon Bay, Berkeley Pier, Bodega Harbor, Humboldt Bay, et cetera.

EAT THEM UP, YUM

Unfortunately, most people associate anchovies with those stinky, ubersalty canned things that can ruin a pizza like nothing else. Anchovies can be deboned and stuffed or broiled to great effect, but really, the most delicious way to prepare anchovies is à la boquerones.

Anchovies à la Boquerones

Pinch the head at the gills and pull the guts out. Slit the belly. Open the body cavity and rinse. Then massage the spine from the meat (see "How to Debone or Butterfly a Small Fish," in the *Sardine* section of this chapter). Trim and rinse the little deboned patties. Cover the bottom of a plastic container with kosher salt, place a layer of anchovies (in their natural position, not splayed flat), a layer of salt, a layer of anchovies, et cetera, in the container. Refrigerate. After 24 hours, thoroughly rinse the salt off the anchovies. Lay the rinsed anchovies in a plastic tray. Pour vinegar over the anchovies till they are completely immersed and place in the fridge.[15] After another 24 hours, take them out, rinse them again, place them in a glass or plastic container, cover them with olive oil, and place a tight lid on the container. The oil will create an airless environment and, stored this way, the anchovies should keep for at least ten days at room temperature.

---

14 "Sabiki" is angler parlance for a baitfish rig. These lightweight modifications of the common shrimp fly rigs can be baited or simply jigged. The sparkling hooks, flashing, and brightly colored feathers are usually enough to induce small schooling fishes like anchovies and sardines to bite—but some desperados insist on baiting them. For more on Sabikis, check out Swim Bladder 1.

15 A good excuse to try an artisanal champagne vinegar if you haven't yet.

PACIFIC CHUB MACKEREL

Scomber japonicus

I'm not really sure what's up with the "chub" business. But what the hell. It's better than "horse mackerel," which has become the preferred name on the docks here in the last few years. What there is in a Pacific mackerel that would remind someone of a horse (or a chub for that matter) I know not.

THE WHERE, WHEN, AND HOW

Pacific chub mackerel can evidently live to at least twelve years, but it is rare to find one over nine years old. The state hook-and-line record listed on the Department of Fish and Wildlife (DFW, formerly the Department of Fish and Game) website is 2.8 pounds. But Milton Love, in his seminal classic, *Certainly More Than You Want to Know about the Fishes of the Pacific Coast: A Postmodern Experience,* mentions several six-pound lunkers caught in California during the 1930s.

With mackerel, as with sardines, it's all about hook-and-line fishing.[16] But keep in mind that pulling a Sabiki loaded with mackerel onto a boat or kayak can be a truly unhappy experience—hooks whipping around, snagging everything, fish flying all over the place. I've found that three or four hooks is all I can handle when dealing with mackerel on a boat—two if I'm on a kayak. From a pier, or on days when the fish are few and far between, use as many hooks as you like.[17] Also remember that mackerel are big enough to swallow a medium-sized anchovy, so a couple of standard "scampi" rigs (clipped together end to end) or the larger Sabikis are what you want. In our area most mackerel are caught in the summer and fall. Although they will bite at any time in the tidal cycle, your best bet from shore is to fish the incoming tide. On a

---

16 The California Department of Fish and Wildlife regulations book does not list mackerel as an allowable species for throw-net fishermen to take. However (as of this writing), there is no bag limit on Pacific chub mackerel.

17 Except inside SF Bay, where the maximum is three hooks.

boat, expect to do a lot of chasing, as mackerel swim fast and don't stay in one spot for very long. Mackerel like to eat pinhead anchovies (the tiny, one- to two-inch jobs). So if you locate a big school of "pinners," there's always a chance there will be some mackerel working the perimeter of it.

Pacific chub mackerel (okay, that's the last time I'm writing "chub") show up locally in large numbers during warm-water years, which may be one of the happier side effects of global warming. As far as small fish go, nothing fights as hard as a mackerel. So if you're in it for the sport as well as the food, fly gear or light tackle is truly the way to go.[18] My preferred technique is to break a shrimp fly off a scampi rig, crimp a split shot onto the leader, and fish it with a three-weight fly rod. If this sort of bastardized version of fly fishing offends your aesthetics, go with a sinking line and a Crazy Charlie or a modified Boss pattern. But these fish ain't picky. You could conceivably catch a mackerel on anything from a striper fly to a safety pin to a gummy bear with a hook in it.

PACIFIC JACK MACKEREL
Trachurus symmetricus

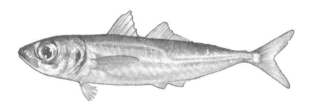

This is another one of those coastal species that's normally associated with areas to the south of the geographic range of this book, but has been showing up in increasing numbers of late. Note its aesthetically appealing blue-green color and slightly spiraling lateral line. For whatever reason (global warming? El Niño? *The End of Times?*) local Sabiki wielders have been catching a lot of jack mackerel (aka Spanish mackerel) in our waters during the last few years. As skimpy as jack macks may seem (in near-shore waters, a seven-incher is a hawg), they evidently come in large and extra-large sizes as well (they get up

---

18   I'm serious about this. Catching big mackerel on fly or ultralight tackle is a blast.

to thirty-two inches). If you're bound and determined to get yourself a trophy jack mackerel, make sure there's plenty of gas in the tank: it's a one-hundred- or two-hundred-mile round trip to where the lunkers hang out. Or you can save on gas and catch the little ones off a local pier in the summer.

THE WHERE, WHEN, AND HOW

In case you're wondering how to catch these guys, here's a hint: the fish pictured on the original Sabiki packaging is a jack mackerel. Jack mackerel often show up in large swarms along the coast, near piers and in harbors and bays. Yes, they will bite at night. Yes, they will bite at low tide. Yes, they will bite at high tide. High tide (plus or minus two hours) seems to be the better of the two. But basically, if you're on them (or in them) they'll bite. No need to bait the Sabiki, just drop it in and start jigging. Usually you will get a few Pacific chub mackerel while you're at it. As far as specifically targeting jack mackerel goes: good luck. Look for birds diving, seals and sea lions going berserk, big flocks of cormorants moving to and fro, and/or, if you're floating on the surface with a fish finder, the usual bait marks on the sonar. Once you drop your baitfish rig in, you'll know in a matter of seconds what type of fish the birds are so excited about.

EAT THEM UP, YUM

Bones aside, jack mackerel are good eating. The best way to cook them is grilled. Sprinkle with olive oil, salt, and pepper and grill for 3–5 minutes per side, depending on size. Squeeze a lemon on 'em and call 'em done. Nothing fancy. Some of my seafood subscribers did a boquerones-style cure (see *Northern Anchovy* above) with jack mackerel fillets and it worked great. The only thing is that these little guys are a tad smaller than your average herring, so filleting them requires a very sharp knife and a high degree of patience. If you have both, the end result will not disappoint you.

TRUE SMELTS: OSMERIDAE

SMELL THE CUCUMBER

Let's just get this straight. If you hear or read the word *smelt* and think immediately of the big, long, nasty basura smelt of SF Bay, think again. Jacksmelt and topsmelt are not true smelts. They're silversides of the family Atherinopsidae, the family that includes flying fish. Their meat is passable, their worms are horrifying, and the black stuff in their guts, whatever it is, does not inspire me to wax haikuic, nor to grill, fry, steam, or broil them (unless I'm desperate or trying to prove they're edible).

Not that I am a smeltist in any way (some of my best friends are silversides), but the true smelts are a superior group of fish. And the people who understand this distinction are likewise a superior group of *Homo sapiens*.

Now, how in the hell do I explain this?

There's something so ... aesthetically appealing about true smelts. No, that's not it ... there's the wading and the throwing of the nets, and the dipping of the A-frame and the ... no, no I'm missing it. Hmmm.

Honestly, I think it's about the cucumber. All members of the Osmeridae family give off the refreshing effervescence of cucumber. Doesn't matter if it's a lake smelt from Wisconsin, a capelin from Iceland, a wakasagi from Japan, or a night smelt from California. They all have that clean, improbable *odeur*. Cucumber is the very definition of a subtle smell ... yet you dip your schnozz into a bucket of "dayfish" (as those who love surf smelt are known to call them) and the scent is anything but subtle. In fact, it's overwhelming ... an overwhelming scent of cucumber. This is a contradiction in terms. And yet there it is, wafting through your refrigerator, the cab of your truck, your kitchen—anywhere those shimmering little fish end up en route to your belly.

I'm still not getting at it ... the fact that any of the true smelts exist at all, let alone exist in decent numbers, strikes me as a bit of a miracle. All members of the family require clean, cold water, and all of them tend to perish very quickly when they are denied it.[19] Can it really be that we've almost wiped out the eulachon, a true smelt par excellence, in California? Had it not been for the Cowlitz Indians in Oregon, this remarkable creature might not even have been listed! As late as the mid-1970s the spawning biomass of eulachon was almost laughably huge.[20] And then ... poof! In a span of five years, they were gone—or almost gone, anyway.

Often, when fishing for dayfish, I stare down into the waves and think: "Are these fish really swimming here? Or am I dreaming? And is this even my dream? Or the dream of a coastal Miwok three hundred years ago?"

By which I mean to say that the osmerid family gives me hope that the ocean is still okay despite everything we've done to pollute and annihilate it, that the sandy intertidal is still reasonably clean, that the beaches are still rea-

19 Populations of longfin smelt, Delta smelt, and eulachon have all been listed as threatened or endangered.

20 This from the *Yurok Tribal Fisheries Program Report: A Preliminary Status Review of Eulachon and Pacific Lamprey in the Klamath River Basin,* by Zachary S. Larson and Michael R. Belchik, April 1998: "The magnitude of runs was so great, according to fishers, that a continuous mass of fish lined the banks and as many fish as one could physically manage were pulled onto the river's bank in dip nets."

sonably undegraded, and that, yes, miracles can still happen—and sometimes they even come swimming in on the waves.

SURF SMELT
Hypomesus pretiosus

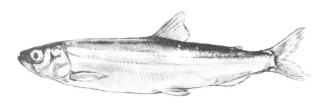

Haiku #3,891

Oh pretiosus !
Sparkle in the foamy waves !
Sizzle in the pan !

It's true, small fish are not for everybody. But I have yet to find a coastal fisher/forager who doesn't like surf smelt. Be forewarned, there are few fisheries that are as addictive as this one. And finding the spawns usually entails considerable driving, walking, and scouting of the coastline.

Surf smelt are found from Alaska to Central California. Males typically live three years and females four to five years. A lunker surf smelt is anything nine inches and over.

THE WHERE AND THE WHEN

As the name suggests, surf smelt spawn in the surf. This is the only time their inshore concentrations are high enough for you to target them. The beaches you're looking for are loosely packed with medium- to large-sized sand grains. Insofar as any fish is ever formulaic, here is the surf smelt formula:

1. Look for large sand grains. These fish must have loosely packed sand to spawn—as fine-grained sand packs too tightly for them to get their eggs down.

2. Show up just before the outgo. The optimal time is one to two hours after max high. But they might run anywhere from an hour before high to an hour after low.

3. Watch for reasonably mellow shore pound, with decent water visibility.

4. Look for the following piscivores in the surf zone (listed in descending order of importance):

    a. Old Portuguese men (most important)

    b. Caspian terns, harbor seals, and/or sea lions (all of equal importance, though Caspian terns are your spotter planes)

    c. Cormorants

    d. Pelicans[21]

    e. Seagulls[22] (least important)

5. Surf smelt spawn between March and October, sometimes earlier and sometimes later. But the peak, in our area, seems to be early summer to early fall.

6. The easiest time to see, and hence to catch, surf smelt is when the sun is high overhead.

Okay, now forget all this. I've caught these fish on brutal windy days, not a bird or marine mammal for miles, in brown turbid water, in the rain, on incoming tides, at flat low tide, and on beaches that had smallish to medium sand grains. The formula above really describes the optimal conditions. So if, for instance, you have a limited window to go looking for smelt, keep the formula in mind—but remember, fish don't give a damn about formulas, and some days they will do unpredictable things.

THE HOW AND THE HOW NOT

You show up at your spot. You look down the beach and see a Caspian tern (yes, even one) hovering directly over the foam. If the bird is diving more than ten yards from shore, the fish have not come in yet or are headed back out. You pull out your binoculars (very important to have binocs when surf smelting)—now, all of a sudden, you can see two harbor seals also in the surf zone. Put on your waders and polarized sunglasses.[23] Grab your bucket, scale,

---

21 Pelicans, due to their size, tend to dive on smelt only when the smelt are too far out to catch with a net from shore. A pelican diving in twelve inches of water would likely break its neck. Often when pelicans are desperate to get at the smelt in shallow water they will paddle inshore and scoop from a seated position atop the waves. Terns, being lighter and more adapted to a belly-flopping approach, have no problem diving in very shallow water.

22 Some smelters will disagree with my assessment that seagulls are anything but a nuisance out there. But I've had many days when terns and seals were completely absent, and suddenly a big group of western gulls starts hovering over the foam, screeching and yammering as they are wont to do. Lo and behold, the smelt start running. In fact, if a large group of gulls is sitting in the sand just above the tideline, staring at the waves, in a spot where you don't normally see them, it is possible that they are clued in to something that you, with your puny human senses, are completely oblivious of. And then of course, they might be looking at a sand crab spawn, a dead fish floating in the water, or a garbage scow going by.

23 Yes, polarized lenses make a big difference.

and casting net.[24] Walk down the shore to the spot where the tern is hovering. Take a deep breath—relax, you could be here a while. Walk up to the water but do not wade deeper than your ankles. Let a few waves pass. Stare into the small, clear windows between sections of foam. The fish will appear as little shadows darting in and out. Wait till you see a school of more than half a dozen fish before you start throwing. And try to avoid "blind-tossing." There's nothing experienced smelters hate more than the person who comes down to the beach and immediately starts blind-tossing. It's okay to do this on a rough day when there is little or no visibility, but on a reasonable day, don't do it. Or do it sparingly. For one thing, blind-tossing is the kind of thing that impatient people do and we all must try to cultivate the great virtue of fishing: patience. Blind-tossing also happens to be a surefire way to scare off the fish before they are actually ready to spawn. It's also dangerous (read "The Bad Day" below). So again, unless the water is very turbid, refrain from the blind toss.

One other thing … bring a net bag. Same type as you would use for abalone or make your own out of A-frame netting (see Swim Bladder 4). Surf smelt (like night smelt) will be covered in sand grains. The net bag allows you to rinse them by dunking them in the surf before you head home.

Though "smelt jumping" technically refers to the act of catching smelt by means of a two-man net (seldom seen these days), I use it here and throughout as a synonym for smelt fishing, whether that be with a throw net or an A-frame.

24 You are required to have a scale while fishing for smelt. The daily bag limit as of this writing is twenty-five pounds. The best nets for surf smelt are the more expensive ones that have heavier lead, and hence, sink faster in the swash.

THE GOOD DAY

In case you were unaware of the total awesomeness of smelt fishing, try to picture the roiling surf, the wind, the Caspian terns hovering, the blue water, the sparkling fish dancing in and out. And then that magic moment when you see the school, time the throw perfectly, pull the drawstring, and fill your net with sparkling golden slivers of pure oceanic joy. That's what a good day of smelt fishing is all about.

THE BAD DAY

Lest you should think smelt fishing is nothing but blue skies and nets full of fish, I offer the following:

Once upon a time, on a stormy Saturday in June, at the very beginning of my surf smelt career, I decided, despite poor conditions and a brutal shore pound, to drive to my favorite smelt spot. I got to the beach and was saddened to see that the shore break was even worse than it had been on the surf riders' webcam. I walked down the beach, picked an area with promising smelt sand, sat on my bucket, and waited for the swell to die down. It didn't. Suddenly I saw two seals darting nose to tail through the curl of a wave. I grabbed my net, ran down to shore, and stared hard into the water around my legs. Still couldn't see anything. I looked down the shore—no fishermen. I stared up at the cliffs—no one watching me. I went back to my bag, pulled out my binoculars, and made triply sure there was no one to witness my next move. Several moments later I hurled my first blind toss of the season. I pulled the rope. Nothing. I regrouped, waded a little further out, thinking *maybe the fish are holding in the trough*. I gathered up my sinkers and my rope and launched my net like Al Oerter going for the gold in the 1960 Olympic Games. I let it sink. I pulled the string. Nothing. *Man, I just can't throw it far enough!* I waded a little deeper, readied my net, and let it fly ... Still nothing ... *If I could only get it a little further* ...

I think you can all see where this is going. Rest assured, if you wade out deep enough into the surf while wearing chest waders you will soon find yourself drowning. In my case, the wave that went over my head and dragged me to my death (I'm writing this now from the other side) was only part of the problem. The other part was the harbor seal that my blind-tossed net had landed on, and the "death knot" I had tied on my wrist to prevent it from slipping off when I commenced the Olympic heaves. I won't write here about the surfer who saved my sorry ass, or the 7.5 gallons of water that I swallowed, or the net that I lost, or the savage rope burn on my wrist caused by a 150-pound harbor seal pulling against it (thank Poseidon it wasn't a sea lion). I will, however, mention that when I got back to the parking lot (a dripping, limping, freezing, wheezing wreck), the passenger window on my truck had been smashed and my cellphone charger and bait-caster stolen. I took this as a sign from the ocean gods: they were annoyed that I had underestimated their powers. In many cultures the ocean is not seen merely as an impartial and uncaring force, but also as a malevolent, vindictive, and angry deity. Poseidon was many things, but he was never a particularly nice guy. It's probably a good idea to remember this from time to time (either that or to offer the occasional hecatomb to the earthshaker).

The above story is completely fictitious (really, I swear it!). I put it here only to illustrate several ways you might kill yourself while "smelt jumping" on the California coast. I should also point out that it is yet another demonstration of why blind-tossing is such a bad idea. It encourages the net chucker to keep wading out deeper and deeper... until she's, as they say, *in over her head*.

EAT THEM UP, YUM

Stuffed Surf Smelt à la Fishwife

Head and gut your fish. Snip off all the fins. Debone. (See "How to Debone or Butterfly a Small Fish," in the *Sardine* section of this chapter.) Take the deboned bodies, making sure they're still "hinged" together at the back, and set aside (preferably in the fridge).

Preheat the oven to 400F and brush a baking sheet with olive oil. In a food processor combine:

> ½ cup fresh breadcrumbs
> 3 Tbsp Parmesan
> 1 Tbsp fresh herbs, whatever you got (cilantro! basil! dill! sage! parsley! mint? Yes, do it! Seriously, they won't clash!)
> 1 tsp minced rosemary
> 1 tsp minced garlic
> Handful of walnuts
> 1 tsp good-quality mustard
> Splash of olive oil

Pulse the mixture until it's nice and sticky. Then toss a handful of raisins into the mix. Yes, raisins!

Pat your fish dry, then pour a tablespoon of olive oil in your hands, rub them together, and rub the fish so that they're coated. Stuff each fish with a bit of the stuffing, arrange them in rows on the baking sheet, and sprinkle with salt and pepper and a little lemon juice. Bake about 15 minutes, until a little golden. Cut up some lemon wedges (or whip up some optional dipping sauce, below) and voila! You're ready to scarf some delicious little fish. This recipe also works well for sardines and other small fishes.

Dipping Sauce

> Juice of half a lemon
> 3 Tbsp mayonnaise
> ½ tsp cumin
> ½ tsp Sriracha hot sauce

Stir ingredients, put in a shallow bowl, dip, and enjoy!

NIGHT SMELT
Spirinchus starksi

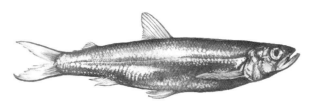

THE WHEN AND THE WHERE

Night smelt (aka nightfish) are only about a third of the size of surf smelt (dayfish) and, obviously, run at night.[25] Like their larger cousins, they prefer outgoing tides, gentle ocean conditions, and beaches with large (but not too large) sand grains. Often the two species run on the same beaches—surf smelt taking the day shift and nighties the night shift. Target them around the least extreme tidal conditions of any month. Often you will have to wait until the sun is completely gone before the fish start running in earnest. The main thing is to show up at dusk and look for harbor seals in the surf zone: they are usually dead giveaways to the imminent arrival of *S. starksi*. Night smelt rarely reach six inches in length and three years of age.

THE HOW AND THE HOW NOT

The primary gear used in night smelt fishing is the A-frame dip net. Although it may be hard to find these nets for sale, making one is a fun project (see Swim Bladder 4). A-frame nets work simply: the fish are caught in the wide part of the net on the incoming wave and then dumped into the "sock." This way, you don't have to walk back up the beach and transfer your fish to a bucket after each dip.

I've used my ¼-inch mesh anchovy net for night smelt several times. The thing works reasonably well, but even so, I find it surprisingly difficult to throw in the dark. What's more, when fishing for night smelt you will often be surrounded by seals. Seals that would never venture to get so close to you in daylight hours. On the scale of the potential hazards of night fishing, snagging a seal with a throw-net has to rank at or near the top. So take the time and effort to make yourself an A-frame net—you won't regret it!

---

25 Fishmonger's editorial insertion: ten to twelve surf smelt = 1 pound; thirty-one to thirty-four night smelt = 1 pound.

As mentioned in the surf smelt section, make sure to bring a net bag for your night smelt, so you can rinse off all the sand and grit before you leave the beach.

Eat Them Up, Yum

Fries with Eyes

Night smelt are the easiest fish in the seven seas to process. No scaling or gutting necessary. Rinse them, toss with flour (do an egg wash if you're feeling adventurous), and drop them into the fryer whole. That's it. Night smelt are usually eaten head, guts (not much in the way of guts in these guys), and all—hence "fries with eyes," the popular term for them in the Bay Area restaurants that serve them.

Note that night smelt can be a bit gritty. This is because sand grains tend to get caught in their gills. So if a bit of sand is a problem for you, don't eat the heads. Some strange smelt fans out there are known to head and gut all their night fish. Seems to me like a lot of unnecessary work, but to each his or her own.

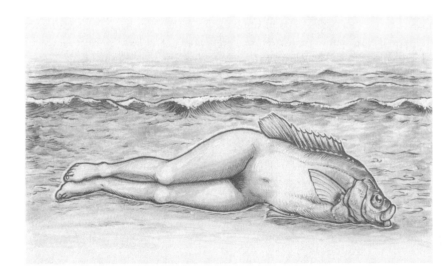

THE CLIFF

Unbelievably, for about six months I lost the ocean. Without getting too deep into it, this loss involved a spinal tap, a CAT scan, an MRI, and forty-five thousand dollars in uncovered hospital bills. It also involved an uncharacteristic period of depression. A brush with mortality—my own—and a sort of all-encompassing fear, a sense that I had lost something, a sense that for the first time in my life, I was, well . . . mortal.

The good news here is that I snapped out of it. The prognosis is now good. The errant bus, the kayak-chewing shark, the Charles Joseph Whitman type, I have no control over. But the thing all those doctors thought I had, *that* can be struck from the list.

And yet, it really knocked me for a loop. In retrospect, I think it had something to do with the florescent tubes in the hospital and the spinal tap. I felt like the experience, my first-ever extended stay in a hospital, had sucked part of my soul away and spat it out somewhere dark and lonely. But what is worse, and what really worried me, was that it took the ocean away from me.

By which I mean to say, I was already feeling weak and puny, and I couldn't deal with feeling any weaker and punier. So I neglected the tides. I heard the fish were running and I did what? I watched Frodo and Sam shivering in the cold of Mordor and then I watched it again. And again. I wrapped myself in blankets and walked around my apartment. Feeling old and tired and weak and vulnerable. At night I told Camilla "The Fishwife" Lombard that I felt a change coming over me. I was ready for a new epoch of my life: a more distant relationship to the intertidal zone, a more meditative approach to things in general.

Mikey, my fishing partner, whipping boy, and brother from another mother, called me before the last tidal cycle and said: "Are we going?" To which this, unbelievably, was my texted response:

"Warm. Watching a movie. Too f-ing tired for that cliff."

In my weakened state, there was simply no avoiding the fact that the night smelt, if they were even running, were running along that stretch of beach whose only shoreward approach included what I had come to view as an agonizing, death-defying, back-wrenching climb down (and then, still more problematically, *up*), a sandy escarpment known to fishermen simply as *the cliff.*

Mikey texted me back: "Are you Lombard of the Intertidal or Lombard of the sofa?"

This struck a chord. I meditated on it for several days and came to the conclusion that my stint in the hospital had left me with what could best be described as a crisis of faith. I tried to remind myself of the beauty of the surf at night, of how magical a smelt spawn could be: seals in the foam, fish washing up on the beach, the moon's reflection painted on the surface of the ocean, the wind, the waves, yada yada. Yet despite my best efforts, I couldn't convince myself that this was anything but a lame attempt to justify a passion that I no longer felt, an activity that I was no longer capable of enjoying, a deity that had fallen from grace with me.

And then, on the last night of the smelt tides, while my brain was busy repeating the mantra *I'm not going fishing, I'm not going fishing,* my body, acting mostly on muscle memory, started gathering up my A-frame and placing it in the back of my truck. Then, strangely, the waders, the bucket, and the net bag were packed, the key was in the ignition, and I found myself rolling toward the setting sun.

Forty-five minutes later, pulling up at the beach parking lot, I was already looking for excuses to bail: the cliff was too steep, the wind too strong, the shore break too rough, the swell too big, the smelt unlikely to run.

I looked down from the cliff—way down. There were three dayfish guys down there with buckets full of nothing and a couple of bass pluggers leaning on their poles and talking to each other. As far as nonhuman piscivores, there were two nonchalant seals in the surf zone and that universal fish finder, a Caspian tern, hovering over the swash. Obviously the tern was keeping the fishermen on the beach—all five of them were staring at it, hoping it would spot something for them. Still an hour till sunset.

Thirty minutes later the tern was gone and the seals were floating on their backs, staring up at the clouds. (In harbor seal body language, this translates to, *We're done for the day, there's nothing here worth chasing.*) Then that awful south wind started to pick up. "I'm so over this!" I yelled. My voice, buffeted by the wind, came out sounding puny and ridiculous, the exact feeling of puniness I was trying to avoid.

A small flock of western gulls flapped past, heading for their nightly roost. I went back to my truck, sat down, and turned on the Giants game.

No solace there. Once again the home nine seemed to be inventing new and infuriating ways to lose. I switched the radio off and turned on the audiobook I'd been listening to: an under-appreciated actor named George Guidall reading *The Odyssey* in warm, somber tones. The fact that I had arrived at Book XXIV was evidence of how little fishing I'd done this summer. Anyway, Homer wasn't getting it done, so I turned it off and watched the sunset. I'm always hoping to see that fleeting greenness everyone talks about, but again, staring right at it, waiting for it, focusing all my energies on it, I saw nothing—no greenness, no flash, just the slow and deliberate death of another day. A cold wind blew from the water. The two bass pluggers turned from the waves and trudged toward the cliff.

At this point I figured it was time to fondle my gear for a minute, even if I had no intention of fishing. My waders, Gus's Discount rubber sales bin jobs, looked like WWI army surplus equipment, cracked and slightly torn between the legs. The big question: to put the waders on pantless, and risk embarrassment, or to keep the pants on and deal with a damp, frozen crotch all night. The wind blew cold again. "Fuck it, I'm leaving," I said aloud.

"Hey man," said a voice behind me. "I see you got an A-frame in the truck. You going down there?"

It was one of the surf smelt fishermen. He had evidently climbed up the cliff while I was sitting in the truck. I stared at him for a while without answering. A tough, handsome, slightly salty and sand-smeared fisherman's face stared back at me. I had harassed this guy maybe four times over the years when I worked for the Fish and Wildlife Department. Did he remember me?

"Are you going for night smelt?" he asked again.

Here was the moment of truth. At the risk of being un-PC, I have to say it like it is: had this fisherman not been Filipino, I might have answered no. But being that he was a Filipino fisherman, and that Filipino fishermen represent to me the very zenith of piscatorial wisdom, passion, and skill, especially where shore fishing is concerned, there was only one way I could answer this question and maintain my dignity as a shore fisherman.

"Yes, goddamn it, I'm going down there."

The guy's name was Angel. (You can't make stuff like this up.[26]) Angel, after skunking all day on surf smelt, was hoping he would run into someone who wanted to go for nighties (he'd left his A-frame at home). But the night smelt runs had been so miserable this year, he wasn't expecting to find anyone he could tag

---

26 Actually you can, but I'm not.

along with, until he saw a curious-looking A-frame with pseudo-Ohlone pictograms carved all over it, sitting in the back of the Ford Ranger next to his car in the lot.

"That's a nice A-frame," he said.

"Thanks," I said.

Having now committed myself to this unhappy venture, I stared miserably at the cliff, then slid into my perpetually predampened waders (with pants *on,* mind you—my friendship with Angel was too young to allow for butt-naked wader-wearing), grabbed the A-frame, a bucket, and the requisite abalone net bag, and with Angel leading the way, commenced descending the dreaded cliff.

"I don't think I can handle this cliff," I said.

"What cliff?" said Angel.

"I hate this fucking cliff," I said. "I see it in my nightmares."

In ten minutes we were on the beach. My knees were fine. My back felt great. No apparent cardiac arrest or embolism. Yet I still resisted the euphoria that was taking hold. I looked toward the waves. Not a seal to be seen. All the relevant birds were nestled down for the night somewhere, like sane fish-eating animals. 8:39 P.M. Twenty-two minutes till true dark. We carried the gear down to the shore and plopped it in the sand.

"This water looks awful," I said.

Angel felt the sand with his feet. "Yeah, but the sand is good."

As I've mentioned above, night smelt and surf smelt require coarse-grained, loosely packed sand. If the sand grains are too small (like, say, the sand grains at Ocean Beach, Dillon Beach, or Capitola), surf and night smelt cannot wiggle down to lay their eggs in it. I grabbed a handful and let it drip between my fingers. Angel, of course, was right. The sand was good. Perfect, in fact. But this was no time for optimism.

"Look, Angel, I gotta leave at 9:15, okay? I don't want to be out here all night."

"No problem," said Angel. "It's your gear, leave when you want."

At 9 P.M., I handed Angel my A-frame. If I could get out of this evening without soaking my balls in freezing salt water, so much the better. There was still a faint suggestion of blue on the horizon. Still light enough for us to see each other clearly. Angel took the net, whipped it around, opened it, and slapped the crossbar into the slot—not unlike Odysseus effortlessly stringing his bow before slaughtering Penelope's deadbeat suitors. *Night smelt tremble as this man approaches,* I thought.

Angel marched to the shore and dipped. Nothing. He dipped again. Nothing.

"Too much light still," he said.

For the next fifteen minutes, while Angel nodded politely, I railed on and on about my bad luck of late. How I had lost all interest in the pursuit and capture of intertidal life forms. How there was no financial, psychological, or spiritual justification for recreational fishing. I roughly tabulated my gas expenditures, how much protein I had taken in versus effort expended (the predator's equation), and concluded that it was all a waste of our extremely limited time on earth—time that, I had recently learned, was dearly finite. At the end of this diatribe Angel laughed and said, "It's 9:15, you still wanna leave?"

I stared out at the gigantic ocean, feeling puny and miserable. Again my body and my brain were of two different minds. "Yes," I said. "I'm leaving."

At 9:30, despite fog, total darkness, and lack of a headlamp, Angel said he'd just seen seals about one hundred feet down the beach.

"No you didn't," I said.

"Yes I did!"

"Where?"

"Right there."

A seal splashed in the foam. Another one rocketed through the swash. Angel ran down the beach and dipped. "They're here!" he yelled. "They're here!"

And then everything changed. Suddenly the A-frame was back in my hands. I dipped, I pulled, I looked down. The sound of the waves, which two minutes earlier was a crushing, malevolent heartbeat, was now a glorious timpani of victory; the chilly wind wasn't so much chilly as clean and fresh; the wet spray in my face wasn't a potential source of pneumonia, but a gentle kiss from the naiads. I heard someone laughing and realized it was me.

In twelve minutes we banged out two easy limits of night smelt with our shared net. We ascended the cliff, each of us carrying twenty-five-pound buckets, plus gear and backpacks, in an invigorating seventeen minutes. Edmund Hillary in his prime could have done no better. Alone in the dark parking lot, we divvied up the catch, exchanging high fives and briefly deconstructing the night's adventure—like two Pleistocene cave dwellers talking about the day's mammoth hunt by the side of a roaring fire. After a while I climbed into my truck and said goodbye to my newest fishing partner.

He smiled. "Hey Kirk," he said. "The cliff wasn't so bad, was it?"

"The cliff?" I said, "What cliff?"

EULACHON
Thaleichthys pacificus

Much as I hate to admit it, I've never fished for eulachon (aka hooligan or candlefish). And since they're evidently on the brink of extirpation in California, my chance to do so may have already passed ... but one can dream, no?[27] And since it's such an amazing creature, I am including it here.

The eulachon is an anadromous smelt[28] so full of oil that it can be dried and fairly easily turned into a candle. (Just set the head on fire and watch it burn: there are a few videos online of people—miscreants and sociopaths mostly—doing this.) Evidently the spawning runs on the Klamath were epic affairs as late as the 1970s. Many of the old "Indian trails" throughout the West Coast were originally called "grease trails" because the main item of commerce along them was, you guessed it, eulachon grease. Meriwether Lewis considered it to be "the finest eating of all fishes."

No one knows definitively what is causing the demise of this species, but global warming, changes in the California coastal upwelling, habitat destruction, shrimp trawling, siltation, and destruction of spawning habitat have all been presented as possible explanations. Whatever the reason, the eulachon is nearly gone in California, and we are all the worse for its decline.

GOING, GOING ...

Back in the day, when the stocks were still considered fishable, candlefish were typically caught in the Klamath during the spring, by shore fishers armed with long-handled dip nets, standing in key locations on the bank. It was evidently not uncommon for a dip netter to bag twenty-five pounds of fish in two or three minutes of such dipping. Recent net surveys at the mouth of the Klamath have shown little evidence that eulachon will be returning anytime soon.

THE WHERE, WHEN, AND HOW NOT

It is currently illegal to take eulachon in California.

27 I should point out that the eulachon disappeared from the Columbia River for ten years and then suddenly and unexpectedly showed up in massive numbers in 2012. I await a similar resurrection in California ... though at this point it would be nothing short of a miracle. They've been virtually (though not completely) gone for over thirty years.

28 And as such, the only critter in this book caught exclusively in fresh water.

"FALSE SMELTS":
ATHERINOPSIDAE, NEW WORLD SILVERSIDES

JACKSMELT
Atherinopsis californiensis

Okay. Let's get this straight. We have a lot of jacksmelt in California. Despite the roundworms and the nasty-looking black stuff in their guts, many people eat these creatures.[29] Many people also eat fat innkeeper worms ("penis fish") and monkey brains. If you absolutely must go get yourself some jacksmelt, you want to fish spring and summer, though they appear to be fishable from shore year round. There is no limit on them, so you can fill up bucket after bucket.[30] And if after cleaning these fish you are not traumatized by all the worms crawling around your sink, and the thick sticky scales stuck to your sleeves and your fingers and the walls and everything else, well then you're a better piscivore than I.

The thing to remember is that a jacksmelt isn't, technically speaking, a smelt at all. It's a silverside, family Atherinopsidae—closer to a flying fish than to a smelt. The only person who seems to care about this distinction, however, is me. It can be difficult to convince anyone familiar with jacksmelt that there is anything worthwhile in a fish that has "smelt" in its common name. And yet, surf smelt and night smelt are two of the cleanest, most delicious fishes on the coast. Guilty by faulty association, I guess.

THE WHERE, WHEN, AND HOW

Jacksmelt can reach twenty-two inches in length and live for eleven years. Most jacksmelt fishers use a big ol' bobber or a piece of Styrofoam. The hooks are

29 Not that I'm squeamish. Like anyone who's been in the seafood biz for more than a week, I have a thicker skin on this issue than most people.

30 As of this writing.

suspended vertically below the bobber (see Swim Bladder 1). Some people set up elaborate mooching rigs,[31] throwing a heavy sinker out, then sliding the bobber with leader attached down to the surface, but this is really way more work than is necessary. Jacksmelt can be caught on any tide, but they seem to like the flood, and it's probably a good idea to fish for them two hours before high water and two hours after it.

Shore angler par excellence Champion de la Banana and his South Bay cronies refer to jacksmelt as "basura smelt." And this is coming from a group of guys who commonly extol the virtues of deep-fried inner-city pogies. That should say something for the gastronomic qualities of jacksmelt meat.

Monster Ling Bait

If, however, you are fishing for lingcod to the exclusion of all other fishes, a big, live jacksmelt is the ticket. (Lingcod will also slam fresh dead ones drifted from boats or kayaks.) There are very few other local game fishes that can swallow a big jacksmelt whole. I know of at least one commercial hook-and-line lingcod fisherman who uses jacksmelt so that he can specifically select for hawg lingcod and avoid the rockfish species that he isn't allowed to catch.

The Bright Side

Seriously, though, worms and scales and funky black stuff in the guts aside, this is a very cool and important species. It is a staple in the diet of virtually all our local piscivores, from fish to marine mammals to birds to all the different people of various stripes who fish on shore. It is also quite the harbinger of spring. I never really feel that herring season is over and spring is upon us till I see a few buckets of jacksmelt caught on one of the city piers. Jacksmelt are also a great starter species for kids. Did I mention that they fight hard? Well, they do. When I first moved to the Bay Area back in the Pleistocene (I'm older than I look), I used to fly fish for jacksmelt and, frankly, it was a blast. My favorite spot for this was near Candlestick Park, but you can pretty much catch jacksmelt anywhere along the California coast on any sparkly fly that looks like you cut it off a Sabiki rig.

31 For more on shore mooching rigs, see "On the Pier" in Swim Bladder 1.

I've actually had very good steamed jacksmelt courtesy of one Mrs. M. Tran (ginger and green onions, yum!). But as good as those fish were, I just couldn't get over the idea that I was munching on copious quantities of nematodes. This may or may not have been the case. I have heard rumors that jacksmelt are less wormy when caught outside of SF Bay. And, as my good friend Mikey "Caveman" Dvorak points out, "a little extra protein won't kill ya." Kill me, no. Gross me out? Kind of.

GRUNION
Leuresthes tenuis

The grunion is usually considered to be one of the emblematic species of Southern California. In fact, in our geographic area, grunion are uncommon enough that I left them out of the first two drafts of this book. Even when they do run in this area, the runs tend to be … uninspired … or maybe non-committal is the word. Kind of like a transplanted Dodger fan tentatively donning the orange and black for opening day in San Francisco. Which is to say, all the grunion spawns I've seen north of Santa Barbara have been positively unsexy, the fish seemingly content to hang out in the trough, not committing to full coitus in the foaming waves and sand.

And then, this past June, Sea Forager advance scout and tiny home builder par excellence Lloyd Kahn (Agent 009) called to tell me that there were small silvery fish washing up late at night on a local San Francisco beach. I initially figured he was speaking about night smelt, but the moon was wrong, and that particular beach is known for its fine-grained sand. As if to confirm my suspicions, Lloyd sent me a video the next day of a very robust (read: sexy) grunion spawn near the time predicted on the Department of Fish and Wildlife grunion page. So I drove out on the last night listed there, and soon realized that at least *some* grunion have fully embraced Northern California as a place worthy of kinky fish sex on the beach.

To summarize grunion for the uninitiated Northern Californian, it might be best to compare it to that other, more northerly, nocturnal beach spawner in our area, night smelt (see *Night Smelt* above). The salient differences/similarities:

1. The spawning behavior of grunion is remarkably formulaic (night smelt, not so much). Once you figure out what beach they're on, the rest is quite literally like clockwork. However, if you have trouble remembering formulas, the California DFW offers an extremely helpful "Expected Grunion Run" page on their website. Just be advised that the times on that page are based on tides at Cabrillo Beach in Los Angeles.

2. Grunion are a tad bigger than night smelt (at least the females are) and have a proportionately smaller mouth, comparatively thick scales, and no adipose fin.

3. Grunion are not true smelts but belong to the silverside family (like topsmelt, jacksmelt, and flying fish)

4. Insofar as night smelt spawning can be predicted, they seem to favor mild tides and ocean conditions, while grunion (rather famously) spawn on new moons and full moons, and the three to four evenings following these lunar phases.

5. Both species like outgoing tides, which makes sense if you think like a beach spawner for a minute.[32] On both new and full moon cycles, grunion may start running at any time within the first two hours after high tide. Their spawns last between thirty minutes and three hours.

6. Unlike night smelt, which rarely condescend to beach themselves, preferring to perform the procreative act in the relative privacy of trough and backwash, grunion rather hedonistically roll up onto the sand and go at it like ancient Romans at a Viagra convention.

7. Grunion prefer fine-grained sand, night smelt prefer coarse.

8. Whereas night smelt spawns may last for many hours, and may linger on for a while after peak activity, grunion are prone to sudden arrival and disappearance.

9. As far as fishing regulations go, you are not allowed to use anything other than your hands to gather grunion—no A-frames, casting nets,

---

32 If beach-spawning fish laid their eggs on incoming tides, the eggs would be more likely to be pulverized or pushed upslope than on falling tides.

beach seines, or depth charges.[33] Also, you are not allowed to dig troughs, canals, or ditches in the sand to trap them. There is no bag limit on grunion (the limit for night smelt is twenty-five pounds), but only take what you need.

10. Whereas night smelt may run early or late in the evening, grunion almost always spawn at ungentlemanly (read: miserable) hours that will leave you wandering the beach at times when no sane person should be out of doors.

11. Grunion do not smell like cucumbers. In fact, they smell exactly like jacksmelt (read: fishy) And unlike night smelt, each fish has to be scaled before eating.

As beautiful and awe inspiring as grunion are, all the things that make harvesting and prepping them a pain in the ass are nonfactors for night smelt. No need to scale night smelt, no need to wander the beach after midnight, no need to grab them with your fingers, and then… night smelt smell like cucumber perfume. It almost seems like they were designed to eliminate the challenges associated with grunion fishing. Like a sort of new and improved grunion (grunion 2.0?)

THE WHERE, WHEN, AND HOW

Because grunion are infrequent visitors to our local beaches, finding where they are spawning is akin to finding the proverbial needlefish in a kelp stack. So intel is the key here. There's really no use walking sandy beaches at midnight in this area hoping to chance on a grunion run. I would never have found them locally if I hadn't, over the years, cultivated a loyal group of scouts and informants who call me when they see cool stuff (thanks again, Lloyd).

So once you've determined that the grunion have been spawning in a certain location, get there at the top of high tide (aka midnight) and wait at least two hours. Keep a sharp eye out for silvery fish sparkling in the waves or (ahem) *dancing* in the sand.

---

33 I should point out that grunion grabbing is much easier when you use both hands. So bring a bucket, and a net bag. Put the net bag in the bucket as a liner, so that its mouth is wide open. When you see a nice pocket of fish, run over to them, plop your bucket down, kneel in the sand, and start grabbing grunion and throwing them in the net bag/bucket—with both hands. My buddy Mikey did not have a bucket last time out and so he had to hold his net bag with one hand and grab grunion with the other. Because of this I absolutely destroyed him in our manly competition to produce the largest sack. When the spawn is over and the grabbing done, take the net bag and thoroughly rinse it in the surf just as you would for sand-covered osmerids like *S. starksi* and *H. pretiosus*.

EAT THEM UP, YUM

As far as cooking goes, small grunion can be breaded and fried just like night smelt; the larger ones can be de-boned and stuffed or fried like surf smelt. The major difference in prep, as mentioned above, is that you have to scale them first.

KINGFISH (WHITE CROAKER)
Genyonemus lineatus

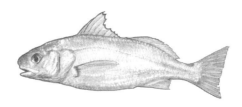

In Cantonese, *wong fa*. In Korean, *chogie*. In Latin, *Genyonemus lineatus*. And in Amer-slang, the white croaker goes, inexplicably, by *kingfish*. Whatever you call them, these fish are similar to jacksmelt in the number of nematodes one tends to find in their guts and meat. There is, however, one salient difference: kingfish meat is quite good and it is understandable that someone might want to brave the worms in order to eat it. The heavy metals I'm not so sure about. That is, despite being relatively short lived and low on the food chain, kingfish evidently bio-accumulate toxins at an alarming rate.[34] In fact, they fall into the red zone (fish to be avoided) on the health department list of local fish species.

There was a time when shore fishers caught a lot of kingfish inside San Francisco Bay. The water seemed to be absolutely loaded with them, but sadly, that time seems to have passed. Canvassing the Bay Area shorelines as a fisheries observer ten years ago, I came in just as the kingfish were on the way out. I still remember the groups of elderly Korean anglers with their platform rod holders fishing *chogies* on the Marina Green wall on Saturday mornings. But slowly the bite died off, and lately it's become rare to see a shore-caught kingfish in SF Bay. Nevertheless, offshore populations in Pacifica, Half Moon Bay, and Monterey Bay appear to be extremely abundant.

WHAT'S IN A NAME?

"Kingfish?" I mean *really?* As in *king of fishes?* With all due respect to the *wong fa* aficionados out there, you gotta be kidding me. *King* salmon? That makes

---

34 They have a hard time metabolizing toxins.

sense. *King* mackerel? Sure, why not? But *king*fish for the white croaker? My own impression is that a more fitting nickname would be a few steps down from the top rung of the human social ladder. In fact, I'm thinking maybe "pauper fish" or "peasant fish" would be more apt. It has occurred to me, of course, that the person or persons who started this *kingfish* business may have meant it sarcastically. In which case, all I can say is: *I get it.*

THE WHERE, WHEN, AND HOW

If you feel inclined to throw health advisories out the window and go nab some kingfish, you might want to consider a baitfish rig loaded with pieces of squid or squid tentacles. Several other fishing books suggest pile worms, and certainly a large percentage of the kingfish diet consists of marine worms, but it seems to me that pile worms, at twelve dollars a dozen, should be saved for something a tad more … *exciting* than kingfish. Target kingfish two hours before and after the top (or bottom) of the tide. And remember that these fish like the bottom, especially sandy or muddy bottoms. The average kingfish fights about as hard as a wet sock but they are adept at stealing bait from a hook—which is another good reason to forgo the pile worms and bait your rigs with squid. (Squid is both cheaper and harder to peck off of a hook than a pile worm or a piece of one.) Oh yeah, kingfish live to be at least twelve years old. Anything over fourteen inches is a hawg kingfish. Mikey Dvorak, Caveman of the High Seas, reminds me to mention that live kingfish make an excellent lingcod bait. But then so does anything that swims.

SAND DAB
Citharichthys sordidus

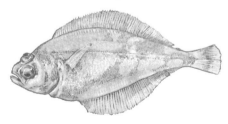

In our area, the principal sand dab caught by hook and line is the Pacific, *C. sordidus,* as opposed to the longfin and the speckled, both of which occur more frequently in the central to southern areas of the California coast.

Like almost all members of the flounder clan, the sand dab is deeply delicious. And yet its popularity seems to be restricted primarily to California—

and more specifically, to the area from Santa Barbara to San Francisco.[35] Go to a fine seafood restaurant anywhere else in the United States and ask the chef when they will be getting sand dabs in, if you want to understand the very definition of a blank stare. Most of the sand dabs consumed in our area of the state are caught by deep-water trawlers, or "drag" boats, and are thus caught by the ton. In many cases these "dragged" sand dabs will be in a sorry state by the time they've been scraped off the seafloor, crammed into the cod end of the net, suctioned from the hold, dumped into containers, trucked to warehouses, sorted, iced, delivered, trimmed, and (oh yeah, one more step) cooked. In short, the difference between the fresh, unsmashed, unabused sand dab that you catch with hook and line and the bottom-trawled fish can be significant in terms both of appearance and texture.

THE WHERE, WHEN, AND HOW

Sand dabs can live up to ten years and can evidently attain sizes up to sixteen inches and two pounds. Anything over twelve inches and one pound is a veritable *toad*. Dabs are typically caught year round by small-skiff fishermen on sandy bottoms, fishing from thirty to three hundred feet—very often in the same areas where Dungeness crabs are caught. Hence the popular "crabbing and dabbing" trips offered by party boats in the winter, when other near-shore sport fisheries (i.e., rockfish and salmon) are closed. The typical setup is a large Sabiki rig or "sand-dab" rig, baited with small pieces of squid or squid tentacles (see Swim Bladder 1).

If you don't have access to a boat, fear not. In the winter and early spring, sand dabs are commonly caught from shore by hook and line. The best spots for this in our area tend to be public piers and jetties, which can get you out into deeper water than you can otherwise reach from shore. In some years the inshore abundance of dabs can be remarkable. In the winter of 2007 and again in 2008, sand dabs came into SF Bay in vast numbers. Shore fishers nabbed them by the bucketload from all the piers between the Golden Gate and the Bay Bridge. Even during off years, one can usually wrest a dinner's worth of sand dabs (three to twelve, depending on size) from the wintry shoreline of SF, especially on the north side of the city (the closer to the Golden Gate, the better). Further south, Capitola Pier, Santa Cruz, and Monterey Wharf are good spots to get your winter dabs. When the dabs are running, tide and time of day do not seem to matter much. However, several of my sources suggest that the best tide for dabbing is a mellow, incoming one—around dawn or dusk.

---

35 Sand dabs are as San Francisco as sourdough bread.

EAT THEM UP, YUM

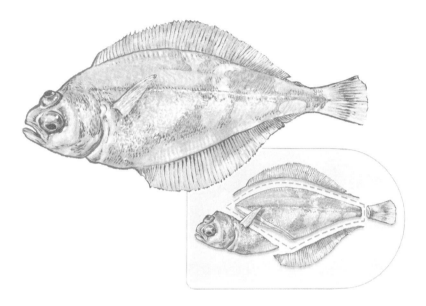

As far as prep goes, cleaning a sand dab is about as easy as it gets. Just follow the dotted lines (see diagram) for "pan-ready" sand dabs. If you cut exactly as pictured, the meat will lift right off the bone after you cook it. If you leave the fins intact, the meat will not lift easily off the bone and eating the dab will be a bony, unhappy experience. Sand dab meat is extremely delicate and subtle and requires a hot skillet and a sensitive touch. In my humble opinion, there is no better eating fish in our area. And again, until you've caught your own dabs, or eaten someone else's hook-and-line-caught ones, you won't really understand what you've been missing.

Yuck

The strange, white, tick-like things crawling around in your sand dabs' gills are parasitic isopods distantly related to the pillbugs (aka "roley-poleys") found under logs and in backyards throughout North America. These isopods are harmless to humans and actually make for a good surfperch bait if you can get over the yuck factor of handling them. Anecdotally speaking, whereas these critters are commonly found in sand dabs throughout our waters, the sand dabs caught inside SF Bay are particularly infested with them.

SURFPERCH

"There is much more pleasure in hunting the hare, than in eating her."

Izaak Walton, *The Compleat Angler,* 1653

The surfperch family took up approximately one-third of the first draft of this book. It was the first section I wrote and I poured a truly absurd amount of detail into it.[1] But ultimately, despite my high opinion of these noble creatures, it was hard to justify such a grandiose expenditure of words on a family of fish that has such … mediocre culinary properties (there, I said it). Especially in a coastal foraging book.

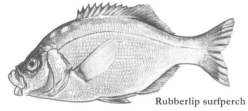

Rubberlip surfperch

Now, before all the ardent surfperch hunters out there start sending me indignant letters, this is not to say that the inherent mushiness of perch flesh can't be overcome, embraced, or at least mitigated to some extent.[2] But for those of us who see deep-frying as a form of cheating and who do not have the patience to soak their fish in lime juice for three days, or who aren't overly excited about the prospects of inner-city rubberlip sashimi (given surfperches'

---

1 By the way, I am forgoing the whole "sea perch" versus "surfperch" nonsense in favor of the more common and less confusing "surfperch." If I have offended any "rainbow sea perch" or "striped sea perch" fans, I extend my deepest apologies.

2 Of these, the best option is to embrace the mush and go the "Asian steamed fish on a plate with green onions and ginger" route. See *Rockfish* in chapter 4 for how to correctly steam a whole fish.

high toxicity ranking on all the health department lists), it's kind of difficult to justify treating them with the type of veneration due a littleneck clam, a surf smelt, or a thresher shark. Nevertheless, surfperches are very popularly eaten in California. In my experience the best way to go is to fillet them and

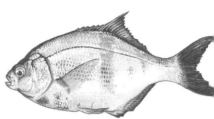

Pile surfperch

turn them into ceviche (for ceviche instructions, see *Monkeyface Prickleback* in chapter 4). You can also slice them up, "candle" them, and go the sushi route (see Swim Bladder 3). But honestly, eating surfperch sashimi has always struck me as an act of desperation. One I don't tend to engage in unless there's absolutely nothing else available.

Now, if I may be permitted to backpedal here, for many years I have extolled the virtues of fishing for pogies, pileys, rubberlips, and redtails. Given

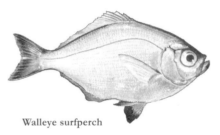

Walleye surfperch

a free afternoon to go do any type of fishing for an hour, especially in an urban setting, I would probably go perch fishing. All the members of the surfperch clan, from the lowly shiner to the exquisite redtail, are fun to catch, relatively easy to find (compared to, say, a white sea-

bass or a sturgeon), and aesthetically appealing to look at. How shall I describe the bizarre pleasure of hooking a lunker pogey while fishing in a concrete drain (the urban California version of ice fishing)? Or the first charge of a pile surfperch on ultralight tackle? Or the graceful, athletic flight of a big barred surfperch in the trough? In haiku, that's how:

Haiku #3,962

Surfperch take the grub.
Surge, shimmer, sparkle, and dance !
Crown prince of our shores.

In short, no person who calls him or herself an angler (or who is at least inclined to think he or she might become one) could fail to enjoy the nuanced fight of the redtail or the dogged perseverance of the striped perch. No person with any sort of appreciation for the miracle and beauty of fish could fail to marvel at the delicate patterns of the rainbow surfperch (*Hypsurus caryi*) or the Dada-esque absurdity of the rubberlip. That is why, despite the culinary failings of this family, I am taking the time to give them a proper sendup, albeit a shorter one than originally intended.

THE WHERE, WHEN, AND HOW

Surfperch are one of the mainstays of beach, bank, and pier fishing in our area. Here are the most commonly caught species, and the habitats where one is most likely to find them.

Structure Perches

(These surfperches are generally associated with rocks, kelp, wrecks, pier pilings, and other underwater structures.)

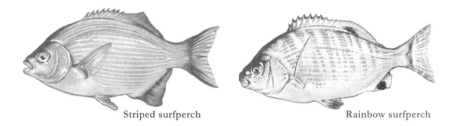

Striped surfperch   Rainbow surfperch

Black surfperch, *Embiotoca jacksoni*

Rubberlip surfperch, *Rhacochilus toxotes*

Pile surfperch, *Rhacochilus vacca*

Striped surfperch, *Embiotoca lateralis*

Rainbow surfperch, *Hypsurus caryi*

Calico surfperch, *Amphistichus koelzi*

Redtail surfperch, *Amphistichus rhodoterus*

Dwarf surfperch, *Micrometrus minimus*

Shiner surfperch, *Cymatogaster aggregata*

Sandy Beach Perches

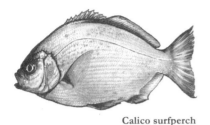

Calico surfperch

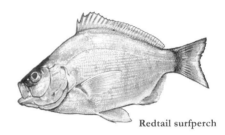

Redtail surfperch

Barred surfperch, *Amphistichus argenteus*

Redtail surfperch, *Amphistichus rhodoterus*

Calico surfperch, *Amphistichus koelzi*

Walleye surfperch, *Hyperprosopon argenteum*

Silver surfperch, *Hyperprosopon ellipticum*

Striped surfperch, *Embiotoca lateralis*

As you can see, there is some overlap here. Occasionally one will catch a big (lonely) rubberlip cruising over a sandy beach with no structure anywhere, or a barred surfperch by an outcropping of rocks. But these fish seem to be the rare eccentrics, and the above list should prove to be a useful, if somewhat generalized, guideline.

Tide and Month

Speaking to a quorum of seasoned surfperch fishers on the subject of the best tides and times of year for surfperch made one thing clear: they all had their own opinions (fancy that). Some folks swore they got their fish on incoming tides, some on the outgo. Some tend to fish for surfperch in the summer, some fish only from August through March, when DFW regulations (inside SF Bay) permit. So here's what I've been able to extrapolate from this varied information: although surfperches are caught year round, and it is certainly possible to have banner days in the summer and spring, the most productive seasons for catching surfperches on local beaches appear to be fall and

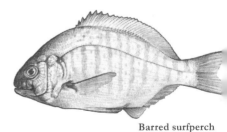

Barred surfperch

winter. This also seems to be the case with "structure surfperches" on rocky reefs and kelp beds and inside harbors and bays. As far as tide and time of day are concerned, I defer to surf-perch.net mastermind Mark Won, who has converted his catch logs into a really cool (and appealingly OCD) series of pie charts and graphs. From these he speculates that although surfperch may bite on any given tide, "in general, the statistics seem to suggest the [most productive time is the] one-to-two hour period prior to and following each high and low tide." Mark is the first person to point out the imperfections in his data sets, but fishermen are accustomed to going on word of mouth and tips from friends, and as far as that stuff goes, Mark's information is golden.

PERCH RIGS

Most surfperch in our area are caught by bait soakers and grubbers using either Hi-Los or Carolina rigs (see Swim Bladder 1). Obviously, the details—like length of leader, type of sinker, and bait—will vary based on ocean conditions, bottom type, and the species being targeted.

Artificials

As far as artificials go, a motor oil–colored grub on a Carolina rig is de rigeur for perch fishers, though it seems to me that pieces of Berkeley "gulp" worm work better—either on a Carolina rig or on a two-way. If you are fishing around pilings or other structures, a small Kastmaster jigged off the bottom works like a charm for black perch, rubberlips, and striped perch.[3] In turbid water, trout spinners work well in the surf, though to my knowledge I'm the only one using them.

Fly fishing for perch, especially in the surf, has become very popular in recent years. The flies of choice are bead-heads, but various shrimp and sand crab imitations also work well. However, before you break out the waders and six-weight fly rod, be forewarned: if shooting heads and stripping baskets ain't your thing, this is going to be a frustrating experience for you. (See "On the Beach" in Swim Bladder 1 for more on fly fishing in the surf.)

---

3   The surest way to guarantee success while perch fishing inside local bays is to "chum the water" by scraping mussel- and barnacle-encrusted pilings with an oar, clam rake, or long stick. Whether a local warden wants to cite you for a "waste of resource" violation while you are thus engaged is up to his or her discretion.

Bait

These are the most commonly used baits for the surfperches listed above, in descending order of effectiveness:

1. Live grass shrimp (most effective)

2. Sand worms, pile worms, and blood worms

3. Sand crabs, especially soft-shelled sand crabs (for perches of the sandy beach)

4. Ghost shrimp

5. Pieces of mussel

6. Pieces of market shrimp (fresh or frozen)

7. Small shore crabs (for pile perch and rubberlips)

8. Small pieces of squid (least effective)

Most of these are discussed at length in the *Invertebaits* section in chapter 3.

PARTING SHOTS

Some things to keep in mind: surfperch give birth to live young. You may want to consider this if you catch one that is abnormally fat—especially if you're fishing in the spring or summer. There's nothing more depressing than cutting open a surfperch to find twenty perfectly formed little perch babies that would have happily spawned a few hours or days later had mama been returned to the water.

Surfperch may live anywhere from two years (shiner) to ten years (rubber-lip). For some reason most of them are listed by the ever-cumbersomely titled Office of Environmental Health Hazard Assessment (OEHHA) as fish to be avoided. Which seems strange, as they are low on the food chain and not particularly long lived.

And with these two pages, I make my editors happy and trim twenty pages from this self-proclaimed "Sea Forager's" guide. If I sound a tad bitter, it's because I am. Nothing makes me happier than writing endless descriptions and haikus and anecdotes about species that no one in their right mind gives a damn about. Like, for instance, spotfin surfperch.[4] In any case, they are allowing me to keep my "pogey" chapter (see below) for posterity's sake.

---

4 Apologies to Michael Westphal.

EAT THEM UP, YUM

Below, please find one of the more common ways to prepare surfperch.

Mark G's Barred Perch à la Med School Chinois

Mark says:

> Lately, we've been eating barred. We are poor right now (she's in med school, my work is slow), so sometimes I'll go to the beach and grub a couple up. I clean and scale 'em, give 'em a couple slashes, and dredge them in chickpea flour (this is the secret). I fry them and the big ones I finish off by steaming with soy sauce and/or lemon juice. I serve them with a dipping/drizzling sauce of soy sauce, lemon juice, and shaved ginger, and top with cilantro and/ or green onions. Kinda Chinese style. Usually served with stir-fried veggies or hot-and-sour cabbage. To deal with the soft texture, I clean them and then salt them generously before putting them on crushed ice in a colander. They get firmer after a day or two and stay fresh with the ice. Just remember to rinse them before frying or they will be too salty.

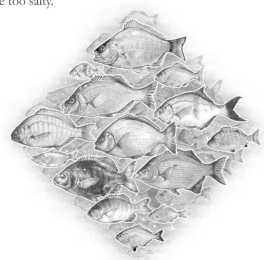

BLACK PERCH (POGEY)
Embiotoca jacksoni

OF POGIES AND MEN

Weighing in at a maximum of three pounds and measuring no more than sixteen inches, the black perch—colloquially, the *pogey*—is the welterweight champion of the Embiotocidae, the surfperch equivalent of a young Manny Pacquiao.[5]

By which I mean to say: this is one tenacious little bugger. Last year, as I kayaked around the old pilings off China Basin (near the Giants ballpark), a black perch bit my offering of grass shrimp and pulled me upwind for about twenty feet before wearing itself out.[6] The fish probably weighed two pounds. Think about that for a minute. If this same fish were, say, marlin-sized, it could tow an aircraft carrier upwind against an ebbing tide. Imagine all the idiots who'd be out there herniating themselves, trying to prove their inner Hemingways against the black perch.

---

5 Manny is the perfect anthropomorphization of a black perch. However, his recent bid for political office suggests he seeks cleaner waters, and is not content with the rugged and more humble shores of his youth. Black perch have no highfalutin airs and are perfectly happy to live out their lives in whatever waters (polluted or otherwise) they happen to be born into.

6 Kayak fishing in SF Bay for pogies is one of this author's favorite pastimes. A kayak allows a fisher to get into serious pogey habitat, areas into which no sane person would ever take a motorized vessel: in and around broken pilings, underneath abandoned piers, amidst jagged rocks, in two feet of water, et cetera.

Not Tom Stienstra

With all due respect to the Marcel Proust of outdoor writers, the typical pogey hunter represents a sort of anti-Stienstra outdoorsmanship.[7] Floppy sun hats, manicured beards, and multi-pocket fishing vests are unknown to him. Thugism, old-English font neck tattoos, and/or what might charitably be called a "rough around the edges" look are the dominant trends for pogey hunters.

In other words, this is a fish of the urban wasteland. The kind of place where old pier pilings of bygone years abound, where rusted train tracks end abruptly at the shore, where sewage outflow tubes dump their toxic loads into the water. In SF Bay, think of the Third Street Bridge, Hunter's Point, the Agua Vista pilings, Islais Channel (aka "Shit Creek"), the Point Richmond Ferry Pier, Point Molate, the Fruitvale Drawbridge, the Fifth Avenue Marina, PG&E outflow tubes—these are the kinds of places where the black perch seems to thrive.[8] Of course, they can also be found close to shore in some compara-

---

7 Stienstra is Proustian at least by sheer volume of words—in his various columns, guidebooks, radio shows, et cetera.

8 Make a list of all the coastal spots where you are most likely to get mugged while fishing and there you will almost certainly find robust populations of black perch.

tively pristine waters: Monterey Bay, Santa Cruz, Capitola, Pillar Point, Pedro Point, Agate Beach, Tomales Bay, Sonoma Coast, Humboldt Bay, et cetera. The truth is, black perch like structure. Whether that structure happens to consist of broken chunks of rebar-infused concrete, dilapidated pier pilings, kelp beds, or ancient outcroppings of sedimentary rock does not seem to matter. For this reason, pogey hunters who hug the shoreline, fishing close to the rocks and pilings, tend to catch more fish than those who misguidedly cast their bait far from shore.

DISTINGUISHING MARKS

Did I mention that this is a beautiful little fish? Well, I'm mentioning it now. Note the iridescent blue flecks set against that dark brown-black background. Really, there is no other perch that looks much like a pogey. But just in case you need some more help identifying it, here are its three other salient anatomical features:

1. The upper lip tends to have a mustachioed appearance.

2. There is a distinctive white-blue line at the base of the anal fin.

3. It has comparatively large scales under and below the pectoral.

It is surprising to me how many anglers mistake this fish for the larger and more surreal-looking rubberlip perch. Anecdotally speaking, about half the people I've encountered in the field will refer to their bucketload of black perch as "rubberlips."

TO EAT OR NOT TO EAT

Many Bay Area anglers will attest to the culinary advantages of this species. These people invariably deep-fry their pogies. Taking this into account, I should point out that old sneakers, doormats, and used paper towels are reportedly quite good, or at least palatable, when deep-fried. However, having steamed, broiled, and sautéed this fish myself, I must sadly admit that, like its other cousins in the perch family, there is nothing about the pogey's meat that warrants recommendation.[9]

That said, those two prized trophy species, tarpon and bonefish, aren't very good eating either. In light of this, I've been pushing for a new common name for the black perch: *pygmy sewer tarpon*. As of this writing it hasn't caught on.

---

9 That said, black perch, like several other perch species, make for a decent sashimi. And, I should add, the sashimi we recently made from a stringer of bay perch (pogies and piles) turned out equal to or perhaps even better than the previous month's redtail/barred sashimi.

56

I remember reading somewhere that black perch otoliths have been found in Ohlone shell middens going back thousands of years. Hard to imagine any self-respecting Ohlone eating a black perch with all those salmon and sturgeon swimming around, but evidently they did. Who knows, maybe the pogies were reserved for unwanted guests, dogs, enemies, missionaries?

The black perch, like many small and medium species, is a favorite of the Huck Finn/Tom Sawyer/Pippi Longstocking set, what local fishing guru Keith Fraser famously calls "the shiner patrol" (see *Shiner Perch* in chapter 3). The most pogies I've ever seen in a single bucket were caught by a thirteen-year-old kid named Suleiman on the Emeryville Pier three years ago. He was using a hand line wrapped around a soda bottle, with live grass shrimp on a leaderless bait rig—the hooks were tied directly onto the main line with square knots. This was hardly the high-water mark of bait presentation (or was it?) but three other fishermen were standing within thirty feet of this kid catching nothing. He kept saying, "You gotta use your fingers." So I took his advice, hand-lined for a while, caught a nice-sized pogey, and seriously considered throwing away all my overpriced fishing gear. Moral of the story: pogies seem to favor anglers who use pop bottles and drop lines, especially if they're kids.

As for the term *pogey*, the Sea Forager Center for Shallow Water Linguistics assumes that it is a bastardization of *porgy*, a common perciform fish of the Atlantic coast otherwise known as a *scup* (from the Narraganset, *mishcuppauog*). Both are laterally flattened, deep-bodied fish that can be caught from shore or boat. Though, of the two, scups are much better eating.

BAIT

California is home to a wide variety of little, weird-looking, mud-loving, bottom-dwelling, so-called baitfish species and though they may not all be closely related, they tend to share one notable characteristic: complicated and slightly unconventional common names. It's as if the same eccentric biologist named them all. There's the cumbersomely titled Pacific staghorn sculpin, a tough little species that most of us know colloquially as a "bullhead," though it has nothing to do with the small catfish of the same name. Then there's the longjaw mudsucker, which sounds more like the insult you'd hurl at the deckhand who drops your forty-pound salmon at boatside than the name of a fish. Next is the plainfin midshipman, a talented toadfish, the Pavarotti of the sewers, also known as the Sausalito buzzerfish. I'm including the yellowfin goby in this group, despite its disappointingly humdrum appellation, because it has become the dominant mudsucker of our region.[1]

All of these species are top-quality live bait for larger fish like striped bass, lingcod, halibut, and sharks. "Top quality" in live bait essentially means they do two things:

1. Wriggle and dance when impaled on a hook.
2. Perform these tricks for a comparatively long time.

---

1   The Sea Forager Center for Arcane Cladistics and Taxonomy strongly suggests *Godzilla goby* in place of *yellowfin*. When one considers the potential havoc wreaked by invasive species on our native fish populations, the name seems entirely justifiable.

PACIFIC STAGHORN SCULPIN (BULLHEAD)

Leptocottus armatus

In the pantheon of small baitfish that don't seem to mind being skewered through the face with a live-bait hook and dragged around the bottom of the ocean all day, the Pacific staghorn sculpin, aka the bullhead, has no peer. Make no mistake about it, this is the Jake LaMotta of baitfish—able to stoically endure all forms of abuse. Bullheads are good bait for striped bass, though they aren't quite as good as mudsuckers. Part of the problem is those "staghorn" opercular spines. I mean, what ocean-going piscivore wants to deal with those? (Stripers, I guess.)

THE WHERE, WHEN, AND HOW

Bullheads are typically caught by hook and line in bays, lagoons, harbors, sloughs, canals, and the like. They seem to like mud, but can be found in rocky or sandy areas as well. The bait does not matter. Nor does the tide. They can also be very effectively trapped with a minnow or crawdad trap. Bait your trap with a perforated can of cat food, as you would for mudsuckers (see *Longjaw Mudsucker* and *Yellowfin Goby* below). In any case, the longer the bait soaks, the more likely you are to catch them.

TO EAT OR NOT TO EAT

Bullhead Soup

Having handled my fair share of slimy fishes over the years, I can say with confidence that a bucket of Pacific staghorn sculpins can generate a quantity of slime to equal or surpass anything.[2] This was not evident to me until I met someone particularly adept at catching them. She fished every weekday morn-

---

2   Hagfish not included.

ing on the downtown piers in SF, and her name was Mrs. Lee—but her street name was, you guessed it, "Bullhead Soup." Halibut bite red hot? Jacksmelt leaping from the water? Bass everywhere? No matter, Bullhead Soup had her sights set a tad lower than everyone else. She used two long, skinny spinning rods, each with a pair of Sabiki rigs clipped end to end, every hook painstakingly baited with little pre-cut, pea-sized chunks of store-bought shrimp. Outfitted this way, she could catch a third of a bucket of bullheads (roughly twelve pounds) in one day of fishing. Really think about this for a minute. That's a lot of bullheads.

PLAINFIN MIDSHIPMAN
Porichthys notatus

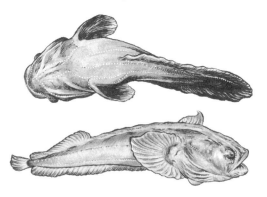

A TALENTED FISH

Of all the strangely named baitfish that live in the mudflats, sloughs, and backwaters of our area, the plainfin midshipman is the star of the lot.

THE WHERE, WHEN, AND HOW

Midshipmen spawn in the spring and summer months, coming inshore from depths of over one thousand feet and establishing themselves intertidally (typically in muddy bays), under rocks. The best time to find them is in June and July.

TWO TYPES

Typically, when you turn over a rock in the intertidal zone, the midshipman you encounter is the Type I male, doing his matrimonial duty: guarding the eggs and keeping them clean.

What's a Type I male? Good question. Evidently there are two types of male midshipmen. Here's what Milton Love, author of that seminal classic, *Certainly More Than You Want to Know about the Fishes of the Pacific Coast: A Postmodern Experience* wrote to me in an email correspondence in 2010: "I assume you are aware that there are two kinds of males? Type I guards nests, lures females, and hums. Type II does not guard nests, cannot hum, and waits for a female to lay the eggs, dashes in and sprays sperm on the eggs, and dashes away. The type II male has humongous testes compared to type I."

Did I mention that Type II males, the ones with the large testes, like to impersonate females? Well, they do. The idea here is that by pretending to be female they can finagle their way into a Type I's lair, and when he isn't looking, give any unfertilized eggs a good spritzing of milt.

A RARE BIRD

In short, this fish is a rare bird. It's odd enough that it has photophores (small light-producing "spots"), but the midshipman also has a few other quirks. First, and most famously, it hums (or, as Love points out, some of them hum, some of them grunt, and some growl). In fact, the humming of midshipmen caused quite a furor in Sausalito a few years ago when houseboat owners could not figure out what that terrible buzzing was: evidently, the buzzing of midshipmen in May and June is so loud the citizenry of Sausalito has a hard time getting to sleep at night. Tsk tsk, poor little Sausalitans.

As if having the voice of a Tuvan throat singer, the uncanny ability to survive at a ridiculous range of depths, and a body covered with lightbulbs were not enough superpowers for one small fish, plainfins come armed with razorsharp gill spines. Again, this is something I've learned about through experience. The lesson was this: if a midshipman ever slips through my hands again, I will not attempt to catch her as she falls. One day, having dropped a midshipman, I tried to catch her before she hit the water and swam away. Wouldn't you know, the edge of her gill cover jabbed me beneath my fingernail?

Of course, shoving anything under your fingernail is going to be unpleasant, but a mucous-covered, razor-sharp gill spine is I think among the more unpleasant of things. Suffice to say, the rest of that particular day was like Inquisition torture camp and I now handle midshipmen with caution, reverence, and the type of respect that a dangerous opponent can inspire in a baitman.

Buttons

If you are wondering how the midshipman got its unwieldy name, wonder no more. The photophores on the belly evidently reminded someone of the buttons on a naval cadet's jacket.

Livin' the Life o' Riley

When used as bait, midshipmen stay alive almost as long as bullheads—the measure of toughness in a fish. They squirm, writhe, dance, and hum. If you're lucky, and they've been eating a luminescent planktonic arthropod known as *Vargula hilgendorfii*, they may even light up for you—though this will only camouflage them to a halibut looking up from below. In any case, given all these attractive qualities, it's a wonder so few people actually use midshipmen for bait. Perhaps I'm not the only person out there who has sentimental feelings for this species.

When you consider that the Type I male spends several months working his butt off, nurturing the eggs, keeping them clean and free of debris, while the Type II male and the female are off living the life of Riley, it's kind of hard to justify flipping the stone over, abducting the midshipman, and destroying the nest. And when you think that these creatures travel from the depths of the ocean (more than one thousand vertical feet), having survived all the hazards California might offer a tiny fish—whales, lingcod, cormorants, sea lions, sharks, skates, rays, sturgeon, striped bass, drag nets, toxic waste, you name it—only to be ripped from a muddy hole near SFO when the finish line (spawning, that is) was so near ... why, it could almost make a baitman cry.

Almost—but not quite. The thought of the monster fish I'm going to catch using live midshipmen for bait usually squashes my sentimental tendencies. You see them squirming and writhing at the end of your line and you're the one that gets hooked. There is simply no way to ignore the lunker potential of a big midshipman. And considering how aggressively the local predatory fish tend to hit a squirmy live bait, it's hard, when you find yourself looking at that vivacious little midshipman, to think he's not going to catch you a big halibut, or a striper, or a ling.

THE DEATH SONG OF THE TOAD FISHES

I'm not sure why, but leopard sharks really like midshipmen, and for a halibut (or anything else) to take your offering of one, it's going to have to get in line behind every leopard shark inhabiting the spot where you're fishing. My last time out on my kayak I caught about half a dozen sharks on a single plainfin. He couldn't seem to stay in the water for five minutes before a leopard shark would slam him and start dragging me into the shipping lanes—and they seemed to like him better dead and chewed than alive and squirming. As anyone who kayak fishes can confirm, however fun leopard sharks are to fight, they are a royal pain in the arse to unhook. Especially the big ones, on a windy day, with a strong outgoing tide, on a ten-foot sit-on-top kayak. But the strange thing was, everywhere I went that day, it was the same. Along rocky shoreline. Under the piers. Out in the open water: leopard shark after leopard shark after leopard shark. It was as if they were following me.

They were.

After fishing for two hours with that one midshipman, I pulled in my live-bait bucket (which usually trails behind me on a rope as I drift) and decided to swap out my wildly popular shredded baitfish for a new live one.

I placed the bucket on the kayak, cleaned the grim remnants of the first midshipman off my hook, and suddenly noticed that the boat was buzzing.

The midshipmen, their nests destroyed, their eggs uprooted, their lives about to be forfeit to the uncaring jaws of a sluggish bottom dweller, were singing. I held the bucket to my ear. What was this song? How often had they sung it? In the depths of the sea? In the polluted sluices of Stege Marsh? In the yuppie flats of

Tiburon? Was it their national anthem? Their rembetika? Their blues? After a few moments I realized what I was listening to ... It was the death song of the toadfishes.

I sat there for a while, staring out at the container ships, listening to this melancholy, monotonal death song, feeling, I suppose, not unlike the Grinch staring down on Whoville before his Yuletide transformation. After a few gut-wrenching moments, my calloused fisherman's heart swollen to thrice its usual size, I paddled to shore and dumped the remaining midshipmen back into the turbid waters from whence they came.

I have little doubt that a sizable school of leopard sharks had been following my kayak all day. It was not a bait bucket, but a leopard shark dinner bell that I'd been dragging behind me.

I guess every fisherman has his weakness, his figurative kryptonite. But how can one justify destroying their nests and skewering their remarkable little bodies, just to waste them on leopard sharks? If you find that they're great for halibut or lings, stripers or seabass ... maybe ... but leopard sharks? Thanks, I'll stick to squid.[3] Honestly, I think the problem here is that I know too much about these little buggers to use them for bait. And now, with any luck, so do you.

Haiku #214

Plainfin Midshipmen,
most talented of fishes !
Why not leave them be ?

3   I'm sure someone out there is going to point out the remarkable life story of the squid, but alas, every species on our fair planet is remarkable. One has to pick and choose, I suppose. For me, the midshipman gets a pass. For you it might be octopus or anchovies or, I don't know ... fat innkeeper worms. In any case, the important thing is to remember they're all remarkable. Even the ones we use for bait.

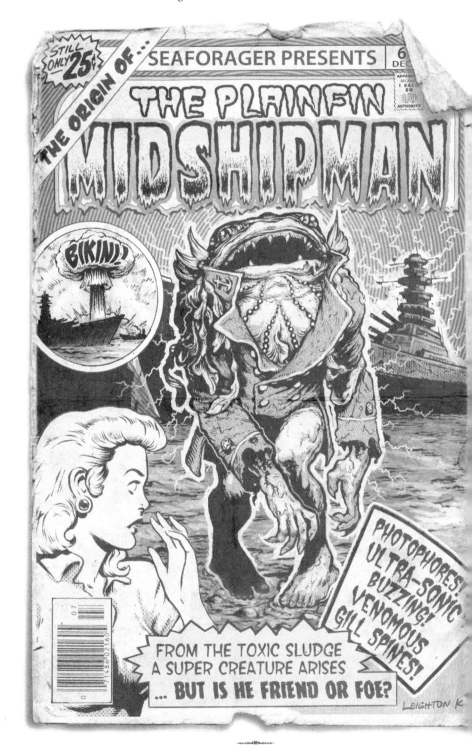

I have long believed that, given its unique talents and special abilities, a mutated, gamma-ray-infected plainfin midshipman might make for a perfect toxic avenger-type superhero: humming its enemies into submission, stabbing them with its nasty spikes, blowing them away with its photophores.

Once again, it looks like Leighton and I are on the same page.

MUDSUCKERS

At this point I think it's safe to say I have a thing for small, ugly fish that live in the mud. Maybe I'm alone in this. Maybe not. Either way, I'm not sure what this obsession portends, what it means about me on a deeper level. But there is no denying it. There is also no denying that mudsuckers are an excellent live bait for the local trophy fish of the everyman: striped bass. But since the term *mudsucker* gets bandied about way too much for my taste, let's get something straight: mudsuckers are gobies.[4] And the two most prevalent gobies in the California bait trade are the native longjaw and the invasive yellowfin.

LONGJAW MUDSUCKER
Gillichthys mirabilis

Ten years ago, while reading through the California DFG regulations, I noticed "longjaw mudsucker" listed among those fish for which there was no numerical bag limit. As this was a unique and slightly pejorative-sounding name for a species of fish, I thought I'd ask around and see if anyone knew where I might catch a few. Everyone I spoke to seemed to agree that longjaws were magnificently abundant and that I'd have no trouble at all finding them.[5] All

---

4 The gobies, or Gobiidae, are one of the most successful fish families currently inhabiting the planet, with over two thousand species and three hundred genuses.

5 In my experience, when someone tells you a fish species is "easy to catch," the opposite always proves to be true.

I had to do, I was informed, was place a few crawdad traps in muddy areas around the bay.

A week of setting traps in muddy areas yielded about two dozen bullheads and a mixed bag of invasive gobies: shimofuri, chameleon, and yellowfin.[6] But no longjaws. This failed mudsucker-trapping adventure went on for another month. Finally an old commercial grass shrimp dragger told me that there were thousands of longjaws in the salt evaporation ponds near the Dumbarton Bridge. So I went down there, snuck across the freeway in the dead of night, and threw a few traps into the salt ponds. Lo and behold, the next day the traps were loaded with longjaws—tiny ones, but longjaws nonetheless.

THE WHERE, WHEN, AND HOW
See *Yellowfin Goby* below.

HISTORY

The longjaw mudsucker was once the king of live baitfish. Caught by trap and shrimp trawl, this versatile goby was *the* go-to freshwater black bass bait in California for many years. As it turns out, in addition to their tolerance for high salinity, longjaws are able to live in fresh water, but cannot reproduce in it, so they're the perfect live bait for freshwater sport fish because they can't escape and colonize freshwater systems.[7]

CANNED MUDSUCKERS?

I should point out that, as unappetizing as the word *mudsucker* may be, they're not bad eating! Gobies are quite popular in Eastern Europe and Asia. Go to any Russian market worth its smoked sturgeon and you should be able to locate a can or two of *bychki* (pronounced "beech-key").[8] (There appear to be thriving trawl fisheries for grass gobies and monkey gobies in both the Sea of Azov and the Black Sea.) Having tasted both species (ours and theirs), I have to say that they're similar enough in flavor to make me wonder why no one in California eats them—not even transplanted Russians.

---

6   I set traps in Stege Marsh, Brisbane Lagoon, and Heron's Head Park.

7   Longjaws were introduced to the Salton Sea in 1950.

8   Frozen and canned gobies are also available in many Asian markets.

YELLOWFIN GOBY
Acanthogobius flavimanus

The Godzilla of invasive gobies, yellowfins are now the most frequently encountered so-called mudsucker at local baitshops. Like everything else in this section, they wriggle when impaled and last a long time on the hook. Given a choice between using one of our native species or this invasive one, we recommend the yellowfin—your native mudsucker will appreciate it.

Bait

TROPHY GOBY

Strange as it might seem to most California anglers, yellowfin gobies are a very popularly pursued (and eaten) sport fish in Japan, where they go by the name *haze*.[9] Party boats target them. Throw netters bang 'em from shore. Specially designed, hollowed-out bamboo cane poles are used to jig them off the bottom. The fish are generally filleted (something that most Western piscivores would never consider doing with a fish so small) and deep-fried.

Having eaten these guys several times, I can't really decide how I feel about all this. They're definitely not terrible. But are they worth all the hullabaloo? Maybe they taste better in Tokyo Bay. But here they have a faint effervescence of mud in their meat. Maybe I got a bad batch of 'em. In any case, if I'm going to eat a small fish I'd rather stick with something from cleaner waters, like a surf smelt or a sardine or a mackerel.

THE WHERE, WHEN, AND HOW

Both of the gobies mentioned above seem to like canals, sloughs, muddy back bays, lagoons, and even drainage culverts. Yellowfins are easier to find than longjaws and work just as well as a live bait. A can of cat food with a few holes tapped in it, placed inside a crawfish or minnow trap, is the traditional way to get mudsuckers (and bullheads), but two ace mudsucker catchers of my

---

9 According to fishingfury.com, an old Japanese adage says that "a saltwater fisherman's life begins with goby fishing, and ends with goby fishing."

acquaintance (both under the age of fourteen) swear by wadded-up slices of Wonder Bread. I have no idea whether mudsuckers swim into the traps at high, low, ebb, or flood. In many of the areas where I've trapped them, there is zero water at low tide, so I imagine they are entering the trap fairly close to the top of the tide—or at least closer to the top than to the bottom.

LIZARDFISH
Synodus lucioceps

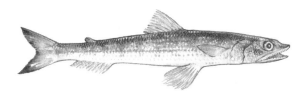

"Can you eat those things?" and "Can you catch anything with lizardfish?" These are the two questions one hears in 99 percent of all conversations between fisherpersons concerning lizardfish. As to the first, inasmuch as any compilation of organic molecules is more or less edible, one can eat lizardfish. I realize there are a few folks out there, bearded men in tight pants mostly, who want to find that strange, off-the-chart species, that "trash" fish that no one *truly* appreciates, the figurative spare rib de mer, lobbed for centuries onto the plantation owner's garbage heap and three generations later turned into the official state dinner of Brazil, the diamond in the rough, the blank canvas to display their culinary genius ... Well, if that's you, here's a news flash: you can have the lizardfish all to yourself.

I tried eating this animal whole once. It had more bones in it than Colma, California. I tried filleting it. The meat ... It tasted like ... like ... words escape me ... like ... *hair*.

Mmmmm.

However, as far as fishing and foraging goes, a live lizardfish is a good bait for any of the big predator species that might be aggressive enough to slam one. Which in our area generally means lingcod and halibut.

THE WHERE, WHEN, AND HOW

Lizardfish are typically caught by baitfish rig. I have noticed that they seem to travel under larger schools of smelt, sardines, or mackerel. Sometimes the ocean seems absolutely loaded with them. In our area, they are seldom caught north of Half Moon Bay, and the best spots for those who want to target them (hey, to each his own) would be all the piers and jetties between there and Monterey.

TRASH FISH

I've noticed over the years a strange tendency for otherwise reasonable fishermen to bonk their "catch and release" lizardfish on the head before throwing them back. "They're trash fish," I remember one of these Neanderthals once offering by way of an explanation. It's my deepest hope that at some point in our continued existence on this planet, the term *trash fish* will go out of use and be buried in the official graveyard of abhorred concepts.[10] Let us take a moment and reflect on the miracle of lizardfishness and think seriously about what a happy animal it must be. I would imagine there isn't a game fish in the entire Pacific Ocean that isn't jealous of the lowly lizard. Being loved by human piscivores doesn't always work out well for ocean fishes—just ask a bluefin tuna. So how can anyone blame the lizardfish for having evolved into a creature that is undesirable to humans? Wouldn't it be far more progressive or enlightened of us to simply throw our lizards back alive? Your local game fish will appreciate it. And the "waste of fish" violation still applies to fish many folks consider trash species.

Bait

TOPSMELT
Atherinops affinis

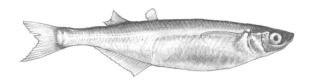

I was going to include topsmelt in the jacksmelt section but the renowned kayak fisherman, salmon slayer, shark attack survivor, and all-around bon vivant Nico "Sharky" Von Broembsen suggested I give the topsmelt its own paragraph—and who am I to thwart such an excellent salty seadog as Von Broembsen? Suffice to say, topsmelt are considered by many anglers (especially the kayak contingent) to be an excellent live bait for halibut. First, they

---

10 Located in the shadow of Shasta Dam.

stay alive a long time when hooked—as long as a shiner but not as long as a bullhead. Second, unlike their close relative the jacksmelt, an adult "toppie" is perfectly sized to fit into a hungry halibut's mouth.

THE WHERE, WHEN, AND HOW

Topsmelt live to at least seven years, and can attain lengths of up to fourteen inches, though most are considerably smaller than that. To find topsmelt, try fishing the mouths of channels that lead to the lagoons, canals, and harbors inside coastal bays. There are a lot of these fish in Monterey Bay, Santa Cruz Harbor, Pillar Point, SF Bay, Bodega Bay, Humboldt Bay, et cetera. Once you locate them, usually near the top of the tide, a Hawaiian casting net is key, though a small or medium-sized Sabiki rig baited with small pieces of shrimp will work well too.

SHINER PERCH
Cymatogaster aggregata

The shiner is a dwarf species and as such offers very little for human consumption in its own right.[11] According to the OEHHA website, shiners retain toxins in high amounts. I'm not sure why this would be, since they live for only a few years and do not occupy a high rung on the food chain, but studies have shown them to be surprisingly high in bad stuff.[12] So don't eat them.

Of course I am not mentioning shiner perch here for their gastronomic potential, but because they make an excellent live bait for California halibut. Often, in early halibut season, before the live anchovy receivers open in North-

---

11   That said, there are those who appreciate them. Back in my days as a fisheries observer, I frequently encountered elderly Cantonese-speaking anglers on the downtown SF shoreline who doggedly fished for and ate all their shiners.

12   One wonders if perhaps the data for this study were skewed or compromised in some way. Like, for instance, with all the larger game fishes only fillets were sampled. Were the shiners filleted? (And who got that job, I wonder—the intern?) Or were they sampled whole? Obviously, a whole fish, with guts included, will have a higher toxin count than a filleted fish. Right? Or maybe for some weird reason shiners are just really high in toxins.

ern California and before the large swarms of baitfish move into shallow water, an angler's only option for quality live halibut bait is the shiner perch. Shiners can be caught by means of bait rig or casting net (see Swim Bladder 1) to the tune of twenty per day (regardless of location, season, or whether the angler has already reached her limit of other perches). Go to virtually any saltwater pier in California and jig a Sabiki loaded with tiny chunks of shrimp near the pilings and you have a good chance of catching shiners. It should be noted that they favor the top of high tide, which can be problematic because halibut do too. Many halibut anglers will go out a day early to jig up shiners for the following day's halibut trip—and keep them alive overnight by means of a battery-operated air pump clipped to the side of the bucket.

Noble Suffering

I would be doing a great disservice to the noble suffering of this creature were I to fail to mention its endurance. There are few baitfish species that will stay alive and wriggling on a hook longer than a shiner—a dubious distinction for this courageous little fish, but one that no doubt has led to its popularity as a halibut bait. Only the toughest of all fishes, the Pacific staghorn sculpin and the plainfin midshipman, can hold a candle to the shiner perch as far as durability is concerned.[13]

There is a fairly robust live-bait fishery for shiners in SF Bay, especially early in the spring. Most of the shiners brought to the local baitshops are caught by means of traps. But there is at least one shiner fisherman who uses baitfish rigs and actually catches a significant number of his shiners by hook and line.

Recreationally, this species is very popular with the elementary school set, what Bay Area fishing guru Keith Fraser has dubbed the "shiner patrol." This is due to the fact that shiners, when they are around, are very easy to catch. Ludmilla Orensen, a ten-year-old shiner fishergirl from San Francisco, interviewed on Pier 7 one rare sunny day in July 2013, informed the author that the reason she likes shiners so much is because they are "so cute and pretty." This statement makes me want to weep every time I think about it.[14] It seems there should be a better fate for a creature so cute and pretty (yet also tough and resilient) than to be skewered through the face by a live-bait hook and dragged around the bottom of the ocean for hours at a time. But alas, that is what we fisherfolk tend to do with shiners. If karma is indeed a valid concept,

---

13 The infamous semi-Boer Nico "Sharky" Von Broembsen protests that "the topsmelt is the toughest of them all, mate. And is way better for doormat hali than shiner perch."

14 Yes, the author weeps for baitfish.

we will return in future lives to experience what it's like to be a noble creature, poorly used.

THE WHERE, WHEN, AND HOW

Shiners are typically caught in bays, near pilings or over muddy bottoms. It's best to target shiners at or near high tide. A "Sabiki rig" baited with little pieces of shrimp is the norm. A hawg shiner is anything over four inches.

Shiners are sometimes confused with dwarf perch *(Micrometrus minimus)* and spotfin perch *(Hyperprosopon anale)*. Rather than try to describe the anatomical differences between the three, I'll direct you to take a close look at Leighton's pictures here. Note the alternating yellow and grey-black bars of the shiner, as well as the distinctive spots of the spotfin and dark mottling of the dwarf. From a legal standpoint, it might be a good idea to be able to tell them apart—lest the angler get stuck with a citation for going over limit. Or for catching what looked like shiners, when all the other perch were off limits in SF Bay.

I'm not sure if there is anything to this, but several live-bait experts inform me that the dwarf perch makes for a lousy baitfish.

Spotfin perch

Dwarf perch

INVERTEBAITS

SAND CRAB (PACIFIC MOLE CRAB)
Emerita analoga

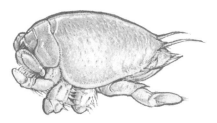

The biggest striped bass I've ever seen in the Pacific Ocean was a twenty-nine pounder caught off Ocean Beach. On that other coast of the American continent, a twenty-nine-pound striper is big but not stupendous. On the Pacific coast, a twenty-nine-pound striper is a jaw-dropping fish (although several stalwart—and ancient—SF Bay bass anglers might disagree). The fact that the gentleman who landed this fish induced it to bite on a soft-shelled sand crab (Pacific mole crab) is kind of cool. All these macho men out there hurling huge bombers and hair-raisers and sixteen-dollar pencil poppers into the sea ad nauseam, and the lunkers are working the surf line for the lowly sand crab.

Normally, bait casters catch their sand crabs with the wire-rimmed minnow nets available for about six bucks at local tackle stores. These "minnow nets" are actually designed for scooping anchovies out of the live wells on boats. I bought one of these things and found it completely unsatisfactory for the job. The mesh was too small, it filled with sand with every dunk, and the wire was not strong enough to withstand the backwash of even the most moderate waves. If you shop around, you can find more heavily reinforced bait nets out there—the skimpy ones are worthless.

Having destroyed my sand crab net and spent the remainder of the day on my hands and knees digging them out of the sand, I returned to the former Sea Forager headquarters in San Francisco and sketched out the ultimate sand crab–capturing device. It would involve heavy-gauge steel mesh and scraps of rebar. I took my rough blueprints to the metal shop of my good friend Jerry Bonafair, who builds fretless banjos and fireplace dampers in Oakland. Even as I was explaining the concept to him, he started gathering up mesh and scraps of steel from the discard bin at his shop. An hour later the job was

Bait

done. Jerry stood back and looked at the beast he had created. It looked like Satan's French fry basket. "What are we gonna call this thing?" Jerry asked.

I looked at my massive, forty-pound sand crab killing device and said, "You can call it what you will, but I'm calling it … Death Hammer."

When Death Hammer hits the beach, baitmen look at me the same way average Joes once looked at DiMaggio when he showed up at Toots Shor's with Marilyn Monroe at his side. Sometimes, in their jealousy, they can be critical:

"Hey man," they have been known to yell, "is your sand crab trap big enough?!"

These detractors can keep on using their dinky little anchovy nets—and keep buying new ones every two months. The beauty of Death Hammer (maybe I should call her Marilyn?) is that she will never die. I guarantee that Death Hammer will be dealing death to sand crabs for the next four thousand years, barring a nuclear holocaust. Plans are already in the works to find a successor, someone worthy of this mighty war tool after my demise.

But really, the nicest aspect of Death Hammer is that, with her wide (yet legal) girth, she gives me a much higher likelihood of encountering soft-shelled sand crabs than the guy with the puny little wire-rimmed net. Anyone who uses the diminutive *Emerita analoga* for bait can tell you that there is a marked difference between the regular hard-shelled variety and its soft-shelled phase. I understand why this is (it's the same reason soft-shelled crabs cost twice as much as regular ones in fancy New York restaurants), though I do not understand how in the hell a surfperch or a striped bass can immediately tell a softshell from a hardshell when it hits the water.

I have stood next to skilled perchmen casting regular hardshell sand crabs without a bite for two hours, stepped into the foam, skewered one of my soft-shells, plunked it out ten feet from the other guy, and banged three perch in rapid succession. Very weird. Like the difference between a live hellgrammite and a dead worm in fresh water.

That said, Marilyn Death Hammer is admittedly a little too heavy (but then again so am I). There is no denying that it is a major pain in the arse to drag her more than twenty feet. That's the maximum distance I can walk (struggle, wrestle, grapple) with her before my back starts to go out. Then there are the pieces of razor-sharp frayed wire from the ends of the mesh basket, which have a tendency to puncture my shins and my waders . . . And worse yet, no matter how much marine finish I put on her, that cold-rolled steel begins to rust the moment it comes in contact with salt water and so she invariably dyes my hands bright orange with rust. Oh yeah, and there is no way to adequately store her . . . And, as I mentioned, beach fishermen laugh at me and mock me (in both English and Tagalog) as I heave her to the shores … And then of course, sometimes, no matter how big your trap is, there just aren't any decent-sized sand crabs.

I was just wondering if any of you readers might like to buy the miserable contraption. I'm selling cheap: twenty bucks and the Death Hammer is yours!

Really, catching sand crabs is a clean and wholesome activity—and with Marilyn Death Hammer, a challenging cardiovascular workout for the whole family!

(Twenty bucks, c'mon! Twenty bucks and you too can be the orange-palmed, bloody-legged, laughingstock of your local beach.)

The Where, When, and How

Sand crabs hang out in the trough but move around the beach as the tides change. Personally I prefer the ebb, just after high water. If you are desperate out there and don't have a net, just dig down randomly in the sand and you will probably find a few. They seem to prefer fine-grained sandy beaches. But I've caught thousands of them on gravelly beaches too. If they're small, double or triple them up on the hook.

A Hi-Lo or Carolina rig is the way to go with sand crabs (see Swim Bladder 1). Someone out there is probably wondering: why not just use an A-frame net? Well, most A-frames exceed the legal diameter of thirty-six inches for a sand crab trap.

To Eat or Not to Eat

Sand crabs are edible but they not only pose a PSP risk (see "Health Risks" in chapter 5) but also host a nasty acanthocephalan (a big word that means "thorny-headed") parasite linked to high mortality in sea otter populations, *Pro ilicollis* sp. I would think that this same parasite might cause a human mam-mal significant problems, burrowing as it does *through* the stomach wall of otters and into their intestines, but I have never heard of humans getting sick from eating sand crabs. Then again, this may simply be because so few people eat them. I have no idea if cooking minimizes the risk.

There isn't a whole lot of meat in sand crabs. In fact, eating them is kind of similar to chewing on fried shrimp heads. But they do have a distinctly crabby, shrimp-like flavor. One thing you might want to consider is de-pooping them by turning them on their backs, carefully unfurling the abdomen (or "tail") and pulling it out. Usually when you do this, their digestive tract comes out in one piece with the "tail."

I've cooked these little buggers exactly twice. The first time I kept looking at my lovely fishwife and asking, "They're pretty good, aren't they?" To which she would continue chewing and give a sort of pained semi-nod of near assent. The second time, we added bacon fat and enjoyed them. Or maybe *enjoyed* is a bit strong. Certainly, chomping on their little helmet-like bodies belongs to a different category of enjoyment than say, eating a broiled and stuffed surf smelt, slurping a bowl of cockle chowder, or scarfing a pound of pickled herring fillets. Nevertheless, if you really *(really)* like chewing on shrimp heads and absolutely must dine on sand crabs, de-poop them and stir-fry them whole with olive oil, garlic, mushrooms, and whatever else floats your boat.

PILE WORM (CLAM WORM)
Alitta succinea/Alitta brandti

FEELING DIRTY INSIDE

Gathering sand crabs in the roiling surf, jigging shiner perch off the pilings of a local pier, and chucking a casting net onto a school of topsmelt all strike me as relatively clean and wholesome activities. But gathering pile worms in the Brisbane mudflats, or the shadow of Candlestick Park, or the back end of the Richmond Harbor, or … or … really *anywhere*, strikes me as a uniquely depressing enterprise. Maybe it's the putrid gunk under the rocks, maybe it's the scrawny quality of the worms, maybe it's the depressed neighborhoods surrounding the areas where worms seem to abound, or the shattered glass in the streets where I park. Maybe it's the fact that I am the only person with both incisors in San Francisco who engages in this putrid mudflat hunting. Or maybe it's the fear that I will run into a former fisheries department colleague or ex-girlfriend (can't decide which would be worse) while thus engaged. What kind of self-respecting adult wakes up at 5 A.M. and turns stones in the toxic shallows of Hunter's Point on his day off? For what purpose? To what end?

Well, pile/clam worms are an excellent bait for surfperch, rockfish, monkeyface pricklebacks, starry founder, sturgeon, and striped bass. *Alitta succinea* are an invasive species. The invasive nereids only exist in California because bait slingers routinely dump the contents of their partially used bait boxes into the water after fishing. Nevertheless, invasive or not, a wild-caught Candlestick pile worm is to its store-bought counterpart what a native Sierra rainbow trout is to a farm-raised pellet eater. Look at a store-bought pile worm: big as a monkeyface, sure, but the sucker is *subdued!* Compare these soft, plump, well-refrigerated annelids to the vicious little bastards under the rocks at Candlestick Park, each fighting for its own exclusive chunk of dioxin-saturated mud. Skins tough as tires, parapodia undulating, chitinous teeth bared, ready to bite holes in a baitman's fingers.

I mean no disrespect to the imported pile worms of the bait world. Few creatures suffer so valiantly. Imagine the terrible transit of a pile worm across the great North American expanse. How many dark nights jammed into a cardboard box with only a few strands of eelgrass for cover? Who knows what thoughts and fears, what acts of sacrifice and heroism occur under these conditions? I have no doubt that pile worms have their champions, their martyrs, their folk tales and songs (all of these involving copious quantities of mucus). But by the time the poor creatures arrive in local bait shops they are, understandably, a tad subdued (that and overpriced). For me personally there are some things I am not willing to do. Paying a dollar per worm for twelve worms is one of them.

Happily for me I am willing to trudge through the sludge to get my own. If you are equally penurious when it comes to bait, read on.

THE WHERE, WHEN, AND HOW

Pile worms can be found on any tide marked "0.3" and lower in a tide book. The best areas for this are inside muddy bays. You're looking for rubble and rocks sitting on mud. In these kinds of dirty, back-bay areas, the last thing you want to do is cut yourself on a jagged piece of rebar or glass. So break out your nitrile gloves and clam rake, and use them to turn over large rocks (see Swim Bladder 5). If the worm is not visible beneath the rock, rake the mud a bit. Sometimes lunker worms are waiting just under the surface (and sometimes they're just too deep to be caught). Occasionally an avant-garde worm will cling to the bottom of a rock, so keep an eye out for that—and remember, the pile worm bites by everting its pharynx![15] Yuck.

15 *Evert* is a great word that doesn't get nearly enough play ... it means to turn inside out, as in "the everted pharynx of polychaete worms."

Sand Worm (Shimmy Worm)
Nephtys californiensis

Sand worms (aka shimmy worms) live on fine-grained sandy beaches of the open coast, while pile worms live under rocks in the muddy areas of bays.

The Where, When, and How

The happy solution to the drawbacks of digging mudflat worms in semi-toxic areas is digging sand worms instead. I have seen these creatures only on the San Mateo County beaches (Gazos Creek is a sort of mecca for worm hunters), Ocean Beach in San Francisco, and Stinson Beach in Marin County. The trick to finding this worm is in locating its distinctive track.

The challenge here, of course, is that this worm track is really, really subtle. It's why you always see worm hunters bent over, staring intently at the sand. Before I learned the Way of the Sand Worm, I assumed that the correct method for getting them was to randomly dig the sand about ten to twenty feet up from the low tideline on a low minus tide. That's what the worm hunters appeared to be doing from a distance. Actually, no wormer worth his stringer of redtails starts digging before he sees the telltale worm divot pictured at right. My most excellent Pinoy fishing gurus have a term for the type of wild man who walks up and starts digging indiscriminately for sand worms. They call this person a "farmer." As in, "that guy must be farming the beach for tomatoes because he sure as hell ain't catchin' any worms."

The sand worm is a super bait for any fish that frequents the surf—especially perch and striped bass. They are tough and lively and instill confidence in the bait soaker who uses them (half the battle). If you cast a nice-sized sand worm into the waves and fail to get a bite within thirty minutes, move to another spot: no self-respecting perch is inhabiting that stretch of shoreline.

FAT INNKEEPER WORM
Urechis unicinctus

In Korea, where they are commonly referred to as "penis fish," fat innkeeper worms are thought to have aphrodisiacal powers. Nature's Viagra, they call it. I actually tried eating one myself and I will say this for it: if projectile vomiting is sexy, then penis fish are a great stimulant for the male libido.

All joking aside, I totally get that some cultures look at monkeys and bats and worms and cockroaches as possible items for the day's lunch menu. I've been on Andrew Zimmern's show and read enough Anthony Bourdain to appreciate the overlooked and the undervalued. But I suspect that the "penis fish" phenomenon is not really about discovering hidden flavors and textures in an overlooked creature. More likely it's about eating something that bears an uncanny resemblance to the male procreative organ—for the dubious purpose of transferring sexual potency to the eater. Someone once remarked to me that the fat innkeeper was the most disgusting creature they'd ever seen. To which all I can say is: imagine what they think of us.

As a bait, innkeeper worms seem to work quite well for rockfish. I've seen innkeepers in the stomachs of bat rays, leopard sharks, and, strangely, cabezon.[16] Hooking them is somewhat challenging, as they sort of pop and ooze when skewered (nice, eh?).

One curious anatomical feature worth mentioning is the weird golden tusks or bristles of the innkeeper—two on the bow and a ring of them on the stern. Take a close look at either end and you'll see what I'm talking about.

THE WHEN, WHERE, AND HOW

Fat innkeeper worms are typically found by bait hunters pumping ghost shrimp in the mudflats, on minus tides. They build U-shaped burrows, the

---

16   I say "strangely" here because I associate cabezon with rocky areas and innkeepers with mudflats.

ends of which are usually two to three feet apart and capped by a distinctive sand chimney. Curiously, they don't seem to mind providing free room and board to other mudflat species (namely gobies, scale worms, and pea crabs). In human terms, they would get a five-star Yelp rating for these innkeeping services, providing immaculate rooms and free food to all guests.

GHOST SHRIMP
Neotrypaea californiensis

One of the best marine baits in California, the ghost shrimp is found in muddy back bays and harbors all over the state. They are best targeted on minus tides, but can be "pumped" on many moderate low tides as well. Look for a mudflat perforated with thousands of small holes, all about the diameter of a pencil. Sometimes these holes will have chimneys or mounds (often described as "volcanoes") around them, but often they will not. Most anglers think of ghost shrimp as a bait for sturgeon, and they are that, but they will work for almost anything else on the Pacific Coast, from rockfish to steelhead.[17]

Because their bodies are so soft, the primary challenge in using ghosts for bait is keeping them on the hook. For perch, use small ones or pieces of big ones. For everything else, you will want to bind them to the shank of the hook by using small rubber bands or the elastic thread sold in many bait shops—unless of course you're more inclined to feed fish than to catch them.

IMPRESS YOUR FRIENDS

Ghost shrimp are popularly featured in museums and aquariums on the West Coast, and like their neighbors the fat innkeeper worms, they don't seem to mind sharing their tunnels with other creatures: gobies, worms, and pea crabs.

The ghost shrimp's life is one of ceaseless toil.[18] As Ricketts and Calvin

---

17 Mikey "Caveman" Dvorak, commercial salmon fisherman and river guide par excellence, says: "I've caught at least twenty steelhead on ghost shrimp, and several were huge."

18 And a surprisingly long life it is. Ghost shrimp evidently live to the ripe old age of eighteen years.

put it in *Between Pacific Tides*, "they are obsessed with the Puritan philosophy of work." Much of this involves cleaning themselves and their burrows. The legs of the ghost shrimp have evolved to perform specific functions. The first two are for digging, the middle legs are for passing detritus backward, the back legs for propelling the ghost shrimp forward or back.

PUMP

In California we have a thriving cottage industry for ghost shrimp pumps. And, predictably, every pump maker insists that his or her pumps are the best. I have experimented with various designs, including the "threaded rod to rubber ball" type, but the one I am personally happiest with is my own take on the "Champion de la Banana" model pictured at right. (El Champion uses a rubber ball; I prefer rubber gasket material … See Swim Bladder 4 for instructions on making your own).

Bait

THE WHERE, WHEN, AND HOW

Pumping ghost shrimp should really be called "sucking" ghost shrimp, since what you're doing is sucking them out of their holes with a giant syringe. But I guess "pumping" sounds better. In any case, be advised that you typically have to put the pump into the hole three to six times in order to get to the shrimp. So don't make one or two pulls and walk away.

While conducting coastal tours, I am often asked if the tiny ghost shrimp that invariably get sucked out of the holes along with the larger ones will survive the ordeal. The answer is, probably not. Sadly, if ghost shrimp do not stay in close physical proximity to the walls of their burrows, they perish.[19]

This is a low-tide, mudflat activity. There are usually a lot of ghost shrimp inside coastal harbors and back bays. A clam gun (see Swim Bladder 5) will also work well for sucking them out of their holes.

---

19   The Sea Forager Center for Improved Vocabulary suggests you look up the word *thigmotaxis,* for there is nothing more positively thigmotactic than a ghost shrimp.

BLUE MUD SHRIMP
Upogebia pugettensis

News flash: blue mud shrimp are in trouble. Their West Coast populations have been in free fall since the early 1990s due to the sudden appearance of a highly parasitic invasive isopod *(Orthione griffenis)* that lodges in their gills, sucks their blood, and prevents them from reproducing. There have actually been several recent attempts to list blue mud shrimp under the Endangered Species Act, but none of these have gained much traction. Protecting a species from human depredation or habitat destruction is one thing; protecting it from a tiny invasive parasite to which it has no natural defense is next to impossible.

It took me years to figure out how to catch these guys[20] and then poof! I started reading about the very real possibility of their imminent extinction and I felt too guilty to take them. If there was ever a holy grail of bait gathering, it involved the pursuit and capture of this elusive and highly effective bait species. Imagine a ghost shrimp that actually stays on the hook (and squirms) without rubber thread. That's the blue mud shrimp.

THE WHERE, WHEN, AND HOW

Perhaps someday they'll rebound. Miracles can happen. Should that occur, gathering blue muds is similar to gathering ghost shrimp, except that it is best done on very low minus tides, all the way out at the extreme edge of the tideline. I've also collected a few while turning rocks in the muddy intertidal zone in SF Bay. And remember, as the name suggests, they seem to like mud more than sand or sandy mud. I should also add that many locations that would seem to offer perfect habitat do not hold any blue mud shrimp at all. Whether this is due to the ravages of parasitic isopods or to the finickiness of blue mud shrimp about what they're looking for in a housing complex is anybody's guess. The only blue mud shrimp for sale in California bait shops are caught in Oregon and shipped

---

20   This is a bit of a stretch. I didn't really figure it out. I simply found a couple of locations that have a lot of them. And those locations are only reachable during very low minus tides. If I haven't made this clear: these creatures are really, really difficult to find.

down. The main recipient of this supply is Loch Lomond Bait and Tackle, in San Rafael, the headquarters of Bay Area legend and baitmaster Keith Fraser.

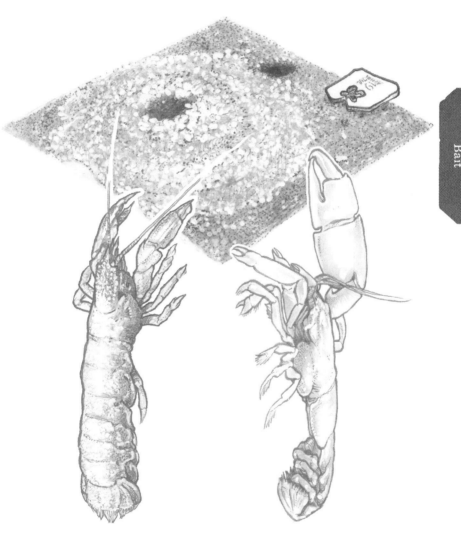

The
Mainstream

The fish in this chapter are the ones that seem to generate the most attention. The ones with websites and chat boards and millions of fans. The ones that inspire people to go out and spend a lot of money on gear, boats, hotel rooms, charter services, et cetera. So that's where the designation "mainstream" came from. I couldn't really figure out one term that encompassed them all, and I've always found "game fish" to be strangely off-putting and inadequate. In any case, I've spent most of my adult life as a tuba player in an avant-garde band that makes its own instruments and plays on street corners... so I tend, naturally, to distrust the mainstream and the hype it generates. Nevertheless, in California our so-called mainstream fishes are beautiful, magnificent, and worthy of all the attention they get. Here's a little more.

KING SALMON
Oncorhynchus tshawytscha

And Poseidon looked out upon the earth and had his first genuinely friendly thought in several eons. "Wow," he said, "I, Poseidon, Earth Shaker, brother of Zeus, master of the seven seas, lord of the swell and the wave and the seaborne tempest, will perform an uncharacteristic act of charity." At this he cleared his throat and waved his trident for emphasis. "In appreciation for the kindnesses rendered unto me by a comely mortal who has shared my clammy chambers, I will now design a perfect fish, a fish to nourish and make human beings happy. It will be bright as silver but happily speckled and somehow reminiscent of … let's see … what's the most beautiful of all things? *The rainbow*. Yeah, that's right. I can do this. No problem. I'm Poseidon. This fish is going to be so beautiful, many people will go insane over it, dedicate their lives to it, pray to it, make their livings off it, subsist off it, and follow it to remote areas of the globe. Ha ha! In fact, *whole cultures will do this*. I'll make the meat … hmmm … what color do human beings really appreciate in their meats? How about … pinkish red? Or occasionally, deep, dark red. And sometimes even *ivory white* … for the few who prefer white meat to red. Because *why not*. I am, after all, Poseidon."

And having thought all this, Poseidon leaned back on his trident and hammered out the details of the thing …

"What else? How can I *really* do this right?

"I know! I'll make this fish fully accessible to people who are not fated to live in close proximity to my wonderful oceans. Let any of the simple river gods resist me in this if they have the audacity … but I think they will appreciate the rich, deep-ocean nutrients my perfect fish will bring inland. And I'll make sure it isn't particularly hungry when it enters their pitiful streams and rivers, so it doesn't deeply impact their juvenile fish populations as it swims to its spawning grounds.

"What else? I'll sugarcoat this … I'll make sure this fish lives a fast life and has a natural tendency toward abundance. I'll make sure it doesn't bioaccumulate toxins the way tunas and other predators do … In fact, I'll jam its meat with all kinds of nutrients and omega-3s and I'll make it among the healthiest, most delicious things a human being can eat—and especially well suited to the flavors of smoke and grill. I'll even make its life cycle reasonably predictable so that, in the future, if they want to, they can re-create its spawning behavior in an artificial setting. And lastly, I'll make it a smart fish (as fish go) and a strong fighter so that lowly mortals will enjoy the challenge of pursuing it. And it will be worthy of their tall tales and songs. And it will be like unto a god to them. Yea, even the gods will revere this fish as one of the great miracles of the world."

And with one more wave of his mighty trident, Poseidon (and ten million years of evolution) created salmon (king, Coho, and the rest, each with its nuances and peculiarities). And he looked upon his creation and he wept, for it was so beautiful. Then, gesturing toward a distant estuary on the western coast of a great continent, he said, tellingly, "I, Poseidon, Earth Shaker, shore pounder, master of the oceans, have made this perfect thing. Now all you humans have to do *is not screw it up*."

REASONABLE ECOSYSTEMS

… and yet sometimes that seems to be what we are bound and determined to do. The thing to remember here is that salmon need fresh water and there's a limited supply of it in California. It doesn't really matter how effective our hatchery system is or how well regulated the sport and commercial fisheries are if there isn't enough water in the rivers for the salmon to safely reach their spawning grounds, and for young recruits to get back out to the ocean. As anyone who's seen the film *Chinatown* (or opened a newspaper) can attest, the question of who gets the water (and when) is a highly charged political and social issue in California—with the fishing public (commercial and recreational) typically on one side and the agriculture industry on the other.

In 2008 and 2009, when DFW closed the salmon season statewide because of terrible returns and abysmal jack counts on the Sacramento, things looked impossibly bleak. Then, two decent years of rain, a good offshore upwelling, and a more reasonable water allotment policy combined to give us three epic salmon seasons in a row. This should serve as a reminder that the bulk of our sport- and commercial-caught salmon are products of the state-run hatchery system. In order to maintain this system, the rivers do not need to be perfect; they just need to be *reasonable*.

HATCHERY PROS AND CONS

And what about our hatchery system? There are eight major king salmon hatcheries in California. These hatcheries were put in place to mitigate the problems caused by dams. The idea was to place hatcheries below the dams, and thereby provide artificial spawning locations for fish that would formerly have traveled further upstream. Today the bulk of sport- and commercial-caught salmon in California were born in hatcheries. Advocates of this state-managed system tend to downplay the genetic difference between hatchery fish and wild ones. They also point out that the salmon hatchery system, for all its faults, has been in place for sixty years, and has managed to sustain important (and lucrative) sport and commercial fisheries—albeit with drastic boom and bust cycles.

Adversaries claim that hatcheries favor fish that succeed *in hatcheries*—not in the wild. They also warn that hatchery fish (which the more vociferous among them refer to as "clones"[1]) compete with out-migrating juveniles and degrade

---

1 This pejorative term stems from the idea that hatchery fish, which do not mate naturally but instead have their eggs and milt squeezed out of them by hatchery workers into one common centrifuge (thereby skipping the last steps of their evolution-perfected life cycle), lack the complicated genetic variation of wild spawners. Studies have shown that wild spawning populations may do better than hatchery-spawned fish in ocean waters, and may be less susceptible to the drastic boom and bust cycles that appear to be the trend with hatchery fish.

the wild gene pool. To the rhetorical question "Well, what can you do?" the hatchery adversaries propose four basic solutions:

1. Put the hatcheries in harbors or at the mouths of rivers, to decrease the likelihood of stray hatchery fish breeding with wild fish further upstream.

2. Take out the dams, close the hatcheries (or some of them), and restore salmon access to their former spawning grounds.

3. Tag *all* hatchery fish and clip their adipose fins (currently only 25 percent of hatchery salmon are clipped and tagged) so that wild and hatchery populations can be easily differentiated.

4. Create a brood stock genetically distinct from wild fish and selected for traits (especially timing of migrations) that will make them unlikely to spawn in natural conditions.[2]

To those who argue "if it ain't broke don't fix it," one might point to the mercurial boom and bust cycles and the overall salmon declines in the past century as evidence that the system is, indeed, broken. Or, conversely, one might argue that the current system is good enough, providing jobs, food, and great fishing opportunities for California's citizenry. Whether you're pro, con, or undecided, it's probably a good idea to understand the dilemma, so you can choose sides intelligently.

SUSTAINABILITY (THE "S" WORD)

Even the most hardcore salmon activists would probably admit (under torture) that fishing is of secondary importance to water usage in discussions about the recent decline of salmon stocks.[3] Our sport and commercial fisheries are closely watched and fiercely regulated. If you are concerned about going out and legally killing a salmon, don't be. Your tax dollars paid for the hatchery that most likely raised that fish, and it would be absurd for you not to benefit from it. At the same time, just because you caught a couple of thirty-pound hawgs on the *Wacky Jacky*, don't assume that everything in Salmon Nation is peachy keen.[4] Stay abreast of salmon-related issues and figure out where you stand. An educated and involved public is fundamental to a wise management strategy.

---

2 Drop everything and read Jacob Katz and Peter Moyle, "Have Our Salmon and Eat Them Too: Re-thinking Central Valley Salmon Hatcheries," on California WaterBlog, http://californiawaterblog.com/2012/02/29/have-our-salmon-and-eat-them-too-re-thinking-salmon-hatcheries-in-the-central-valley/, accessed November 18, 2015.

3 Though one could make the case that by specifically targeting (and catching) large, mature salmon, sport and commercial fishermen thereby remove the fish that are most likely to succeed in spawning.

4 The *Wacky Jacky* is a well-known (and loved) party boat in SF Bay.

Keep in mind that because a salmon's life cycle is predictable, and because the lion's share of salmon spawn in hatcheries, population estimates are much more accurate for salmon than they are for many other fish species. Rest assured that if the populations are considered to be in crisis, the fishery will be shut down and you won't have a chance to catch them unsustainably.

IMPORTANCE

Salmon is the most important fish, if not the most important *thing,* to the original people of the West Coast of the United States. The Yurok word for salmon, *nepu*, translates as "that which is eaten." In other words, salmon is a synonym for *food.* To this day some Native Americans subsist on salmon, much as they have for the past seventeen thousand years. And of all the meats to subsist on, salmon is probably the best—it's so high in all the good stuff and low in all the bad.

The sport and commercial salmon fisheries of California are also deeply important to the descendants of later immigrants to this coast (like me, for instance). A fisher-kid's "first salmon" is still one of those rites of passage that retains its significance in the face of all the schlock rituals spat at us by the great maw of civilization. And the opening of salmon season, as blustery, windblown, and disappointing as it tends to be, is a time of great spiritual importance to thousands of salty sea dawgs, whether they want to admit it or not.

THE WHERE, WHEN, AND HOW

Ocean salmon season in California begins in the spring and ends in the fall. Most recreational salmon are caught on party boats or by anglers in small skiffs, trolling anchovy popsicles (or white hoochies and watermelon apex lures) behind flashers and/or dog whistle sinkers (see Swim Bladder 1 for rig/lure diagrams and a reasonable translation of all this).[5]

As far as catching them in the ocean is concerned, you've got two choices: trolling and mooching. Since the advent of circle hooks, mooching has fallen out of favor. But mooching is kinder on gas, and, in my own humble opinion, a lot more fun in terms of hooking and fighting the fish.

For catching salmon from shore (from pier or river bank), there are similarly two options: mooch or lure. Mooching rigs for pier fishing are a separate and distinct species from the mooching rigs used on boats (see Swim Bladder 1).

---

5 Dog whistles, also called "quick release" sinkers, do just that. Try to imagine for a moment how much lead there must be on the floor of the Pacific Ocean in heavily trolled areas like Duxbury Reef.

Once salmon are in spawning mode, the most popular artificials are the big, ugly, wiggly jobs that flutter, dance, and shake in the face of a salmon, thereby pissing it off and inducing it to bite. These lures are typically used in the fall by the folks fishing on the banks of salmon rivers or stretches of SF Bay or the Delta where salmon pass within casting distance of shore.

Salmon can be caught during the day on big tides, small tides, and in-between tides. Mornings and evenings are always the preferred times to have your hook in the water but salmon will bite all day. That said, early morning around the changing of the tides is your optimal time.

As of this writing it is illegal to take Coho salmon *(Oncorhynchus kisutch)* in California, so it's probably a good idea to be able to identify them. (The California Fish and Wildlife department has a helpful flyer to assist you in this.) The main difference between the two species is the gums. But it isn't just a matter of grey gums versus black gums, as some anglers seem to think. In Chinook salmon, the gums are uniformly black. In Cohos, the outside of the gums may be black but the area at the base of the teeth (from whence they erupt) is usually grey or greyish-white. Often Coho are caught higher in the water column than Chinook and the way they fight can be distinctive—with lots of leaps and typically a more frenetic escape plan.

Flossing

Salmon are exceptionally vulnerable as they enter the mouths of rivers at high tide. Flossing (also called snagging or lining) is a popular method of catching them at these times. This technique (involving a very long leader and a cork or bead) is frowned upon by many anglers, especially those with a strong (or moderate or infinitesimal) sense of ethics, but seems to be tolerated by law enforcement as long as the fish is hooked *in close proximity* to its mouth.[6] While "lining" these fish may be a reasonable method in harbors and bays where "net pen" fish are not traveling upstream to spawn,[7] it sure seems unsporting in a coastal river, where salmon simply *have* to swim upstream and the relatively shallow depths and confined space make them easy targets. Ultimately it comes down to that basic question posed at the beginning of this book: what kind of citizen do you want to be?

---

6 In flossing, the salmon, with its mouth open or partially open, swims upstream into the leader. Its forward motion, the current, and the wielder of the rod then do the rest, "flossing" the line steadily through its mouth until the outside of the jaw gets "snagged" by the hook at the end of the leader.

7 "Net pen" fish are hatchery fish released from net pens far from our main spawning rivers. The sole purpose of these fish is to provide fishing opportunities for the public. If they aren't taken by anglers they are going to die, unspawned and unutilized by anyone other than rock crabs and seagulls.

LIFE CYCLE

The life cycle of a salmon has been described in an infinite array of confusing diagrams and charts. Rarely before, in a fishing book, has it been described in verse. I hope I'm not starting a trend:

> The salmon starts in gravel beds,
> The eggs are laid upon the redd,
> The male swoops in to fertilize,
> And soon the eggs develop eyes.
>
> In several months the alevin,
> With yolk sac in between its fins,
> Leaves the gravel, develops bars
> And soon transforms from fry to parr.
>
> The smolt phase is the next you see
> (Smolts are aged from one to three).
> At some point in this phase they smell
> The ocean, and head out there to dwell,
>
> For one year, two, or up to five,
> They roam and try to stay alive
> Avoiding sharks and whales and seals,
> And folks with nets and rods and reels.
>
> And then (great mystery of this earth!)
> They seek the river of their birth,
> And finding it, they make the nest
> And from this point ... you know the rest.

The Mainstream

EAT THEM UP, YUM

Remember that carcasses, scraps, and collars—portions of the fish that are often (unbelievably) thrown away—can make for excellent meals...Here's one my lovely fishwife Camilla Lombard uses for salmon collars and carcasses.[8]

---

8 To get the meat out of the carcass without filling the soup with bones, lay the carcass on a flat surface and use a fork to scrape out the meat. This is also a good way to go when making ceviche.

The Fishwife's Coconut Salmon Soup

(Can be made by Fish Husband while Fishwife relaxes after a long day at work.)

3 stalks celery, chopped
1 onion, diced
1 Tbsp chopped ginger
1 Tbsp cooking oil
2 sweet potatoes, peeled and diced
1 box (3 cups) chicken broth
1 can coconut milk
3 Tbsp soy sauce
1 salmon carcass, including attached meat
2 Tbsp chopped Thai basil
2 Tbsp chopped cilantro
½ teaspoon Sriracha hot sauce, or more if desired

Sauté celery, onion, and ginger in cooking oil for 5 minutes. Add sweet potatoes, sauté for 5 minutes more, then add broth, coconut milk, and soy sauce. When the sweet potatoes are cooked, add the salmon carcass and simmer until cooked through. Turn off the heat, remove any remaing bones, throw in chopped herbs, ladle into bowls, and add Sriracha to taste. Easy and delicious!

And for those more experimental types, my friend, employee, and fishing buddy Brian Haller offers the following tidbit on the French cooking technique known as sous vide... which is considered by many to be the absolute perfect way to cook fish. Here's Brian:

Sous-vide cooking (French for "under vacuum") is a revolutionary cooking technology. Invented in France in the 1970s, but popularized in the early 2000s alongside the molecular gastronomy movement, the method works by submerging food in vacuum-sealed bags into a temperature-controlled water bath. The cooking process is utterly simple. Step 1: The temperature of the water bath is set to the desired final temperature of the food. Step 2: The vacuum-sealed food is submerged and allowed to slowly reach the same temperature as the surrounding water bath. For salmon, cooking times are usually between twenty and forty minutes, but the variable of time is never critical.

Since the food can only ever get as hot as its surrounding water bath, perfect cooking is guaranteed!

Sous-vide cooking is very accessible to the home cook but it does require some specialized equipment. You will need an immersion circulator: a device that regulates the temperature of the water bath. It both precisely heats the water and circulates it around the pot, ensuring an even temperature throughout the bath. At the time of this writing, budget immersion circulators sell for around two hundred dollars. A vacuum-sealing machine is helpful but not entirely necessary. A sufficient vacuum can be created by carefully removing as much air as possible from food placed in an ordinary plastic freezer bag.

Simple Sous-Vide Seared Salmon

Heat a water bath to 122F.

Place a seasoned, skin-on salmon fillet in a plastic bag and vacuum seal with a machine or by hand.

Cook the salmon fillet sous-vide for 40 minutes (or until it reaches 122F).

Remove the salmon fillet and dry its skin with paper towels.

Quickly sear the skin side in a hot, well-oiled pan.

Remove and serve skin-side up.

STRIPED BASS
Morone saxatilis

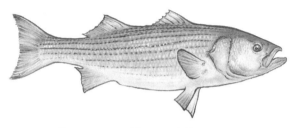

IMPRESS YOUR FRIENDS

Brought to California from New Jersey in the late nineteenth century, "stripers" are the most notorious invasive fish species on the West Coast. Many purists (along with farmers and water managers) like to blame the striped bass for declines in salmon and steelhead stocks. Meanwhile, striper fanatics point out that the bass have been here since 1879 and for most of that time have coexisted reasonably well with salmon.[9] In fact, the beginning of the precipitous declines in salmon stocks, they say, coincided with a marked drop-off in striper populations—which even a striper hater would have to admit might possibly have something to do with water management. Anyone who has caught a Delta striper and found its belly teeming with salmon smolts is not going to deny that stripers eat salmon. The question is, how much does that predation really impact salmon populations? UC biologist Peter Moyle points out that removal of striped bass from the Delta could have unforeseen consequences. And that, although it is true that stripers prey on salmon, it is more likely that the real culprit for declines in salmon stocks is water diversion.[10]

Striped bass spawn from April to June in brackish Delta water. Teenage fish hang out in estuarine environments for a while, then migrate to the ocean as adults. The biggest striped bass ever landed on hook and line was an 81.88-pound super lunker caught in Long Island Sound. The California hook-and-line record stands at a more modest (but still chest-thumping) 67.5 pounds.

HEALTH CONCERNS

No mincing of words: striped bass are mercury magnets. This should come as a surprise to no one. Translated into terrestrial terms, eating a striper is

9 Over much of that time there were thriving commercial fisheries for both species.
10 See Peter Moyle and William Bennett, "Striped Bass Control: The Cure Worse Than the Disease?" on California WaterBlog, californiawaterblog.com/2011/01/31/striped-bass-control-the-cure-worse-than-the-disease/, accessed November 18, 2015.

roughly equivalent to eating a leopard. It's a species that is very high on the food chain and, unlike a salmon, lives plenty long enough to bio-accumulate toxins (stripers can evidently live to about twenty years of age). Although they are often caught in the surf, bass really love the Sacramento Delta—which isn't the cleanest water in our area. In any case, regardless of whether you caught your striper on Stinson Beach or by the Rodeo oil refinery, follow the health restrictions. Women aged eighteen to forty-five and children under eighteen: no striped bass! Women over forty-five and men over seventeen: don't eat stripers more than twice per week.

THE HUNT

Wherever it occurs in California, the striped bass is really the great game fish of the everyman/everywoman. Let's face it, Jane and Joe Blow have no real chance of catching a sturgeon or a salmon from shore—not really. But they might just land a striper, by dumb luck, on their lunch breaks. A twenty-five pound hawg. A fish so beastly and awesome that Joe and Jane might just step away from the battle, even having lost it, and think a little more highly of themselves. It's a fish so unmistakably alpha—and yet sort of aesthetically dainty, with its neat rows of black stripes. Sort of reminiscent of the New York Yankees, sideways. A fish that lends itself to successful taxidermy, Christian glam bands, and two-fisted haymaker street fights outside Bukowski-type bars with blinking neon martini glasses lighting up the bloody glass shards in the street (I am describing a fight outside a bar in Crockett in 1999, when I watched a former fishing partner and salmon activist drubbed into the dirt by a striper fan who took offense at her totem animal being disparaged. I should add that hardcore striped bass enthusiasts [male or female] will punch you in the face if you say unsavory things about their favorite fish. This of course cannot be backed up by anything other than anecdotal data).

It's a fish that turns human beings into birds (perched with binoculars at Mussel Rock) and terns into spotter pilots. Turns mean-faced, leather-throated, whiskey-swilling salts into wide-eyed ten-year-old kids in a matter of 1.5 seconds—or as long as it takes to yell "Fish on!"

It's a great fish. Great in the *terrible* sense. Like Attila the Hun was great. The striped bass is the Lana Turner or Montgomery Clift of the great sexy mainstream game fishes of the Pacific Coast. Why Lana and Monty? Because they were both terrible beauties. Because they swam through some pretty dirty waters, consumed some questionable mudsuckers, and died proudly bearing the scars of their misadventures. But still, no matter how high in heavy metals (e.g., mercury, platinum), the striper remains one of the most beautiful game fish that ever swam the oceans of this or any other planet.

Where was I?

The striper is not quite worth its weight in salmon smolts... and yet, a more worthy adversary is hard to imagine. With polycyclic aromatic hydrocarbons and mercury to defy Hans Geiger. With fan clubs from San Quentin to Greenwich, Connecticut. With calendars and books and magazines devoted to it. Is the fetishization of this species as extreme as it is for salmon? Not on this coast. But still, it's a very important fish to a lot of people here.

The Where, When, and How

Striped bass season in our ocean waters runs from April through October, peaking around June and July. During this time stripers can be caught in the surf on all the local beaches from Santa Cruz to Point Reyes and from virtually every point inside SF Bay, from Alviso to the Carquinez Strait. But the Sacramento Delta remains the mecca for local bass anglers.

I fish for stripers in the surf, two hours before high tide and two hours after. That's me. Everybody has his or her own formula. Some people swear they catch all their bass on outgoing tides. Some only fish the last hours of the outgo. Bass will hit at any time, but for my money, it's that four-hour window around the top. The most popular bass lure in our area is the white hair-raiser–rubber grub combo. But top water lures can be equally effective, as are swim baits and spoons. Did I mention fly fishing in the surf? Stripers are the main beach-caught big game fish targeted by fly fishers in the Bay Area. And then, of course, there's bait. Stripers will hit anything from a pile worm to a sand crab to a bullhead to a frozen anchovy popsicle. Equal opportunity predators, these fish (see Swim Bladder 1 for more on rigs and bait).

Parting Thoughts

It seems like someone (usually a beleaguered state water manager, farmer, or salmon activist) is always proposing less restrictive regulations in an attempt to rid the waters of striped bass. But as of this writing, the minimum size is eighteen inches, and the daily bag limit is two.

One could make the case that killing striped bass is one of the more sustainable things a piscivore can do on the Pacific coast of North America. It's not just salmon smolts that stripers like to chomp. It's anything that can fit into their gaping mouths. But here's a question worth considering: at what point do we stop referring to something as an invasive species? Certainly, the striped bass has been here long enough to earn *some* native credit, hasn't it?

THE CHAMPION OF BRISBANE, CALIFORNIA

You've been sitting in a cubicle staring at a screen for two years, watching your life flash by you in the shadowless fluorescent lighting of your office. Down below, the bay sparkles in the summer sun. Today, just for the hell of it, you grabbed a rod out of the closet and brought it to work. You've got one lure, a slightly rusted red and white "daredevil" spoon you bought for large-mouth bass twenty years ago. At twelve noon you march downstairs with your rod and your bag lunch. Some idiot from the third floor makes a joke about you bringing a rod and reel to work. You sneer at him and continue out the door across the parking lot and stop by a bench along the shoreline. Weird how ten years ago you used to fish all the time—once a week at least. It's crazy how you just stopped doing that, considering how much you loved it at the time. Never once, in the two years since the company moved to Brisbane, have you thrown a line into the bay. You've thought about it though . . . every day. *Every single day.*

You tie the daredevil onto the line, no swivel, step onto a rock, click the bail, and fire your first cast in ten years. Not bad. The old Ugly Stik still has some spring. You look down in the water and wonder whether any self-respecting striped bass would hit a daredevil. A rusted, twenty-four-year-old daredevil at that. But still, it sparkles fairly well in the water and the wobble sure seems enticing. You pull it out and cast again.

After eleven casts, you start feeling relaxed in a way you haven't felt in months. You're breathing easier. You start noticing things: how clear the water is, the heron wading along the rocks, the big flock of cormorants to the immediate north—what are they chasing? You keep casting. You start to get into the rhythm of it. You look at your watch. Oh man. Fifteen minutes till the meeting. Better pack it up and get back inside. That elevator at lunch time can take up to seven minutes to get to the twelfth floor. One more cast, just one more.

You reel in the spoon, flick it back, and fire it straight out into the bay. Best cast of the day. You start to reel. Something surges in the water behind your daredevil. You hear yourself say, "No way!" You keep reeling. "Is that a..."

Wham!

A twenty-five-pound hawg bass has just slammed your rusty daredevil. You no longer care about the meeting. The fish is surging like you've snagged a Jet Ski. Your heart is pumping like it hasn't in years. You follow the fish along the rocks. How can this be happening? You slip briefly and your left leg slides into the bay up to your knee. You don't give a damn. To hell with these punk-ass designer shoes. You hold the rod tip up.

The fish surges again. You start wondering about the strength of the line—it's been on this reel for what, ten years? Now the fish lightens up. You're gaining on it, reeling it toward you. Are you too soon? Is it going to surge again? Does the drag even work on this old reel? The last (and only) striped bass you ever hooked (in Sag Harbor on your friend Cindy the dentist's boat, back in 1987) surged and snapped you off after an epic but heartbreaking fight. So you're on the drag with deep sensitivity.

And then all of a sudden the thought enters your mind that you are going to lose this fish. Like all the dreams and the shadows of the dreams that have evaporated under the fixed and pitiless gaze of those cold fluorescent tubes. One more dream inevitably dashed on the rocks of reality, one more god-awful disappointment. You haven't prayed in years. Not even when you thought the plane was going down last Christmas with the in-laws in Milwaukee. But all of a sudden you find yourself praying. "Please god, please let me catch this fish. Please . . ." As if in direct response to this query, the line immediately goes slack. The whole thing is over. Of course it is. Of course the things you really want will always remain out of reach.

Stunned and defeated, you grimly turn the handle of the reel. Yep, it's slack all right. Incredibly slack. How could it be so slack? You keep reeling. You reel faster. Wait a minute, you feel a bump. The fish isn't gone, it's just swimming toward you! You reel faster. Now all of a sudden the line is taut again—the fish is twelve feet in front of you. You stare down into the water. You see a gigantic flash in the murk. Your heart is now doing double duty. The fish thrashes the surface. "Oh my God!" you scream. "What a fish!"

You walk into the office holding this massive, dripping creature aloft and every single person on the floor comes over and slaps you on the back. Fifty people in the place and not a single one of them could've landed it.

On the drive home, the traffic isn't bothering you as much as it normally does. Today, for the first time in years, you stepped off the grid and wrested your (mercury-laden) protein from mother nature—and made a few salmon happy while you were at it. Your smile is flexing facial muscles that you haven't used in years. The world and everything in it has changed significantly. Today you're the *Homo erectus* who killed the mammoth with one lucky toss of a spear, the Cro-Magnon woman who felled the cave bear with a rock. Which is to say, today, for a little while, you were the champion of the world . . . and if not of the world, at least of Brisbane, California.

Eat Them Up, Yum

Once you've tasted freshly caught striped bass, it sure becomes a lot easier to throw the health department warnings aside and get down to some hardcore, urban estuary scarfing. Generally, the way I cook striped bass is the way I prefer all large fillets: grilled.

As far as cutting them goes, striped bass are much like any large fish. The main thing is whether you want to take out the red meat or not. Strangely, when I'm going to bake, broil, or pan fry them, the first thing I do is remove the red parts. But when I'm grilling my striper fillets (with skin on), I never even think of the red meat.

Grilled Striper Two Ways

Fire up the grill to medium/high heat, score a few slices into the skin of the fillet (about two inches apart), add a little salt and pepper to both sides, spritz the grill with spray-on olive oil, and throw that bad boy on there. Sizzle. Depending on the size and thickness of the fillet, it could take anywhere from 3 to 10 minutes per side. But don't go by that. Just take a fork and probe the fish a little: if it flakes, it's done. Remove from the grill with a spatula, squeeze a lemon on it, grab your favorite brewski, and voilà, a meal for royals!

Fishing buddy and seafood gourmand extraordinaire Brian Haller of Berkeley suggests grilling striped bass fillets on a cedar plank. Soak the plank for an hour so it won't burn, put it on the grill, and throw the fillet on it. Close the lid and cook for 20 to 30 minutes, depending on the fillet's size and thickness. The wood adds a smokiness to the fillet, but you can also throw alder or applewood chips into the hot coals. No need to flip the fillet: with the plank in place and the lid closed, it will cook all the way through quite nicely.

White Seabass
Atractoscion nobilis

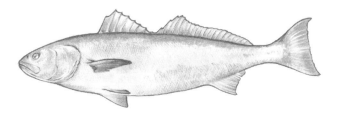

The first thing everyone seems to want you to know about white seabass is that they are not bass, they're croakers. In California, where a surfperch is not a perch, a lingcod is neither a ling nor a cod, a jacksmelt is not a smelt, and a monkeyface eel is not an eel, this shouldn't surprise anyone, but nevertheless, it does. So, if you were wondering what all that excited radio chatter about "croakers" and "really big kingfish" on the shortwave was, now you know. Guys with sixty-thousand-dollar Grady-White powerboats do not, as a general rule, get excited about kingfish. In any case, white seabass belong to the fraternal order of croakers, a perciform family of fish that gets its name for its members' notable ability to produce an audible grunting or croaking sound (by vibrating their abdominal sonic muscle fibers against their swim bladders). White seabass live to at least fifteen years and some of them are sexually mature at two. They evidently eat a wide variety of schooling fishes, crustaceans, and the like, but in our area, they're rather famously associated with squid. In fact, a local seabass angler using anything else for bait is downright eccentric.

The DFG Status Report from 2001 points to an apparent downward trend in California white seabass populations. But 2001 was a while ago, and in the last fourteen years anecdotal information would seem to indicate that there are: (a) more seabass north of Monterey than there have been in recent times, (b) more people targeting them north of Monterey, or (c) both.

How to Lose a Seabass: A Three-Part Study

There sure is a lot of online verbiage about how to catch these fish—chatboards, forums, websites, and blog posts (ad nauseam). But before we delve into the overly familiar territory of how to catch white seabass, let's start with the easiest ways to lose them.

Part 1: Drag Too Tight

Often, because it's hard to determine where in the water column these lunkers are hanging out, you will want to fish one to four rods, each one at a different depth. When fishing multiple rods, it can be difficult to keep track of all of them. On a recent kayak outing, my deep line snagged a rock. I cinched my drag down tight, to unsnag it. Just as the sinker came loose from the bottom, my mid-water reel's clicker went off. I quickly put the bottom rod back in its holder, grabbed the other one, and reeled in what turned out to be a small lingcod that had come way up off the bottom almost to the surface to grab my squid. After trying to measure and untangle this ferocious little bugger I finally got it free, let it go, and rebaited my hooks. Just as the bait went back in the water, a mackerel hit my top-water fly-line rig. I reeled it in, clipped its gills, threw it in the bucket, and rebaited. I then sat back to focus on my four lines. Something was wrong. I had the palpable sense of having forgotten something, left something unfinished, *but what was it?* An hour later I noticed my boat suddenly veering to port. I looked back at my bottom rod, which was behind and to the right of me, and saw it bent and surging at an impossible angle. Fish on! But why was no line playing out and why wasn't my clicker going off? Alas, after that earlier snag, I hadn't reset the line—it was locked down tight. Rookie mistake (and I've been doing this for how many years?). They say the sound of my screams can still be heard echoing across Soquel Canyon. But the sound that echoes in my ears to this moment is that resounding *sssssnap!*

Part 2: Sharp Body Parts

According to John Han, commercial fisherman and croakerman extraordinaire, breaking off a seabass is most apt to happen at the leader. "Sometimes, when they're mouth-hooked near the gills," John says, "their gill rakers will cut your line. And sometimes, when they inhale the bait and get gut-hooked, the sawing of the line back and forth across their teeth breaks you off." As for preventing this, John says that "fluorocarbon line tends to be more abrasion resistant than regular mono[filament line]. And when you fish at night you can bump up the line strength because they can't see it. I've fished with line as heavy as one-hundred-pound test at night and as light as twenty-pound test in the daytime."

Part 3: Predatory Animals

The only creatures that are big enough to grab a white seabass off your line are sea lions and great white sharks. Anyone who's been robbed by a great white can at least show a really awesome photo of the aftermath. But when a sea lion breaks off your fish and then proceeds to fondle it, nip at its gills and mouth, toss it around for a while, and then … *let it go, dead* … well … it's something quite different than thrilling.

THE WHERE, WHEN, AND HOW

1. See "On the Boat" in Swim Bladder 1 for seabass mooching rigs.

2. The best months in our region for white seabass are July, August, and September. The best places are anywhere that squid are present in large numbers.

3. A mint-condition, fresh, dead squid appears to be the preferred bait—even over live squid. However, a quick perusal of the Internet will show you that anglers in other (read: more southerly) areas of the Pacific coast use a wide assortment of baits and lures for seabass, and one wonders why this is not done more regularly in our waters. Recent examination of the contents of some locally caught seabass bellies found them absolutely loaded with medium-sized anchovies and sand dabs! And yet everyone was still using squid for bait—go figya.

4. This is not a fish that you are likely to catch from shore, though it has been known to happen from time to time. And I know of at least one fly fisherman who bagged a thirty-eight pounder while fishing for redtail perch.[11]

5. A loose drag is important to the successful capture of this species. These are big, powerful fish, and you are not likely to stop them on their first or second charge, so loosen the drag and let 'em ruuuuuuuuuuun! Seabass typically will give two or even three runs before cashing in their chips and coming to the boat with little resistance.

6. Catching a white seabass represents the crowning glory of a kayak angler's career—at least in our waters. Since they are often reasonably close to shore, it is possible to reach white seabass fishing grounds from many of our local beaches and harbors. Seabass are normally caught by "mooching" (see "On the Boat" in Swim Bladder 1).

7. As far as time of day is concerned, the two professional seabass killers interviewed for this book both confirm that they catch most of their seabass at dusk, at night, or in the wee hours of the A.M.

11 Mark "Surf-perch.net" Won … and guess what he did? He released it!

8. For your leader, use six to fifteen feet of twenty-pound test fluorocarbon; for hooks, use a double hook rig with a 4/0 octopus hook up front and a treble of the same size in back.

9. Since seabass can be anywhere in the water column, you may fly-line or use up to ten ounces of weight—depending on where you think they are. When fishing in the ocean for white seabass, you can use as many rods as you can handle. Nico "Sharky" Von Broembsen uses five rods on his kayak. (This is really something to see, especially considering that the "man in the grey suit" didn't leave him much of a left hand to work with.) One tidbit that Sharky shares is that when fishing this many rods, you may sometimes want to drop your lighter lines down deep very quickly, either to get them out of the way of the fish you're fighting or to suddenly get them down to where the baitfish or squid are registering on your sonar. In these moments, having your sinkers on a clip or double snap is key. Just clip the sinker to the line and let it slide down till it takes your leader to the depth you want.

10. When white seabass go into kelp beds to spawn, they are next to impossible to land on hook and line. The most effective way to get them during these times is to don the flippers and mask and break out the old speargun.

11. White seabass otoliths are cool, and can make for some interesting jewelry. It might be a good idea to check out a fish anatomy book before you attempt to dig one out of a seabass skull, however.

Eat Them Up, Yum

Grilled Seabass Collar

Some of the best meat in large fish like seabass and halibut is located in the collar and head. A 40-pound white seabass has a collar that weighs about 3–4 pounds—most of which is premium-quality meat. While everyone else is *ooh*ing and *ahh*ing over their fillets, grab a collar and rub it with olive oil, salt, and pepper. Grill that puppy over high heat for 10 minutes a side or till the meat on it flakes. Slurp a cold beer, squeeze a lemon on it, and call it done.

WHITE STURGEON
Acipenser transmontanus

Herewith the yin and the yang of sturgeon, in six key points:

1. Sturgeon meat is delicious.

2. Sturgeon meat may be full of heavy metals and toxins.

3. It's really fun to catch a sturgeon.

4. It's not particularly fun to sit in an anchored boat all day staring at your rod tip, waiting for it to pump.

5. When one considers the time and effort that goes into catching a single keeper-sized sturgeon, one feels a great sense of achievement at having caught one.

6. When one considers the potential age of the fish and the decline of the sturgeon population from its historical levels of abundance, and the fact that they have irregular spawning behavior and take a long time to reach sexual maturity, one feels a great sense of . . . something other than achievement at having caught one.[12]

I go through this song and dance every year. And still, I inevitably go out there in my kayak in January, paddle into the shadow of the Dumbarton Bridge, and sit for ten hours on my numb arse, soaking ghost shrimp and waiting (and waiting and waiting), mostly in vain, for the big pump.

If you are the quiet, contemplative, and philosophical type, sturgeon fishing is the perfect activity for you. If, like me, you suffer from a bit of attention deficit disorder, can't sit still for more than an hour at a time, and prefer a guarantee of coming home with *something* (seaweed? rock crabs? snails? mussels?), give up on this species now.

Sturgeon fishing is about patience and faith. Faith that eventually, if you sit there long enough, one of these giant, cartilaginous "dinosaur catfish" is

---

12 Sturgeon can live to at least 126 years, and perhaps longer.

The Mainstream

going to inhale your ghost shrimp and (if you're sitting in a kayak when this happens) take you on the Nantucket sleigh ride of your life.[13]

THE WHERE, WHEN, AND HOW

If you consider that sturgeon do not mind swimming into shallow water and that on a public pier or jetty you are allowed two rods instead of one, you might want to consider the advantages of fishing for them from public piers and jetties inside San Pablo and lower SF Bay. The best of these, if we follow the advice of pier guru Ken Jones in his epic tome *Pier Fishing in California*, are (in San Pablo Bay) Paradise Park Pier, McNear's Pier, and Loch Lomond Jetty, and (in the lower SF Bay) Dumbarton Pier, Coyote Point Jetty, Robert Wooley Pier, Oyster Point Pier, Sierra Point Pier, and Candlestick Park Pier.

The epicenter of white sturgeon fishing in California is the Sacramento Delta and any of the major tributaries of the Sac (namely, the American and the Feather). If you want to increase the likelihood of catching one, go to these places. In the South Bay, Alviso Slough and Coyote Creek are twin meccas for *Acipenser* fans.

The universal bait for sturgeon is the ghost shrimp, bound to the hook with rubber thread, followed by a big clump of grass shrimp, followed by herring and herring roe, followed by lamprey eels—though this last bait seems to be used exclusively in fresh/brackish water. Often, one will encounter sturgeon during the winter herring spawns: they like to come into the shallows of lower SF Bay to gorge on herring eggs. Another reason to follow the herring spawns is that a whole dead herring, especially a pregnant female oozing eggs, makes a deeply excellent sturgeon bait. It is also possible to grab a big wad of herring eggs from a recent spawn, bind them up with cheesecloth, and hurl them into the bay as bait.

What else? Sturgeon are one of the few large game fishes that are typically targeted around low tide…

Honestly, I'm thinking all this could be better done in verse.

Okay. Here it goes:

> The sturgeon is a mighty fish,
> And if it is your fondest wish
> To capture him by hook and line,
> Remember please this simple rhyme:

---

13 Of course sturgeon have nothing to do with catfish, but "dinosaur catfish" has become a common nickname for them… and I kind of like it.

As you ponder ebb or flow
Don't forget : *his tide is low.*
For bait, a herring serves you well
(Jingle goes the clip-on bell),
Grass shrimp, and of course the ghost
A sturgeon really likes the most.
But if you plan to fish some brook
Put a lamprey on your hook.
A slider rig will work the best,
With braided line of sixty test
(For leaders you should go with wire,
two ferrules, and some crimping pliers).

Here are places you might try
To catch a sturgeon by and by :

Dumbarton Pier (out at the end),
But heed you this fair warning, friend :
The anglers there are very tough
(Although it may just be a bluff).
Avoid the pitbull on the chain,
And only go there when it rains.
Coyote Jetty and the flats,
Behind the yacht club there (in back).
Oyster Point (if you're a thug
And have no fear of getting mugged).
Candlestick, out on the pier,
Was really pretty wild last year :
Twenty sturgeon, I've heard them say,
Were landed there on Christmas Day !

If you seek more gentle piers,
Try China Camp and McNear's,
Paradise will break your heart
When the sturgeon closure starts.
But if fresh water is your tack,
Try the Feather and the Sac.

As far as fighting is concerned,
Await two pumps, and this I've learned :
Upon the third, quick, seize the pole !
And set the hook with all your soul !

The sturgeon's mouth is very thick
And you must pull to pierce that lip,
And then hold on for all you're worth,
And try here to control your mirth ...

For sturgeon are both big and bold
And some of them are very old,
For trickery they're quite astute,
They'll cut your line with their sharp scutes.

And laugh and leap at your despair
(As in defeat you rend your hair).

Now get thee to some muddy spot
And cast your line, and cast your lot !
Good luck, my friend—it's my last wish
That this helped you catch your fish.

More Stuff

The white sturgeon is the largest anadromous fish in North America. Though the hook-and-line record (caught in the Carquinez Strait in 1983) stands at 468 pounds, they probably attain much larger sizes—up to and perhaps surpassing 13 feet and 1,300 pounds.[14]

The big females are the major egg producers. According to the California DFG's 2001 *Status Report*: "smaller females (under five feet) contain about 100,000 eggs, whereas a 9.2-foot 460-pound female contained 4.7 million eggs." In an attempt to guard against the removal of these super "hens" from the population, the California DFW has established a slot limit of forty-six to sixty-six inches. Which is a good thing for the fishery but a very aggravating thing for the sturgeon fisher. If you ever want to see a grown-up cry, watch a person who just landed an eighty-four-inch sturgeon throw it back.

There is no (legal) commercial fishery for this species. In fact, there hasn't been one since 1917. So if you go to a restaurant and see sturgeon on the menu, it is most likely farmed. Whereas farmed sturgeon often has a muddy flavor, there is no superlative too grand to describe the flavor and quality of wild sturgeon meat. Also, white sturgeon roe can be rendered into some very high-grade caviar. Sturgeon, especially the lunkers, are high in mercury. But really, how much wild sturgeon are you going to eat in your life?

Like abalone, this is a species that has traditionally been slammed by poachers, due to the high potential return on a low risk. Several years ago the California DFW busted an illegal sturgeon fishing operation out of Vallejo. These lovely fellows had trotlines set across the Carquinez Strait, and a bottling facil-

---

14 See California Department of Fish and Game, *California's Living Marine Resources: A Status Report,* 2001.

ity in their garage.[15] They evidently caught many hundreds of our beleaguered sturgeon, gutting them, stripping out the eggs, and leaving the wasted carcasses on the shore to rot. Which, no doubt, some loser is doing even as I write this. (Did I mention that sturgeon can live at least eighty years, and probably longer?) Imagine that somewhere out there is a fish that was born in pre-earthquake San Francisco.

A final note: it is estimated (by the Sea Forager Center for Dubious Claims) that it takes thirty to one hundred hours of fishing to produce one shore-caught sturgeon in SF Bay—and that one might not even be of legal size.[16] If you're fishing from a kayak or boat, your likelihood of catching one improves, but still, it's an anchor and wait (and wait and wait) type of deal. My suggestion is to pick a spot that's visually stimulating (or bring a good book with waterproof pages): you're likely to be there a while.

EAT THEM UP, YUM

Here are two no-frills tips for making the most of your sturgeon: a sturgeon jerky recipe from ace sturgeon hunter Loren Wilson, who's been catching sturgeon on his *Sea Ray* since 1968, and a classic baked sturgeon from Allen "O to Be Pelagic" Leepin.

Smoked Sturgeon Jerky

First, fillet the sturgeon. Then you have choices: you can get rid of the skin (or not) and/or trim out all the dark meat and fat (or not; some people like it). Cut the fillets into quarter-inch pieces and brine them in a solution consisting of 3 cups salt, 3 cups brown sugar, and 6 quarts of water (reduce the amount if you're working with less than a whole fish). Place the fish and brine in a stainless steel or glass container (never use aluminum) and soak overnight. The next day, take the fillet pieces out, rinse off the brine, pat them dry, spread them out, and let the glaze (pellicle) form. You can speed this up by putting a fan on the meat. The time needed will vary with the humidity in the air: plan on around 20–40 minutes with a fan or 60–90 minutes without one. Always make sure there are no flies or cats around . . .

15 Lest you should think that using trotlines to ensnare sturgeon is a new concept, here's a paragraph from Jack London's *Tales of the Fish Patrol:* "By a simple system of floats and weights and anchors, thousands of hooks, each on a separate leader, are suspended at a distance of from six inches to a foot above the bottom … These hooks are only a few inches apart and when several thousand of them are suspended just above the bottom, like a fringe, for a couple of hundred fathoms, they present a formidable obstacle to the fish that travel along the bottom … Such a fish is the sturgeon, which goes rooting along like a pig … pricked by the first hook it touches, the sturgeon gives a startled leap and comes into contact with half a dozen more hooks. Then it threshes about wildly, until it receives hook after hook in its soft flesh … because no sturgeon can pass through … the device is called a trap in the fish laws; and because it bids fair to exterminate the sturgeon, it is branded by the fish laws as illegal."

16 The percentages are much better in San Pablo Bay and the Sacramento Delta.

Next, acquire some applewood chips. (Loren says, "I make these myself by putting my neighbor's apple tree trimmings into a wood chipper and then spreading them out to dry in my garage.") You can also use alderwood. Throw a handful of applewood chips in the pan in the smoker (if you want more smoke, add more chips). Smoke for around 12 hours, depending on the size of the fillet pieces and how dry you like your jerky. Loren uses a Big Chief smoker.

Baked Sturgeon

> Nonseasoned crackers, such as Club Crackers Original
> Sturgeon
> Quality mayo

Put the oven rack in the highest position and preheat the oven to 400F. Line a flat cookie sheet with aluminum foil.

Place crackers in a clear bag and smash up into coarse pieces, not as small as cornmeal, but chunky, then transfer to a bowl.

Cut up chunks of fresh sturgeon as big as allowable, aiming for about 1 ½-inch cubes. If your fillets are smaller, try to match the same total of mass. The same goes if they are longer or wider or whatever. You just want them to all have the same cooking time.

Here comes the part that will gross most folks out. Slather the fish chunks in quality mayo (not Miracle Whip).

Dredge the mayo-slathered pieces of fish in the cracker crumbs and place on the cookie sheet, leaving plenty of space between each piece to allow the oil to flow away from each piece (wrinkling the foil up to form peaks helps with this).

Bake until the cracker crumbs brown a bit, usually about 4 minutes. Turn over each piece and bake for about another 4 minutes. (You may want to adjust these times a bit, depending on the size of your cubes.) The mayo should melt away, leaving a very moist fish inside a crunchy shell. Don't over-cook! A little undercooked is better, as with any fish. Serve immediately, since you want the coating to stay crunchy.

The idea behind the mayo method is to keep the fish moist. As for not seasoning, sturgeon is a delicate fish with a dense texture. You really want to taste the actual fish, not a seasoning. That said, if the fish was previously frozen, you may want to grate a *small* amount of fresh ginger over the cubed fish before dredging.

CALIFORNIA HALIBUT
Paralichthys californicus

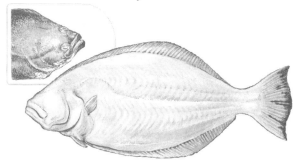

The California halibut is one of the three most popularly targeted game fish in our area. In addition to being popular among the boat and kayak contingents, halibut are also frequently caught from shore and pier and will readily take the same lures and baits as striped bass—although they famously tend to prefer live baits.

THE WHERE, WHEN, AND HOW

News flash: if you're new to this, just because the California halibut is flat and designed for hanging out on the bottom does not mean that it's a sluggish, laid-back, bottom dweller. Cali halibut are ferocious predators—just look at those teeth! Generally, halibut lurk on the bottom, camouflaging themselves (as many flatfishes are wont to do) and waiting for a mouth-sized forage fish to swim by. Which is why you either want to troll, drift, cast, and retrieve, or use live bait for them. Movement is the key (see "On the Boat" in Swim Bladder 1 for halibut fishing tips).

Live topsmelt and small jacksmelt work well as bait for halibut, as do shiner perch, sardines, anchovies, et cetera. Halibut are evidently not as given to hitting bullheads, midshipmen, and mudsuckers as are striped bass, but will readily take a frozen herring, sardine, anchovy, or even squid.[17] There are probably resident populations of halibut in SF Bay, but many seem to come and go, from the bay to the ocean and at least as far back as the Carquinez Strait (further evidence that the flow of the Sacramento is but a shadow of its former self). An old oceanography professor of mine once told me that California halibut

The Mainstream

---

17 Though I have never caught a halibut on bullheads, midshipmen, or mudsuckers, I commonly find partially digested midshipmen and bullheads in their stomachs. Frozen herring, sardine, anchovy, and squid are usually referred to in angler parlance as "popsicles," and are normally used while drifting or trolling. I should also add that several top-notch halibut anglers fish dead squid, herring, and anchovies from shore.

are high in methyl mercury. But frankly, so are many large predatory fish, with the exception of salmon. Your ever-vigilant health department (oehha.ca.gov) suggests one meal per week of halibut for kids under sixteen and women in their childbearing years. For everyone else: two meals per week. Compared to some other local species (kingfish, surfperch, leopard sharks, sturgeon), local halibut seem like the poster child of healthy seafood consumption.

Good halibut tides tend to be gentle ones. Huge displacement of water seems to adversely affect the bite. This may have more to do with what a high flow of water does to your bait presentation than with actual halibut feeding patterns. Generally, your most productive times are the last two hours of the flood and the first two of the ebb. Although they are commonly caught on soft sandy bottoms, halibut are also known to like structure. And they will lurk near rocks, pilings, sunken wrecks, slopes, and the like.

THANK POSEIDON FOR PLAN B

To comprehend how awesome our halibut are, try to imagine how dull the local fishing scene would be without them. In our region of California, fishing trips (even shore-fishing trips) often have to be canceled due to big swell and/ or a nasty shore pound. But since halibut are found inside calmer bays and estuaries, having them for plan B is sort of the fishing equivalent of having Lou Gehrig batting behind Babe Ruth in your lineup. In other words: a strong case could be made that your plan B is actually as good as or better than your plan A.

THE FIGHT

Halibut are notorious for gently taking the bait into their mouths and rather compliantly swimming along with it while they're being reeled in. Be fore-warned: don't set the hook—they'll do it themselves. And be advised: as soon as the halibut wakes from this self-induced trance (often as you are lowering the landing net), it will go berserk. So make sure you're prepared for an explosive finale. When halibut are lost they tend to be lost at boatside.

EAT THEM UP, YUM

As strange as it may seem, I have met several chefs over the years who eschew the local halibut in favor of the larger, more northerly Pacific halibut. I'm not sure what's wrong with these individuals—dropped on their heads at birth? I guess the one knock against California halibut meat is that it's really (really) easy to overcook. And when it's overcooked, it can taste, well … kind of dried out. But it seems to me that this is the case with anything that's overcooked.

I must say that Camilla "The Fishwife" Lombard has this halibut broiling down to a science. Says she: "Actually, the secret to not overcooking halibut is in checking it a few times and not walking away and getting distracted with something else—like the risotto, or the salad dressing, or the baby." Many local chefs and sea foodies insist that California halibut meat is best eaten as sashimi. If you are an inattentive cook, or can't figure out how to cook local hali without drying it out, just eat it raw—you won't be disappointed.[18]

The Fishwife's Cali Hali with Caper Vinaigrette

Treat your beautiful California halibut fillets to this simple caper vinaigrette. The flavor of the fish shines through and the sauce keeps it succulent.

    1 lb. halibut fillets
    1 Tbsp vegetable oil
    2 Tbsp mayonnaise
    1 clove garlic, crushed
    1 lemon, half of it juiced, the other half sliced in wedges for serving
    2 Tbsp champagne or red wine vinegar
    2 Tbsp capers
    1 tsp mustard
    1 tsp fresh thyme, chopped

Season your fillets with salt and pepper.

Fire up the stovetop, get your pan super hot, add the vegetable oil, and swirl in pan. Sear the fillets, starting with the skinless side, until golden, about 3–4 minutes.

While your fish is searing, whisk together the mayonnaise, garlic, lemon juice, vinegar, capers, mustard, and thyme.

Flip your fish and continue cooking, skin-side down, for 2 minutes. Lower the heat to medium-low and pour on some of your sauce. Simmer until the fish is opaque and cooked through.

Plate, topping with more of the warm sauce, and enjoy!

18 Just make sure you "candle" your fillets for larval roundworms (see Swim Bladder 3). I have never seen a halibut that didn't have a few worms, especially around the belly.

ROCKFISH
Sebastes genus

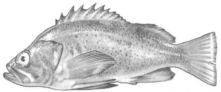

Black rockfish

The rockfish genus, *Sebastes,* is one of the most inspired families of fishes that evolution has to this date produced. On the Pacific coast of North America, there are over fifty species of rockfish, in a wide array of sizes, shapes, and colors. From the eccentrically striped to the daintily spotted, from the coarsely mottled to the strikingly vivid, they are all beautiful to behold, fun to catch, and good to eat.

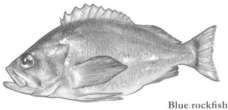

Blue rockfish

Rockfish also tend to be slow maturing and long lived, which has presented challenges to fisheries managers (and fishers) intent on ensuring their sustainable harvest.[19] All of which has become the source of a highly charged political debate, as some of the best rockfish habitat on the California coast has been closed to fishing by the Marine Life Protection Act (MLPA).[20] And make no mistake about it, these closures had a lot to do with rockfish.

POLITICS, UGH (A DIATRIBE)

Most (not all) people who fish our shores seem to resent the closures and downplay the impact of recreational fishing on near-shore rockfish species. Most (not all) biologists feel that the closed areas are essential to the revival and healthy continuance of these near-shore rockfish stocks.

19 Many rockfish species live long (up to or over a hundred years) and take a decade or more to reach sexual maturity.
20 Passed in 1999, implemented 2009–2013 in our area of California.

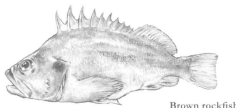

Brown rockfish

There can be little argument that the rockfish species caught by recreational anglers today are generally smaller and less numerous than they were in our grandparents' era. My own grandfather, as avid a sport fisherman as California has to this date produced, would have scoffed at the ten-inch gophers and black-and-yellows that comprise a good portion of today's recreational catch. At the same time, one wonders (okay, maybe "one" doesn't, but I sure do) if the current situation, in which hundreds of boats pile up on the few available reefs and fish them day in and day out, somehow reduces the benefits provided by the protected areas.[21] And one issue that seriously ought to be revisited is the closure of shore fishing areas.[22] Are seal and sea lion populations really so vulnerable to stress (remember that at some point in the not too distant past they were pursued and hunted on a daily basis by grizzlies and Native Americans) that whole stretches of shoreline should be closed to fishing and foraging?[23] Even it we take into account degradation of Turkish washcloth beds from human foot traffic, seagulls caught in fishing line, and the occasional startled seal, it would seem to me that the impact of shore fishing is fairly small. When I monitored the local shores as a professional fish checker, I found that on a busy summer weekend, you might find twenty people fishing the rocky shoreline inside areas that now prohibit fishing. Of these, maybe one-third might actually have a fish or two, maybe a striped perch or a few rock crabs or a monkeyface eel. Is the loss of the bonding experience and the mental health benefits provided by a few hours of fishing and living off the grid factored into the MLPA equation? (They tell me it is but it must be fairly low on the list

21 The idea, of course, is that these locations will take a hit initially, but that over time, when fish populations in closed areas have rebounded, surrounding areas will get a boost in fish numbers. Given how long it takes rockfish to mature, I guess we'll have to come back in a future life to ask future generations how it all worked out!

22 I'm sorry ahead of time for this diatribe. But there's nary a fisherperson on the coast who can accept the coddling of sea lions. Harbor seals, okay maybe. But fur bags? You gotta be kidding me.

23 Okay. I'm really bitter that I lost my secret horseneck clam spot because there happens to be a seal rookery across the channel from it and the "shareholders" evidently felt that my digging a few clams three times a year would cause undue stress to the inordinately plump harbor seals that wallow there and occasionally look up, snort at me, then go back to wallowing. I'm taking it personally because, to my knowledge, I was the only person who ever clammed in that location.

of priorities.) If so, then I guess the stressing out of sea lions and trampling on a few acres of a very common and resilient seaweed are more important than the mental well-being of the local *Homo sapiens* population.

But I suppose everyone has an axe to grind on this issue, and ultimately something has to be done to ensure that our coastal resources can be sustained over the long haul.[24] The MLPA (as aggravating as many coastal fishers and foragers may find it) and its network of closures are a very real attempt to do this. And despite the qualms we all may have, we should try to remember that its ultimate goal is to protect the resources that we all supposedly love so much.

AHEM, BACK TO THE FISH

As indicated above, there are a lot of rockfish species. A whole lot. For the purposes of this book I am going to focus on those most commonly caught from shore or kayak.[25]

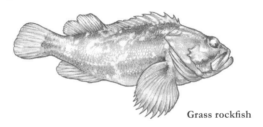

Grass rockfish

The ten rockfish most commonly caught from shore or within a hundred yards of shore are:

1. Brown rockfish (aka bolina cod), *Sebastes auriculatus*

2. Grass rockfish (aka grassy, grass bass), *Sebastes rastrelliger*

3. Kelp rockfish (common only from Santa Cruz south), *Sebastes atrovirens*

4. Black rockfish (aka schoolie), *Sebastes melanops*

5. Gopher rockfish (throw it back and *go-fer* something else), *Sebastes carnatus*

6. Black-and-yellow rockfish, *Sebastes chrysomelas*[26]

---

24 Remember that most of California's ever-burgeoning human population lives within an hour of the ocean.

25 If you want more information on rockfish species, drop everything and get a copy of Milton Love's *Rockfishes of the Northeast Pacific*, and, if you don't have it already, his *Certainly More Than You Want to Know about the Fishes of the Pacific Coast: A Postmodern Experience*. The latter is: (1) certainly not more than you want to know, and (2) a fantastic resource that all fish lovers should own.

26 Despite being of equal size, similar appearance, and, to my palate, identical flavor, black and yellows, strangely, do not have the same bad rap as gophers regarding the texture and flavor of their meat.

7. China rockfish (aka Chinese rockfish), *Sebastes nebulosus*

8. Blue rockfish (aka schoolie), *Sebastes mystinus*

9. Copper rockfish (aka hardhead), *Sebastes caurinus*

10. Vermilion rockfish (aka red rockfish), *Sebastes miniatus*

It's odd that, despite the countless hours I have spent floating around on the Pacific Ocean—or standing on rocks, or poke poling—for rockfish, I have so little to say about them. Perhaps this is because they've been so exhaustively and expertly covered by the giants of ichthyology.[27] Or perhaps it's because the hunting of each species of rockfish is more or less similar to all the others. In contrast, there is a noticeable difference between the way one fishes for redtail surfperch and for rubberlips. Same thing with night smelt and surf smelt. But the difference (other than bottom depth) between catching a gopher, a black-and-yellow, a China, a copper, or a brown is not particularly noteworthy.[28] Same rig, same lures, same motion of the rod. That's not to say you can't target a particular species effectively, but you will most likely catch a bunch of other rockfishes that you weren't targeting.

The Where, When, and How

As far as the more notable species-specific particulars go:

> 1. Black rockfish and blue rockfish are sometimes referred to as "schoolies" and are often (but not always) caught in the middle of the water column. In fact, at times it can be nearly impossible to drop your bait past them, which is a gold-plated problem if you are targeting rockfish anyway.

> 2. "Grassies" are typically caught in shallow water (forty feet and less). The grass rockfish, like the cabezon, has an infamous tendency to grab the bait and take it back down into the hole or crack or cave it calls home. This is another reason why it's a good idea to use a fairly thick leader when fishing the rocky shoreline—or better yet, a poke pole! Over the years, I have caught far more grass rockfish while poke poling than fishing on skiffs, party boats, or kayaks—though the grass rockfish one catches while poke poling tend to be smaller than the ones caught in deeper water.

> 3. The brown rockfish, or bolina cod, is often caught close to shore by bait casters and poke polers alike. Again, these intertidal and subtidal fishes are usually much smaller than their offshore counterparts but

---

27 Definitely the name of my next band.

28 There's probably a commercial near-shore guy out there pulling his hair out as I write this, but the two that I spoke to grudgingly admitted that I am more or less correct here.

every now and then you will surprise yourself and bag a hawg "brownie" in very shallow water. This is probably the most commonly caught rockfish inside SF Bay.

You'll never guess where rockfish tend to hang out . . . around rocks! Fancy that. As far as tide goes, if you're fishing from shore it doesn't really matter, though I have noticed that I get more rockfish (and eels) on the flood than the ebb. The rockfish bite often goes dead at slack water. These are bottom fish, so as a general rule, drop down to the bottom or a few cranks up from the bottom. If you're offshore in a boat or kayak, the main thing to consider is that a big movement of water will make your drift impossibly fast—if you don't have six to twelve ounces of lead down, your bait's going to come up off the bottom. I don't know about you, but fishing with that much lead sort of kills the fun of catching rockfish for me, so I try to pick days where the wind and the tidal flow are moderate.

Any dead or live bait commonly used in California will work for rockfish. The standard is squid. But anchovies, ghost shrimp, grass shrimp, herring, sardines, et cetera will work well too (see "On the Rocks" in Swim Bladder 1 for rockfish rigs and lures).

Eat Them Up, Yum

Whole or Filleted?

The best fillet man I know, Sammy Garcia, is able to cut a big black rockfish at about 40 percent yield. If you aren't a professional fish cutter, you will probably cut rockfish fillets between 23 and 33 percent. The yield goes up when the fish are bigger. Keep this in mind if the fish in your bucket are on the small side. If your aim is to throw down some awesome rockfish tacos, the larger fish are the ones to fillet. But don't throw out your carcasses! Rockfish carcasses (sans gills and guts) are good for making soup stock; scrape the meat from between the bones and you've got the makings for ceviche.

Of course the best and least wasteful way to eat rockfish, especially the smaller ones like Chinas, starries, and gophers, is whole (gilled, scaled, and gutted). A whole rockfish, baked or steamed with green onions and ginger, is a pretty tough dinner to beat. See below for details.

Steamed Whole Rockfish à la Fishwife

Steaming your fish whole is a fantastic way to get the most out of it. You'll be amazed at how much meat you can get from the nooks and crannies, and this tasty Asian recipe is easy and sure to impress. Dressed up with ginger and cilantro, your rockfish never looked so good.

2 whole rockfish, gilled and gutted, 1.5–2 lbs each
4 scallions, trimmed, chopped in half, white parts thinly sliced lengthwise, green parts sliced into 2-inch pieces
White wine or sake
2–3-inch knob of ginger, peeled and sliced into matchsticks
1 bunch cilantro, loosely chopped
2–3 Tbsp canola oil
Soy sauce

Score three slices on both sides of your fish and salt it, inside and out.

Arrange the scallion greens on a plate, place the whole fish on top, pour a little white wine or sake over it all, and top with half the ginger pieces.

Put an inch or so of water in a wok, and place your steamer basket on top. Bring the water to a boil, place your plate of fish atop the steamer basket, and cover the wok.

Let it steam for about 10 minutes, then turn the heat off and let it sit, covered, for 3 minutes.

Remove the plate from the wok and pour off the steaming liquid (careful—it's hot!).

Remove the ginger pieces from atop the fish, replace with fresh ones, and scatter the cilantro on top.

In another pan, heat the canola oil. When it's hot (but not smoking), pour it on the fish (yes, really!). It will sizzle and that's exciting. Drizzle on some soy sauce, top with the scallion whites, and serve. It goes nicely with rice.

The Mainstream

LINGCOD

Ophiodon elongatus

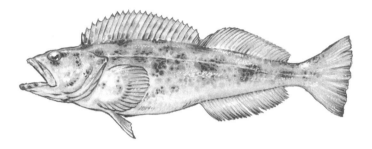

When I first moved to California, I read somewhere that one of the traditional Native American methods for catching lingcod was to drop a fish-shaped lure off the side of the tule canoe, let it sink to the bottom, then quickly retrieve it.[29] When the ling appeared at the surface, having ravenously pursued the lure up from the depths, it was promptly speared by the canoe's deckhand, who evidently sat in position, poised for the kill.

Even having heard rumors of the aggressive behavior of lingcod, this spearing of lings from tule canoes seemed implausible to me. That is, until I booked passage aboard a party boat, bound for the Farallon Islands for a day of bottom fishing. About fifteen minutes after dropping in, the guy next to me screamed "Hitchhiker!" at the top of his lungs. I looked down and saw a large, bright blue fish clinging to the caudal peduncle of a small, bright red fish. The blue fish was shaking the red one like a big dog with an old piece of rope. But what was most remarkable was that it did not appear to be hooked. In its ferocity it had seized the small rockfish and refused to let go—in other words, it had hitchhiked (unhooked) to the surface from ninety feet down. The blue fish, against all reason, held on till it was gaffed (after two missed attempts) by an excited deckhand, and suddenly the spearing of lings from tule canoes no longer seemed like such an outrageous concept.

THE WHERE, WHEN, AND HOW

The lingcod is one of the top coastal game fishes of California and catching one is the highlight of any bottom fishing trip. Lings are notorious lurkers.

29 Coastal Native American tribes in California evidently used ground iris fibers to make their fishing lines. If you've ever seen the size of a ground iris leaf, you will understand the amount of labor that must have gone into making a line—or for that matter a net, or the cordage for binding a tule canoe.

They hang out in crevices and caves until an unsuspecting fish swims by and then … gulp! This is a big, aggressive predator fish, the kind of fish that certain types of alpha humans like to get tattooed on their biceps. Unlike many of the rockfish species that it's normally associated with, the lingcod does not possess a swim bladder. In other words, it doesn't implode halfway up to the boat and phone in the last 50 percent of the ride—it fights from the moment it's hooked to the moment it's landed.[30]

Lings will hit a variety of dead and live baits (see chapter 3). And pretty much anything that swims in front of their jaws. Several years ago, while hanging out at the fish-cleaning station in Bodega, a former fishing partner of mine saw a whole, partially digested common murre come out of the belly of a hawg lingcod.

It is also possible to catch lingcod from shore in very shallow water. The preferred method employed by the people who do this most successfully is to hike out to the end of a long jetty, or to climb up on a rock somewhere along the coast, and jig swimbaits in and around rocks and kelp beds. It is a good idea when doing this to bring a long-handled landing net. And be forewarned: not only is the typical lingcod armed with a set of chompers to make an alligator green with envy, but its gill rakers are perfectly designed to shred the fingers of any human unwise enough to hold it by its gills.[31]

Kinda Blue

At the fish warehouse where I work, I'd say that approximately one out of every four lingcod has either bright blue, blue-green, or kinda blue skin, with bright blue or blue-ish meat. This blueness may be linked to a bile pigment called *biliverdin*. But no one is particularly certain about it, and in any case the blue color disappears with cooking. Blue ling meat is highly coveted by my seafood subscribers, and every time we offer lingcod, we get special requests for the so-called "smurf fillets."

Eat Them Up, Yum

Lingcod with White Wine Cream Sauce

Chris "Clayman" Mayes contributes this variation on an East Coast striped bass recipe. As he says, "It works great with any white-fleshed fish, especially lingcod. Best part is, it's all cooked in one pan and it's really easy!"

---

30 Fish with air bladders suffer barotrauma when brought to the surface from deep water.

31 To be clear, it's no problem shoving your hand into the gills of a lingcod. Pulling your hand back out is where the problem lies.

2 Tbsp butter, or more if desired
¾–1 cup yellow onion, finely chopped
1 cup white rice
½ cup dill, finely chopped
½–¾ cup white wine (Chris prefers Pinot Grigio)
½ cup heavy whipping cream
2 medium-sized lingcod fillets, cut in half if desired

Melt the butter in a skillet on low-medium heat. Add the onion and cook until it is caramelized. In the meantime, get the rice steaming in a separate pot or in a rice cooker.

Add the chopped dill to the onion (you can add a bit of additional butter too, if you like).

Once the dill is soft (usually 1 minute or less), add the wine and cream. Stir, then cover and simmer until bubbling.

Season the lingcod fillets with salt and pepper, and lay them on top of all the other ingredients in the skillet. They'll likely be submerged in the sauce—this is perfectly fine.

Cover and cook on medium heat for about 10 minutes, or until the fish flakes easily with a fork. Remove from heat and serve over steamed rice.

KELP GREENLING (SEA TROUT)
Hexagrammos decagrammus

The rap on greenling is that they ...

1. Are loaded with worms

2. Taste kind of weird

3. Have too many bones

4. Have mealy flesh

As I think I have shown here, I have no qualms about calling a perch a perch. Or stating for the record that some fish, despite their popularity, should be thrown back in the water. Greenling is the leading example of this. Despite the fact that they commonly show up in the live tanks at Asian markets selling for exorbitant amounts, the meat of this fish is just sort of lacking. Whoever likened it to a trout was either insane or trying to improve it by suggestion (or both). On the other hand, as far as worms go, if most of the seafood-eating public saw the worms that are ground up in their fish sticks, or their beer-battered Pacific cod fish and chips, they'd think of greenling as the next closest thing to wormlessness. Still, years ago my good friends Mike "The Salty Czech" Dvorak and the sour semi-Boer Nico "Sharky" Von Broembsen (when they still spoke to each other) started the dockside meme: "Friends don't let friends eat greenling." Having prepared it several different ways for this book, I have to say … I wish one of them had stopped me.

Eating aside, greenling are a really fascinating species and one of the few visibly sexually dimorphic fish in our area. Although they're rather disappointingly conformist in their coloration—girl greenling have pinkish-orange-yellow spots, boys have blue. They are often caught in shallow water (two to forty feet) and they seem to really like the same little pieces of cut squid that monkeyface eels bite on. Greenling offer a smaller, untoothed, G-rated version of lingcod.

THE WHERE, WHEN, AND HOW

As far as targeting greenling goes … one tends to catch greenling when going for something else. In the intertidal zone I have noticed that, given a choice between a narrow, deep, dark, inshore hole that goes way down into a subterranean cavern (i.e., the kind of hole a monkeyface eel likes) and a relatively wide-open hole or even a semi-protected ledge with a good deal of flow, a greenling will opt for the latter. I'm not sure why this would be, or whether I am the only person who has noticed this, but that's my opinion for what its worth. Offshore you will catch these guys at any point in the tidal cycle. Inshore, especially while poke poling, the two hours after the bottom of low tide are the best. Greenling seem to relish squid, pieces of mussel, and marine worms with equal zest. Like the pile perch, they will also happily inhale a small shore crab.

ROCK GREENLING
Hexagrammos lagocephalus

Everything I've mentioned about kelp greenling also applies to the rock greenling. In our area you will catch approximately twenty kelp greenling for every rock greenling you chance into. The rock greenling, though, is a remarkably beautiful creature. Dig that crazy bright blue mouth and the blood-red spots on its sides. I have only ever caught rock greenling while poke poling. And I have caught them so rarely, I can't really offer any advice on how to specifically target them. They're always an exciting catch. Check 'em out, snap a photo, and throw 'em back—their meat is the same as kelp greenling.

CABEZON
Scorpaenichthys marmoratus

There is something about pulling an eight-pound fish from under a rock in fourteen inches of water that is not unlike pulling a rabbit out of a hat. Thanks to the cabezon and its proclivity for hanging out in very shallow areas, this magic trick is within the capabilities of anyone able to wield a poke pole. Did I mention that cabezon are very good eating? Well, they are. Before you get too excited, however, keep in mind that a substantial portion of this creature's overall body weight consists of head and fins.

THE WHEN, WHERE, AND HOW

Cabezon can be caught from shore or boat by using all the same jigs, shrimp flies, plastics, bars, and baits that rockfish seem to like. They have a renowned tendency to gulp the hook and immediately head for a rock, crevice, or hole. When cleaning cabezon, you will often find whole rock crabs or even abalone in their stomachs. How they are able to dislodge abalone from rocks remains a mystery but I suspect that their methods aren't quite legal (they scoff at licenses and report cards). Cabezon meat is excellent, and that should come as no surprise. We are, after all, what we eat, and cabezon eat some very delicious stuff.

Like lingcod and rock greenling, cabezon will often have a blue-green appearance, especially in and around the mouth and gullet. If the fillets are blue, trust that they will turn white when cooked. There is also a strange crab-like texture to the meat that some (overly sensitive) people find off-putting, and occasionally you will bag one that has a sort of iodiney flavor. One other note to all you experimental foodie types: don't eat the roe. It's poisonous.

Cabezon Skinners Have More Fun

Years ago when I dabbled in the lost art of home bookbinding, I experimented with tanning the skins of various local fishes. For all my efforts, I didn't actually produce a true leather so much as a stiff parchment-like dry preserve. Nevertheless I took the resulting cardboard-like sheets and pressed them into binder's cloth using C-clamps, cellophane, and boards. The resulting product was a tough, reasonably pliable leather-like strip perfect for the spines of my zines. Since the title of this scurrilous little publication was *The Monkeyface News,* I normally used monkeyface skins for the covers.[32] However, cabezon skins proved to be tougher, easier to deal with (because the strips were usually wider), and, due to the handsome mottling that remains even after the skins are salted and dried, much more aesthetically appealing than eel, lingcod, rockfish, or anything else. Again, I never really produced actual fish leather, but for the purposes of my bookbinding ambitions, these sheets of dried, clamped skins worked perfectly, and I would imagine that a master tanner could work wonders with cabezon skins.

Eat Them Up, Yum

A nice, tasty, healthy alternative to frying big cabezon is to cook them whole in a convection oven.

Convection Oven Cabezon

Heat the oven to 375F, and turn on the convection setting. Gut the cabezon, cut slits in its skin, and sprinkle with salt and pepper or Tony Chachere's Creole Seasoning. Place in an oiled baking dish and bake for 45 minutes (for a 22-inch cab) or 45–50 minutes (for a 24-inch cab).

Once the meat is cooked, you can pull it apart and use it in fish tacos, or serve it whole on a platter.

The Mainstream

---

32   It was a handmade, hardcover, eelskin-bound book before it was a blog.

MONKEYFACE PRICKLEBACK
Cebidichthys violaceus

ME, MYSELF, AND THE MONKEYFACE EEL

Warning: this is gonna get strange.

The monkeyface prickleback (aka the monkeyface eel) is not for everyone. Its meat is often described (by haters) as having a rather off-putting iodiney flavor. Its guts, usually filled with partially digested seaweeds, are foul smelling.[33] Its steadfast refusal, despite all manner of abuse, to pass on to fish heaven when a poke poler wants it to, is considered by many to be both annoying and kind of scary. Its strange eyes and frowning simian bad looks are the stuff of slimy intertidal nightmares and misguided haikus jotted down in dark, clammy places. Like this one:

> ## Haiku #1,137
> Of what do eels dream ?
> Of life ? Of death ? Of algae ?
> Or do they not dream ?

Then there's the way their fillets contract into a weird rubbery tube when thrown onto a grill. And of course the unique method of catching the monkeyface, with its bamboo sticks and wire hangers and duct tape. It's all so … *strange.*

Thank Neptune! A fish for all the eccentrics out there (or one of them, anyway).

When I first encountered the monkeyface prickleback, I was in free fall

---

33 More foul smelling than the guts of any other fish I've encountered.

from a crushing breakup with a situation called "Betsy." The monkeyface took me in, taught me his lowly (in the benthic sense) ways, and showed me how to move on. A tide pool animal does not have the luxury of feeling sorry for himself and being all depressed and whatnot. Not with the ceaseless crashing of waves, the inexorable ebb and flow of the tide, the constant competition with other greedy organisms. The monkeyface also showed me something about not rolling over and dying so easily. It was impossible not to appreciate and honor this strange, resilient, and ridiculously named animal. Especially considering that it had become my primary source of protein after I abandoned the trappings of civilization and moved into an inaccessible (from the land side anyway) stretch of local shoreline. In the midst of this transformative period of self-discovery,[34] I one day found myself scrambling along the rocks and came to the sudden realization that I'd been scrambling this way for some time. About a month in fact. Living on goose barnacles and red algaes and, well … eels.[35] Lots of eels. In fact there came a point when, clad in eelskin garb and grubbing on Turkish washcloth, my own skin began to take on a smooth, leathery texture. Orange spots appeared on my shoulders and neck. A thick fleshy lobe emerged betwixt my eyebrows. Yes, I was turning into an eel.[36]

CERTAINLY MORE THAN YOU WANT TO KNOW ABOUT *CEBIDICHTHYS VIOLACEUS*

(Or, Observations Garnered from Two Decades Misspent Hunting the Eel)

Nocturnal Behavior

Yes, monkeyface eels will feed at night, if somewhat less aggressively than during daylight hours. Mike "The Salty Czech" Dvorak is the leading researcher of this phenomenon, about which he states the following: "With a headlamp you can see their little eyes peering out from under rocks. If you want to get a good sense of population density, fish at night. On my last trip I counted about three eels for every rock I fished. But only one in that number was willing to bite the squid."

---

34 They used to call it a "nervous breakdown," but I'm going with "transformative period of self-discovery."

35 Goose barnacles cannot be legally harvested in California.

36 It didn't stop there. Open spaces scared me. I shunned the light. In my dark rooms and on the streets at night my libido knew no bounds. Women saw the eel in my eyes and ran screaming or, conversely, sought me out, writhed with me, locking fins in a slippery ectothermic embrace. I was frequently overwhelmed with a gnawing hunger for red and green algae. Clubbed on the head, and stabbed in the heart by muggers, I resuscitated myself easily, thrashed my assailants, and carried on as though nothing had happened.

The Tides

Contrary to popular belief, huge minus tides are not the best time to capture the not-so-elusive monkeyface. The best tide is anything from a -0.6 to a +0.8. And, I should add, although eels are readily caught on ebb or slack tide, their feeding activity seems to increase drastically on the flood.

The Way They Bite

Monkeyface eels can be divided into three rough classes—gummers, peckers, and slammers—in respect of their attitude toward bait.

Gummers: Setting the hook on a gummer is not easy and may require a hook larger than a 1/0. Some of the biggest eels out there are gummers. For whatever reason, gummers predominate at night.

Gummers very gently take the bait into their mouths and then just sit there gumming it. Although I tend otherwise not to set the hook on pricklebacks (allowing them to set it on themselves), there really is no other way when dealing with a gummer.

Peckers: Logically it would seem that all the peckers out there are too small to actually hook themselves, hence they *peck* at the bait. And although this may quite often be the case, every now and then the pecker you thought was a pipsqueak turns out to be a champion-sized animal. The shark-bit semi-Boer, Von Broembsen, believes that the bigger eels are the ones most adept at robbing the hook—since they have lived longer and have therefore had more experience at it. Dvorak, however, reminds us that a fish's memory lasts only seven seconds (how he knows this I'm afraid to ask). I tend to side with Von Broembsen on this and would venture that a good portion of the human population has far less capacity for memory retention than the average monkeyface prickleback. In any case, many huge eels are expert in the art of removing the squid from the hook—and it is my unofficial view that they learn this behavior after many years of careful practice and study.

Slammers: Slammers see the bait and slam it hard. In many cases they will come up out of the hole to snatch the squid. These are almost all big, strong, and (fatally) confident eels. Slammers are the most fun, and are the easiest to hook. One day I aim to take an eel by dry fly—and it is only because of the existence of slammers that I continue to entertain this ambition.

THE WHERE, WHEN, AND HOW

As you may have guessed, this creature is primarily caught by poke pole (see "On the Rocks" in Swim Bladder 1) at low tide, although shore fishers will occasionally catch them on hook and line.

A long-handled, small-mesh landing net will increase your success exponentially—despite the inevitable hassle of untangling hooks and eels from the net.

Although Brian "Macoma" Lynch, mud clam aficionado and poke poler par excellence, uses mussels for monkeyface bait, my own choice is squid: it's cheap, durable, and, well, pricklebacks like it. Juvenile monkeyface eels subsist on a diet consisting mostly of amphipods, copepods, and worms. But as adults they give all this up and convert to a state of complete veganism. Why then do they so readily take to a piece of mussel rind or squid? I will answer this by posing another question. How many so-called vegans out there are sneaking off to In-N-Out several times per month? Probably a significant number. Maybe there's a similar trend among eels. In my brief time as a prickleback I found a diet consisting entirely of seaweeds to be deeply unsatisfying. Dvorak's opinion that eels are sitting in their holes dreaming about a cheeseburger (or more likely a piece of squid) floating by is, in this eelmonger's estimation, spot on.

It should be noted that whereas eels will slam a piece of squid with reckless abandon, they will not readily bite on an offering of seaweed. Whether this is due to presentation or dietary preference has yet to be determined. Dvorak is right now developing a line of red algae dry flies, using pheasant feathers, turkey plumes, and yarn. But as of this writing these ground breaking new dry fly patterns have not been field tested.

Many poke polers like to tie their hooks to a swivel (see "On the Rocks" in Swim Bladder 1), or forgo the use of line entirely, clipping their hooks directly onto a snap. Whereas it is true that a spinning eel is less likely to get away when the hook is attached to a swivel, the floppiness of presentation is problematic. As with the skinning of cats, there are many ways to rig a poke pole. In other words, some people like swivels, others do not. I personally find that three inches of line from the end of the wire to the hook is all I need.[37] Some iconoclasts out there like more line, some less.

EAT THEM UP, YUM

All the eels I have ever eaten have been filleted. Most reputable chefs up and down the coast simply tempura or deep-fry their eels. As far as soaking the fillets overnight in buttermilk, to lessen what is perceived by many to be a slight

---

37   Haiku #3,490
  All you need my friend:
one hook, three inches of line,
  duct tape, and a pole.

iodiney flavor, to my mind it makes absolutely no difference at all—but many well-respected poke polers swear by their buttermilk.

Eels make a fine substitute for catfish in a fresh Pacific gumbo, and can also be used in cioppino and paella, as they hold up well to boiling or stewing. As far as skinning them goes, you can fillet them off the skin just as you would a bass or rockfish, or you can incise a neat cut around the head and try to strip the skin off like a wet stocking that's been crazy-glued to a leg. If you are saving the skins for use in bookbinding (ahem), this latter method is preferable. But you will likely need two pairs of pliers: one to hold the eel's jaw and one to strip the skin. (Be forewarned—it is extremely difficult to get the skin off without tearing it.) The old catfish trick of driving a nail through the head doesn't tend to work because prickleback skulls are soft.

The Fishwife's Monkeyface Eel Gumbo

¼ pound Italian sausage, sliced
1 Tbsp olive oil
1 small onion, chopped
1 stalk celery, chopped
½ green bell pepper, chopped
1 32-ounce box chicken broth
1 28-ounce can crushed tomatoes
2 Tbsp all-purpose flour
1 Tbsp salt
¼ tsp pepper
1 Tbsp dried thyme
1 bay leaf
½ tsp dried oregano
½ tsp dried basil
1 tsp Creole (or Old Bay) seasoning
1 tsp Worcestershire sauce
4 scallions, finely chopped (½ cup)
½ pound monkeyface eel, cut into chunks
¼ cup chopped fresh parsley

Sauté the sausage in a Dutch oven until lightly browned, then remove the sausage and set aside.

In the same pot, heat the olive oil and sauté the onion, celery, and green pepper until soft. Add the chicken broth, tomatoes, and reserved sausage, cover, and bring to a boil. Cook, covered, for 5 minutes.

In a small bowl, whisk the flour and ½ cup water together, and add the salt, pepper, spices, and Worcestershire. Add this mixture to the pot and keep cooking for 10 more minutes on medium heat.

Add the monkeyface eel, reduce heat to medium, and cook for 5 more minutes.

Add parsley and serve over rice.

The Fishwife's End-of-Summer Herbed Monkeyface Eel and Veggies

This recipe is super easy and fun to assemble and serve. Wrap up those parcels of monkeyface goodness and enjoy the flavors of the season!

> 1 cup mixed chopped basil leaves and Italian parsley
> 2 large cloves of garlic, crushed
> Zest and juice from half a lemon, other half reserved
> ¼ cup olive oil, plus more for tossing with vegetables
> ¾ cup olive tapenade (or chopped olives)
> 4 monkeyface fillets (or 2 large fillets, halved)
> ½ bunch asparagus
> 3 medium summer squash

Combine the basil and parsley, garlic, lemon zest and juice, and olive oil in a bowl and mix well.

Whip out a sheet of tinfoil large enough to enclose one of your fillets. Place the fish in the center, smear some basil mixture on it, top with a bit of the tapenade, and wrap into a secure parcel with the foil. Repeat with all the fillets, dividing the mixture evenly. Place on a baking tray and set aside for a sec.

Turn on the broiler.

Trim the bottom of your asparagus and chop your summer squash into thick slices. Toss with olive oil, spread out on a baking sheet, and sprinkle with salt, pepper, and the lemon zest from the second half of your lemon. Squeeze a little juice on there too.

Broil until the vegetables begin to color, shake the pan a little, toss, then move the veggie pan lower in the oven and reduce heat to 400F.

Pop your fish tray into the oven on the middle rack, bake for about 10 minutes (depending on the thickness of your fillets), or until the flesh flakes easily when tested with a fork. Place the opened parcels on serving plates with the veggies, and enjoy the remnants of summer as you wrap your cardigan around you.

Monkeyface Ceviche

This one was sent to us by legendary kayak angler and poke poler Big Jim Russell, who says, "I think 'monkey' makes great ceviche cuz the meat is so firm that it holds up really well to soaking in lemon/lime juice and doesn't dissolve or disintegrate or get mushy." The quantities are flexible here.

> 1 monkeyface (or several monkeyfaces or a barrel of monkeyfaces)
> Fresh citrus juice (half lemon, half lime)
> Roma tomatoes
> Jalapeños
> Cilantro
> Red onions
> Garlic
> Tabasco sauce

Gut the monkeys ASAP after catching, because, as Big Jim notes, "their bellies are often stuffed full of rotting kelp/algae that can be quite stinky."

Once home, skin the monkeys by scoring them behind the head, then using pliers to rip the skin off each side. Once they are skinned, fillet the meat off the backbone.

Chop the meat up into ceviche-sized cubes. Place the fish in a glass bowl and add enough fresh citrus juice to cover. Cover the bowl with saran wrap and put in the fridge overnight (or at least for a few hours) until the meat turns white.

Drain off the initial juice. (This helps remove any possibly funky flavors from the meat.)

Chop the vegetables and herbs and add them to the fish together with more fresh lemon and lime juice (to keep it juicy and give it a nice crisp taste), some Tabasco, sea salt, and pepper to taste. Big Jim recommends serving it with nice tortilla chips and cold beer.

RAYS AND SKATES

The species of rays and skates that are most commonly taken for food in our area are:

Thornback ray, *Platyrhinoidis triseriata*

Shovelnose guitarfish, *Rhinobatos productus*

Big skate, *Raja binoculata*

Bat ray, *Myliobatus californica*

The thornback ray, shovelnose guitarfish, and big skate are caught in bays and (less frequently) in the ocean proper. In addition, thornbacks are often found (by me, anyway) on very low minus tides in mudflats, where they will bury themselves an inch or two under the sand—often in areas where there is little or no water.

I've only caught two big skates in my life: in one case I was fishing for halibut on a kayak, and in the other I was fishing for leopard sharks from a pier. Both of my skates consumed a whole squid, so I can at least confirm that you can catch them on that bait. I am including them here because the meat was superb.

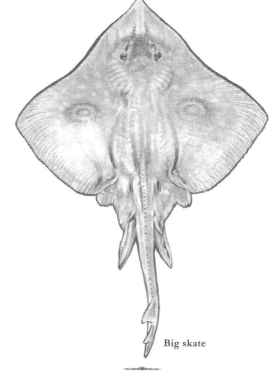

Big skate

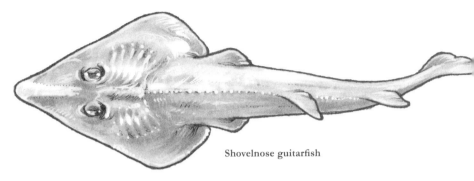

Shovelnose guitarfish

EAT THEM UP, YUM

Here is a recipe (along with prep instructions) for big skate from Chris "Clayman" Mayes. It works well on bat rays too. Chris says:

> Like sharks, skates and rays need to be bled immediately upon capture. Once the skate is bonked and bled (by slitting the gills), use a large fillet or butcher knife to cut away the "wings" from the body. The wings are where the vast majority of the flesh is located. Once they are removed, you can see three distinct layers inside the wing: two layers of flesh separated by a layer of cartilage in the middle. Use your fillet knife to slowly cut away the top flesh layer from the cartilage. After the flesh is detached from the cartilage, flip the flesh over and cut it away from the skin. You will notice the flesh does not come off in fillets, but as loosely connected "ribbons" of flesh. Place these "ribbons" in a bowl. Once all the flesh is removed from the top half of the wing, flip the wing over and repeat the process on the underside. In the end, you should have a bowl full of "skate ribbons."
>
> There are many ways to cook "skate ribbons." I treat them like scallops, as the texture and flavor are very similar. In fact, it can be difficult to tell the difference!

Pan-Fried Skate à la Mayes

1 egg, beaten
Panko breadcrumbs
Skate ribbons
Cooking oil (canola is recommended)

Beat the egg in a small bowl. Pour the panko into another bowl. Lay out the skate ribbons on a plate and season with salt and pepper.

Heat the oil in a skillet until hot (but not smoking!). Take one skate ribbon at a time and dip it in the beaten egg, then coat it with breadcrumbs, and place it in the hot skillet. Be sure to spread the skate ribbons evenly on the skillet.

Fry on medium heat for about 5 minutes, or until the ribbons are crispy and golden in color. Flip once to brown the other side.

Remove the skate ribbons from the skillet and serve. They're a great substitute for "fish and chips" and pair well with tartar or cocktail sauce.

BAT RAY
Raja binoculata

In truth, despite the fact that their meat is actually quite good, I'm sort of on the fence about whether to kill bat rays or not. My thinking here has little to do with science or sustainability and everything to do with sentiment. In the case of bat rays ... well ... what can I say, something about the helpless way they flap their wings when beached strikes me as uniquely tragic. For Poseidon's sake, this is the creature of petting tanks! Despite this (or maybe because of it?) bat rays are probably the most abused of all local fishes. I'm not sure what it is about this gentle and helpless creature that brings out the Hannibal Lecter in certain people, but only a chump willfully abuses a fish before letting it go—and yes, cutting off their tails and stingers is abusing them.

The Where, When, and How

Like leopard sharks, bat rays are easy to find. Just lob a hook laden with squid (or really anything) into the water anywhere on the California coast (especially in back bays and muddy harbors) and you will eventually get one. I've caught these fish at dead low tide, slack water, ebb, flow, high water, et cetera. The big ones are extremely powerful and have the annoying habit of digging down in the mud and refusing to budge. Twanging the line with your fingers sometimes annoys them enough to get them moving again, but not always. As far as the way they fight, bat rays are on the high end of the intelligence spectrum. They will often turn around mid-fight and swim directly toward shore, and are notorious for wrapping fishing lines around pilings.

Eat Them Up, Yum

From a strictly culinary perspective I will add that bat rays are surprisingly good to eat. I say surprisingly because comparatively few modern people eat them. Their remains are common in Native American shell mounds, so we know they were once a popular food source in California. But nine out of ten fishermen will snoot at the very idea of eating bat rays. I'm not sure why this is. Perhaps bat rays are too easy to catch to be valued appropriately. Or perhaps it's the thick, viscous slime on their bodies. Or the fact that they're often seen rooting around in very polluted areas. In any case, a bat ray's diet is no more or less problematic than, say, a halibut's. What do they eat? Among other things: worms, clam siphons, grass shrimp, ghost shrimp, crustaceans, and fish. Yes, they live a long time. And yes, some of them hang out in dirty water. News flash: if you are fishing in dirty water, you will catch dirty fish. I should point out that a lot of folks eat sturgeon, striped bass, and halibut caught along the same "dirty" stretches of shoreline where the supposedly dirty bat rays abound.

Cut the Cookie Cutter

The urban legend about prepping bat ray wings for the skillet has it that all you need is a cookie cutter. But bat ray wings need to be properly filleted and skinned.

Having humanely dispatched your bat ray with several blows of a billy club (it usually takes more than one), score the base of the wings with a sharp fillet knife and remove the skin from the top of the wing with a pair of pliers. (Or you can simply fillet the wing off the skin as you would with any fish.)

Like the skate wing described above, the meat of the bat ray runs horizontally on top of and below the cartilaginous skeletal structure of the wing.

Once the skin is off and the meat is freed from the wing, you can use the cookie cutter you were holding on to all this time to carve out and then bread and fry your "bay scallops." Or you can fry the whole fillet as described above with skate ribbons.

SHARKS

If you have no compunction about eating creatures that are extremely high in methyl mercury and other toxins, the shark family is for you. If you are similarly unconcerned about the ethics of targeting top-of-the-food-chain apex species, again, you may want to consider these fish. And if you put no stock at all in the popular Hawaiian concept that people who eat sharks will, through some sort of divine oceanic justice, be the first ones plucked off the surfboard, kayak, or paddleboard when a hungry shark happens to swim by, then you will have options that the anti-shark contingent does not have.

PREP

I'm putting this here at the top so that no one misses it: if you are bound and determined to eat shark meat, it is of vital importance that you bleed out or gut your fish immediately after capture. Sharks regulate their buoyancy by passing urea through their skins, and if you don't bleed them out, your meat will smell and taste like you pulled it out of a urinal. Inasmuch as it's possible, let's try to empathize with our quarry a bit. Bleeding it properly in the water or bonking it on the head and gutting it seems to me to be the least we can do to ease a shark's passing.

Okay, now that that's clear, here is a list of our most commonly targeted and/or eaten sport-caught sharks:

1. Leopard shark, *Triakis semifasciata*

2. Spiny dogfish, *Squalus suckleyi*

3. Brown smoothhound, *Mustelus henlei*

4. Broadnose sevengill shark, *Notorynchus cepedianus*

5. Soupfin shark, *Galeorhinus galeus*

6. Common thresher shark, *Alopias vulpinus*

LEOPARD SHARK
Triakis semifasciata

THE WHERE, WHEN, AND HOW

Cast any sort of bait, but especially a big chunk of sardine or squid (or a live midshipman) out into the Pacific Ocean or one of the bays or harbors in our range and you will eventually catch a leopard shark. Leopards seem to be most abundant in the spring and summer but they can be caught from shore year round. Tide does not seem to matter much, though I should add that in Tomales Bay and Bolinas Lagoon I consistently get them in the first few hours of the flood tide. If we are to believe the health department warnings, leopard sharks can be very high in methyl mercury and should not be eaten at all by kids seventeen and under and women in their childbearing years. Everyone else is okay to eat them once per week.

Leopard shark meat is very tasty—and especially good when grilled. I have it from several sources that it makes for an excellent ceviche but I gave up on it after a deeply negative first experience, which I relate below.

EAT THEM UP, YUCK

Not long ago, on my day off from fish patrol, I watched a pier fisherman cutting up leopard sharks and turning them into ceviche. That's what he told me he was doing—this friendly faced fisherman who had always struck me as a decent if slightly sodden sort of pier rat.

We were standing on a public pier in a fairly polluted section of southern San Francisco Bay. I wasn't sure what to make of this inner-city, mercury-laced ceviche-on-the-fly—but I harnessed my inner Bourdain, threw caution to the wind, and took the heaping forkful that was offered me. Why, you ask? I will be honest: there are three reasons I did this.

1. I've always wanted to try this leopard shark ceviche they talk about.

2. I figured one bite couldn't really hurt.

3. I figured that taking a bite of delicious (if somewhat sketchy) leopard shark ceviche would show everyone that I was one of the boys today.

So when Jose said, "Hey dude, here you go," and extended his hand with a plastic forkful of what I thought was leopard shark ceviche, I opened my mouth, blindly, and accepted it.

David Mamet once wrote, "A great meal fades in reflection; everything else gains." Despite my gastronomic bent, I have always agreed with this sentiment. Taste, more than any other sensation, is of the now. Of course there are other aspects of a meal that may improve upon reflection—the company, the music, the witty repartee—but as to the taste of the food, after we digest it and poop it out, it doesn't really live on. Not for me. That's all I'm saying. I've always felt this way. I have.

Until the day when that septuagenarian lunatic, Jose, put a forkful of polluted ceviche into my gaping mouth ...Even now, sitting here, the moment expands, snowballs, and blossoms into a heightened sequence of deep personal significance: (1) the briefly terrifying moment when I opened my mouth in a wide-eyed, deer-before-the-headlights sort of way, (2) the pregnant horror of the lukewarm slab hitting my tongue, (3) the reeking foretaste of its sun-drenched, dried-blood, enamel-like crust (hardened slightly more at its edges where the moisture had evaporated first, after sitting in the sun for half the day).

Suffice it to say: A *bad* meal gains.

It Wasn't Ceviche

What it was, was a thick chunk of raw downtown leopard shark upon which someone with a dirty, blood-covered hand had squeezed a lime that had been soaking along with the fillets in a cooler filled with melted ice cubes, spilled beer, dead anchovies, squid, and SF Bay water ... for approximately five hours. After which time it had been pulled out of this solution and left on a paper plate in the sun for another thirty-seven minutes ... That's what "ceviche" was to this lunatic drunk on the end of the pier. This kindly old man, whom I had somehow projected to be an Obi-Wan Kenobi type.

I tasted in that one miserable bite every savage injustice that had been visited upon that lime since it had been plucked. Every sewer that fish had swum through, eaten in, lived near. Every partially decomposed cat's head it had suckled in its fetid natal sluice, every outflow tube it had foraged around, every wad of feces it had (with frightful impassivity) taken in, mouthed, and swallowed ... every used syringe it had actually *considered* eating. Everything. All of it. In that single bite.

Where was I? Excuse my digression. Ahem ...

In short, the leopard shark wasn't very good. Not in that form. Maybe it would be as a proper ceviche, you know, with actual limes, like a gallon of actual limes. Nice, fragrant organic limes, four-dollar-a-pound holistic limes. But surely, not *that* lime! Not *that* terrible, bloodied slab of piss-flavored, poorly skinned bottom feeder. I could taste the rust from the dull blade that had hacked the living flesh from its filthy, worm-pocked flanks! Aaaaaggghhh!

They pee through their skins!

They pee through their skins!

So ... in short, without belaboring the point, the room-temperature leopard shark ceviche, with warm, bloody squid-flavored dirty fingernail lime juice—hey, it's just not for me. Nevertheless, in case there's someone out there you really don't like, the Sea Forager Editorial Machine is happy to provide the recipe:

Room-Temperature Leopard Shark Ceviche, with Warm Bloody Squid-Flavored Dirty Fingernail Lime Juice

> Filthy hands (for flavoring)
> Dull rusty knife (for flavoring/texture)
> Several unbled, rough-cut leopard shark fillets
> 5 gallons tap water/squid slime/anchovy blood/SF Bay-water solution, into which has been poured two cans of warm Budweiser beer
> ¼ bag Nacho Cheesier Doritos, finely crushed
> Limes, cut up however

Take filthy hands, scratch butt repeatedly, fix friend's broken sewer, change oil in truck, drive to pier, pick nose, cut bait, catch shark. Off the ground, pick up dull rusty knife with dried fish blood and undetermined black stains on blade. Using filthy hands and dull rusty knife, fillet shark and rinse in a 5-gallon bait bucket containing tap water/squid slime/anchovy blood/Bay-water solution. With a tough manly gesture, throw open the lid of a large cooler. Into this cooler dump the Doritos, and—as a nod to the original authors of this recipe—*anything else that may be lying around*. Pour bloody fillets and soaking liquid in this cooler, stopping every hour or so to hack off another chunk and pop it down your throat with a couple of swigs of flat beer.

After fillets have soaked for three hours, throw in a few limes and yell: "Hey guys, *ceviche!*" Continue to soak for rest of day, being careful not to stir any more than this solution would be stirred were there various people in the room, say, grabbing a lukewarm beer out of said cooler every five minutes or so.

Finally, reach into the cooler, grab a bleeding chunk of "ceviche," and squeeze a sliced lime on it with filthy hands. Hand this dirty, dripping piece of flesh to some sucker on his day off who's merely trying to blend in. Make sure this person is an optimistic type—the kind of guy who more often than not will give his fellow fisherman the benefit of the doubt.

Not until this last moment, having handed off your filthy morsel to a wide-eyed idiot, can you really be said to have produced a sterling example of Room-Temperature Leopard Shark Ceviche, with Warm Bloody Squid-Flavored Dirty Fingernail Lime Juice.

SEVENGILL SHARK
Notorynchus cepedianus

Think about this for a minute. If leopard sharks are problematic from a health standpoint, and a leopard shark has a wide-ranging diet that includes clam siphons, sea cucumbers, by-the-wind sailors, crustaceans, and small fish, what then are we to think of sevengills, which are known to feed on leopard sharks? I'm just putting this out there. I've killed a few of these over the years but in the end I always regret it. In my mind, there's something intrinsically problematic about hunting down the big piscivorous sharks. In the same way that it seems problematic to shoot tigers and jaguars.

That said, it's legal in California and many coastal fishermen are passionate about their sevengills.

THE WHERE, WHEN, AND HOW

All the sevengills I have seen or caught over the years came from San Francisco Bay. Hot spots seem to be all the deep channels. I should add that they are commonly caught in shallow water too, as many pier and shore fishers can attest. Fish deep and use a stinky bait: whole squid, mackerel, sardine, or anchovy.

If you're interested in eating a sevengill, see the recipes in *Thresher Shark* below.

SOUPFIN SHARK
Galeorhinus galeus

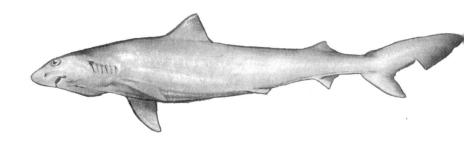

When it was discovered in the 1930s that the livers of soupfins contained large quantities of vitamin A, the price at dockside skyrocketed, fortunes were made, and shortly thereafter the population of soupfins plummeted. Fishermen in our area now encounter soupfins rarely, compared to leopard sharks, sevengills, and bat rays.

THE WHEN, WHERE, AND HOW

This shark is typically caught in the late summer and early fall on whole fish or squid, or big chunks of either. As far as specifically targeting them goes, I have no idea how to do it. And I can't say whether they prefer one kind of bait over something else. I've caught exactly two of these in my life. One bit on a whole squid, the other on a semi-live shiner perch. Both of them were caught in close proximity to the Berkeley Pier (indeed, one was *on* the Berkeley Pier).

SOUPFIN SOUP

I figure at this point most people have read about the unsustainable shark-finning fisheries of the planet. Seventy miles of longline spread over tropical reefs, with a hook every fifteen feet, fins lopped off, dying sharks heaped in piles on beaches or tossed overboard. Hopefully those targeting or randomly catching this species in SF Bay are resisting the suggestion implied by the name and doing something beyond using its fins for soup.

THRESHER SHARK
Alopias vulpinus

THE WHERE, WHEN, AND HOW

Of all the local sharks, the thresher is the one bona fide trophy species, a fish that Ernest Hemingway would've been happy to catch—and eat! As far as shore fishing goes, there is one pier in our area where threshers are occasionally caught: the ever-famous Pacifica Pier (out at the end). Otherwise you will need a kayak or small skiff. Any big bait, like a whole sardine or mackerel, or slow-trolled lure, like a big Rapala or crystal minnow, will work for threshers. Wire leaders are a must. Not only because of threshers' sharp teeth, but because they like to whack at the bait with their tails and tend to get snagged or wrapped up in the leader.

Believe it or not, fighting this fish is easy compared to landing it. In fact, doing the latter without turning your kayak over is a mark of great athleticism and balance. The way most kayak anglers land their threshers is by means of a rope lassoed around the tail. Just be forewarned: it's easier to roller skate on a kayak in heavy surf than it is to tail-lasso a thresher shark.

If you find yourself fighting a thresher shark and you intend to keep it, make sure of several things:

1. That all your gear is tied down.
2. That you do not bring the fish up "green."
3. That you do not bring the fish up "green."

These are big, strong, and extremely awkward-to-handle fish ... and yes, they can take off your fingers if they decide to bite them. So make sure there isn't a whole lot of fight left in your thresher when you bring it up to boatside. And the sooner you can bonk it and bleed it out, the better.

EAT THEM UP, YUM

Here's some more info on thresher shark cuisine from Chris "Clayman" Mayes, and his two best recipes. These recipes will also work for the other large sharks in this section.

> Once a thresher shark is landed, it must be bled immediately: use a knife to cut the shark's gills so that the blood pumps out. After the shark is bled, remove the innards and get to work butchering it like you would any other large fish. I prefer filleting the shark and cutting the fillets into smaller, serving-sized pieces. One extra thing that must be done while butchering the shark is to cut away all dark-colored flesh and discard it. The dark-colored flesh is fatty tissue that can give the shark a strong, off-putting flavor if not removed.

> The flesh is a light pink that turns white upon cooking. The texture is reminiscent of swordfish, though thresher shark is less fishy-tasting than swordfish.

Grilled Thresher

Chris says that this is the easiest and perhaps best method for cooking thresher shark, which "lends itself well to grilling, with its moderate fat content and firm flesh."

> 1 slab of thresher shark, about 1 inch thick
> Fresh dill, finely chopped
> Olive oil

Heat up the grill. If you're using a gas grill, set it to medium heat; if you're using a charcoal grill, push the charcoal to one side of the grill.

Season the thresher shark with salt, pepper, and dill. After seasoning, use a brush to spread olive oil across the shark.

On a gas grill, place the shark directly on the grill over the flame on medium heat. On a charcoal grill, place the shark on the side of the grill that does *not* have the coals. Cover and cook for 8–10 minutes. Occasionally check the shark to ensure it isn't burning.

Flip the shark once and cook on the other side for an additional 5 minutes.

Remove from heat and serve.

Thresher Shark in Curry Sauce

Chris calls this one of his "let's throw things together and see what happens recipes . . . Just another example of the versatility of thresher shark."

> Olive oil
> Chopped veggies, such as yellow onion, kale, and zucchini (the sky's the limit here)
> 1 can of coconut milk
> Curry powder
> Cumin powder
> White rice
> ½ lb thresher shark, cut into 1-inch cubes

In a large skillet, add a splash of olive oil and set to medium heat. While the skillet is heating, add salt and pepper to the chopped veggies in a bowl and mix with another splash of olive oil.

Add the veggies to the skillet. Cook on medium heat for about 10 minutes, or until the veggies are soft, stirring occasionally.

Once the veggies are soft, add the coconut milk and liberal doses of curry and cumin powder. Stir, then cover and simmer on medium-low heat. Start steaming the white rice in a separate pot or in a rice cooker.

While the curry is simmering, heat a medium-sized skillet on medium-high. Add a splash of oil to the skillet, then add the cubed thresher shark. The idea here is that you want to sear the edges of the thresher shark cubes, but not cook them all the way through.

Once the thresher cubes are seared, place them in the large skillet with the curry, stir, cover, and cook for an additional 5–7 minutes.

Remove from heat and serve over white rice.

Note: If you want to skip the homemade curry part, you can substitute the coconut milk/curry/cumin powder with a pre-made jarred alternative.

The Mainstream

SHELLFISH

Shellfish, of course, refers to members of several invertebrate groups, namely mollusks and crustaceans. In this chapter, we will look at some of the most popularly foraged species of shellfish in California, starting with the native bivalves, cockles, and mussels (alive, alive-o!), and ending with the Dungeness crab.

| BIVALVES |

HEALTH RISKS

Okay, let's get this out of the way:

Anyone gathering shellfish, especially filter-feeding bivalves like mussels, clams, and scallops, needs to be aware of the risks involved. As undelicious as these next few pages may be, if they scare you off, you weren't committed enough anyway!

PSP and ASP

Filter-feeding bivalves (plus some of the species that eat them, moonsnails and crabs to name two) and some plankton-eating fish (like anchovies and sardines; see chapter 1) can pick up naturally occurring biotoxins during "red" tides. The insidious thing about California's "red" tides is that, unlike those of other coastal areas around the country, our "red" tides are often invisible. This is because in California waters, the phytoplankton that cause red tides may not reach the densities that they do in, say, the Gulf of Mexico or other warmer coasts. Also, some (not all) visible red tides in California waters are completely harmless.

To be clear, the two conditions I'm talking about here are serious. Paralytic shellfish poisoning (PSP) is every bit as bad as it sounds, and amnesiac shellfish poisoning (ASP) wipes your hard drive clean. Both are potentially fatal. So be aware … *be very aware*. Oh yeah, and contrary to popular belief, cooking your shellfish does nothing to protect you from these conditions. It should also be pointed out that bivalves of the outer coast, especially mussels, rock scallops, and razor clams, tend to be at higher risk for biotoxins than the bivalves of the inner bays. Washington clams (aka butter clams) are evidently quite prone to picking up PSP toxins, which are problematically stored in their siphons.

Given This Sobering Information, How Do We Proceed?

By following the shellfish guidelines of the Office of Environmental Health Hazard Assessment (OEHHA), that's how. Every year from May 1 to October 31, the OEHHA closes mussel season. Dangerous algal blooms are most likely to occur in warmer-water months and by establishing a May through October quarantine, the health department effectively prevents the mussel-eating (and law-abiding) public from endangering itself. In addition to putting a total ban on mussels, the OEHHA *suggests* that the viscera of all other filter-feeding mollusks be discarded during these warmer-water months. Mussels receive special attention because they are such effective filter feeders—if there are any toxic diatoms in the water, they will likely end up in a mussel.

As of the writing of this book, there is a biotoxin monitoring hotline: 800-553-4133. Even if that number changes, the OEHHA (or whatever other abbreviation the health department may someday adopt) will probably keep their monitoring program going, as it is obviously of vital importance to the public.

The Raw and the Cooked

Another potential hazard for the shellfish forager is coliform bacteria. I am told that cooking your shellfish will not necessarily protect you from this either. And in any case many people in California want to eat their wild-gathered clams raw.

Unlike registered mollusk farms, sport pickers do not have biologists checking their clams for biotoxins and coliform bacteria. Local aquaculture facilities, on the other hand, are required by law to test their oysters, clams, and mussels on a regular basis. (This is why it is usually okay to eat farmed oysters and mussels during the quarantine. All oysters legally sold in California are farmed—and thus, tested).

If, after reading this, you are still bound and determined to eat your wild-foraged bivalves raw, avoid gathering them from near the mouths of streams or rivers, or after a heavy rain, as coliform bacteria generally reach estuarine environments by means of runoff. The tendency of many coastal clam aficionados to eat raw gaper clams dug out from the filthy mud next to public launch ramps or other high-use areas at the back ends of busy harbors (where there is little water flow) is highly problematic from a health standpoint.

Months with Rs in Them

A lot of coastal foragers follow the old rule to "only pick your mussels during months with Rs in them." The problem with this is that in our area, September and October can be warm-water months, and warm water is one of the major contributors to toxic algal blooms. The R-month meme (and really that's what it's become) was first mentioned in 1599 by William Butler, personal physician to King James I: "It is unseasonable and unwholesome in all months that have not an R in their name to eat an oyster."

It should be noted that the English coastal ecosystem of 1599 was quite different than the California coastal ecosystem of 2016. So, in short, forget about the "R" months and remember that in California mussel season is closed from May 1 through October 31. This closure was instituted in 1934, and since then, only one person has died from PSP in California and that individual supposedly ate a rock scallop in the summer. Although this closure was put in place by the health department, it is fully enforced by the California Department of Fish and Wildlife.

Shellfish

MUSSELS

Now that I've spent several pages trying to scare you off, it's time for some good news: the people of California have been eating mussels for thousands of years.[1] And there are good reasons for this. Namely, mussels are: easy to find, easy to capture, and delicious.

CALIFORNIA MUSSEL
Mytilus californiensis

THE WHERE, WHEN, AND HOW

California mussels are found on rocky areas of the open coast, statewide. You do not need a minus tide to reach your mussel beds, as you do for many other intertidal invertebrates. Any low tide of +0.5 or lower should reveal a few reachable mussels. Only trophy hunters need to target them on ultra-low tides.

The regulations very clearly state that mussels may only be taken by hand or by hook and line.[2] Nevertheless, it seems like every time I go mussel picking I see people out there with crowbars, screwdrivers, trowels, rakes—in short, everything but the kitchen sink. It's really too bad. The devastation (or the threat of it) wreaked by these folks after a day of ripping the beds apart is probably one of the reasons the MLPA has closed a lot of our coast to shore use. You can't really have a protected

1 Although eutrophication and global warming trends have contributed to increased incidence of toxic algal blooms, the naturally occurring biotoxins that we have in our waters today have been here for a long time. In other words, local Native Americans, who subsisted on mussels, had to deal with these same problematic diatoms.

2 This is a general rule for all mollusks, not just mussels. Since octopus and squid are mollusks and many people like to catch them with hook and line, the rules allow for mollusks (hence mussels) to be caught this way.

marine area that allows people to go at the mussel beds with tire irons and hammers, now can you? So my suggestion (as per usual) is *follow the rules*. Get a thick pair of gloves and pick 'em with your hands. Not only will it look better to the PETA activists standing next to the resource managers and watching you with binoculars from the cliffs, but the fauna of the mussel beds will appreciate it greatly. There's also some room for interpretation where "hook and line" is concerned.[3] The bag limit as of this writing is ten pounds per day, and the mussel picker needs to have an accurate scale to weigh them—"Sorry officer, I thought it was only ten pounds" isn't going to work with most game wardens. California mussels are unquestionably the hawgs of the mussel family, attaining sizes up to ten inches in length.

Big mussels vs. little mussels

Personally, I prefer the medium to smallish mussels. The big ones can be kind of rubbery and there's also something about having a quarter pound of California mussel in my mouth that's a bit too intense for me. Too much of a good thing, I guess. But there are many who prefer the lunkers—to each his or her own.

Eat Them Up, Yum

As far as their culinary properties, it's all very easy with mussels: steam 'em or boil 'em—when they open, they're done. There is no denying that California mussels can be a bit gritty. To reduce this grittiness, soak them overnight in a bucket of clean ocean water. This will allow them to spit out any sand or grit in their digestive tracts. Also, as you might have guessed, mussels plucked from rocks on sandy beaches will be grittier than those plucked in rocky areas or a few feet further up the rock from sandy bottom.[4] Either way, make sure to rinse and scrub them well, and be forewarned: if you dump them into your

3 Again, think about it for a minute but don't go crazy with your interpretation. A crowbar with two inches of line on it is not by anyone's estimation "in the spirit of the law."
4 Steaming mussels is another effective way to reduce grittiness. When mussels are boiled, the rocks, sand, and barnacles all sort of mix around in the pot and settle where they will. Obviously, there will be much less of this mixing inside a steamer.

bouillabaisse without scrubbing them you're likely to crack your teeth on barnacles and grains of sand. These ain't your clean, farm-reared, store-bought mussels! They also have thick, chewy beards that need to be pulled, bitten, or cut off.

The author advocates scrubbing, pulling the beards off, steaming, deshelling, then adding them to the main course. But there's no need to get fancy with mussels. Ten pounds whole comes out to about two solid pounds of de-shelled mussel meat.[5] So you can actually serve them as a main course. Really, nothing beats steamed mussels dipped in a little garlic butter.

Should you feel a little more adventurous, here's a recipe from Camilla "The Fishwife" Lombard's lovely kitchen:

Drunken Mussels with Fennel and Lemon à la Fishwife

> 2 lbs mussels
> 2 bottles light Belgian-style ale (such as Leffe or Duvel)
> 2 Tbsp butter
> ½ medium onion, sliced
> ½ medium fennel bulb, cored and sliced
> ½ cup heavy cream
> 2 tsp lemon zest
> ½ tsp chopped Italian parsley, if you have it (for color)
> Crusty bread to mop up the goodness

First, scrub and "debeard" the mussel shells by scrubbing and tugging the beard off (pull it away from the opening). Then, open a beer for the chef and pull out a big cast-iron skillet, Le Creuset, or any heavy pot with a lid.

Melt your butter until foamy on medium heat, then toss in your onion and fennel. Cook about 5 minutes, adding salt and pepper to taste.

Open another beer, add it to your pot, and bring to a boisterous boil. You may want to start warming your bread in a low oven at this point.

Add the mussels and lower the heat, cover, and simmer for 10 minutes. Shake the pan from time to time—it's fun.

At this point, your mussels should be opening.

When they're open, take tongs or a slotted spoon and put them into two large serving bowls to hang out while you make your sauce. *Note*: If they are not open at this point, discard them.

5 Ten pounds is the legal limit.

Add the cream and lemon zest to your pot and simmer, stirring here and there for a few minutes until it thickens. Taste, adding salt and pepper if it needs it.

Pour your creamy mussel magic sauce over the mussels in the bowls, and break out the bread and another beer. Cheers!

BAY MUSSEL (BLUE MUSSEL)
Mytilus trossulus, Mytilus edulis,
Mytilus galloprovincialis (and hybrids thereof)

Bay mussels are most frequently encountered inside bays and harbors. As you can see in the illustration, the bay's shell is less elongate and more curved than that of the California mussel.

MINUTIAE

The bay mussel is featured prominently on the inventory lists for the various California shell mounds compiled by archeologists in the early twentieth century, where it is listed as *M. edulis*. *M. edulis,* however, is now used exclusively for the non-native European mussel, *M. trossulus* being the new(ish) name for the native bay mussel.[6] In addition, *M. galloprovincialis,* the European blue mussel, has been farmed in California for many years and has established wild populations in several sheltered bays along the coast. All three species of *Mytilus*

Shellfish

---

6 *M. edulis* is thought to be one of the first invasive species of the modern era, having probably arrived here via the hulls of Spanish galleons in the eighteenth century.

are perfectly happy (one might even say eager) to hybridize anywhere they occur in proximity to one another, like for instance in Tomales Bay. So your wild-gathered bay mussel is either a native *(M. trossulus)* or an invasive species *(M. edulis* or *M. galloprovincialis*), or a hybrid of any of the three. Now wasn't that all deeply helpful?

There are plenty of old-timers who still pick bay mussels from inside SF Bay and from the pilings and docks of marinas all over the state, but I advise against eating these inner-city/inner-harbor mussels. Again, since they don't move around much and are such effective filter feeders, mussels may pick up toxins that are in the water where they live.

THE WHERE, WHEN, AND HOW

Of the two main species of mussels foraged on the West Coast (bays and Californias), bay mussels are tastier and less chewy. Unfortunately, due to the fact that they like sheltered coves, bays, harbors, and inlets, and these types of habitats tend to be more vulnerable to pollution than areas of the open coast, it can be challenging to find bay mussels in anything even approximating clean water—challenging but not impossible. Generally speaking, the further you are from major urban centers, the cleaner the water will be ... although in rural areas make sure you are not gathering them from the mouths of coastal streams or rivers.[7] You can reach these guys under docks during any tide, but inner-harbor mussels (especially the big ones) should only be used for bait (see chapter 3 for other "invertebaits"). Otherwise, gathering mussels is a low-tide foraging activity. One excellent way to locate bay mussels is to find out where mussels are being farmed. Then walk along the public shorelines adjacent to these areas at low tide and you are sure to find quite a few escapees growing on intertidal rocks.

EAT THEM UP, YUM

See *California Mussel* above—same deal with cooking them. The only difference is that bay mussels typically have less encrusting growth and smaller beards. Also, they may be more muddy than sandy so soaking them overnight (or at least for a few hours) in an aerated bucket of clean ocean water is probably a good idea. Here's a recipe for them from the illustrious Terry Paetzold:

---

7 Where run-off may be problematic.

Mussel Soup with Saffron Cream

2 ½–3 lbs mussels
4 Tbsp extra virgin olive oil
4 Tbsp unsalted butter
1 leek, white only, cleaned and finely chopped
3 medium onions, finely chopped
2 bundles of bouquet garni (a couple of leek greens folded around a bay leaf, fresh parsley, and thyme and tied with kitchen string or wrapped in cheesecloth)
½ tsp white peppercorns, crushed
½ cup dry white wine
2 carrots, peeled and diced
1 medium celery stalk, diced
1 clove garlic, crushed
Kosher salt
1 large tomato, peeled and seeded, roughly chopped
3 ½ cups fish stock
2/3 cup heavy cream
Pinch of saffron
Freshly ground pepper
Fresh chervil

Prepare the mussels by lightly washing them and gently removing their beards. Place a 4- to 6-quart stainless casserole or pot over medium-high heat and heat half the olive oil and butter. Add the chopped leek and one-third of the chopped onion. Stir gently and cook 3–4 minutes, until translucent and soft. Add the cleaned mussels, a bouquet garni, the crushed white pepper, and the white wine. Continue to cook on medium-high heat and bring the liquid to a simmer for 4–5 minutes to allow the mussels to open, cook gently, and produce their cooking liquor. Uncover to check to see that the mussels have all opened and discard any that have not (these are not safe to eat). Remove the pot from the heat, remove the mussels from their shells, and place the meat in a small bowl and set aside. Discard the mussel shells, and pour all of the cooking liquor remaining in the pot into another small container.

In the same 4- to 6-quart pot used above, heat the remaining olive oil and butter on medium-high. Add the remaining onions and the carrots, celery, and garlic. Salt lightly. Cook on medium heat for 10–12 minutes to sweat the ingredients. Add the second bouquet garni, the tomato, the fish stock, and the reserved cooking liquor from the mussels. Bring to a slight boil and then simmer gently for 20 minutes. While the soup is simmering place the cream in a glass bowl and heat on medium in the microwave for about 2 minutes or until hot (do not boil). Add the pinch of saffron and steep the saffron in the cream while the soup continues to simmer. Strain the cream into the soup and mix well. With an immersion blender, puree the soup until smooth. Taste and correct seasoning with salt and pepper. Strain the soup if desired for a smoother consistency. Reheat on medium. Divide the mussels into six soup bowls and pour hot soup into each bowl. Garnish with fresh chervil and serve immediately.

HORSENECK CLAM (GAPER CLAM)
Tresus capax, Tresus nuttallii

The horseneck is also known as the gaper clam, horse clam, summer clam, great Washington clam, rubberneck clam, longneck clam, and big neck clam. "After this appalling array of popular names," say Ricketts and Calvin, in *Between Pacific Tides,* "it is almost restful to call the animal *Tresus nuttallii.*"

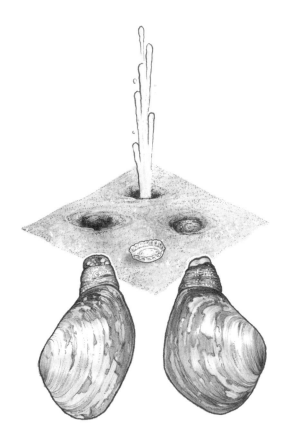

Impress Your Friends

The horseneck comes in two varieties:

>1. *Tresus nuttallii* is the horseneck found inside muddy bays, buried three to four feet deep in the mud. It is the more southerly variety, common from central California to the Oregon border.

>2. *Tresus capax* is often found in sandy mud, or occasionally in sheltered areas along the coast. As a general rule, *capax* becomes more common the further north one goes in California. Though often just as deep in the mud, *capax* on the whole digs a shallower hole than *nuttallii*.

The name *nuttallii* refers to the English botanist Thomas Nuttall, who traveled extensively in North America in the early 1800s and has twelve species of animals and plants named after him. California history buffs will note that he was an acquaintance of writer Richard Henry Dana, and was the model for the character Old Curiosity in Dana's seminal 1837 travelogue, *Two Years before the Mast.*

Like most clams, horsenecks are broadcast spawners. First, the male and female cells mix in the water column. Then, after a brief free-swimming larval stage, the miniature clams settle in the mud and begin the long process of digging down. A two-inch horseneck is about a year old. Horsenecks reach sexual maturity at 2.75 inches and two years of age. At this point their digging abilities diminish considerably. Horsenecks can live to at least seventeen years, but evidently do not reach the incredible one hundred plus years of that other monster clam of the mudflats, the gooey-duck.

Since they don't move around a whole lot, you want to consider the relative cleanliness of your clam grounds before you start digging horsenecks. A clam that has been living next to a busy launch ramp, in an urban area, or at the back end of a marina for seventeen years may not be the one you want to eat for dinner.

Fill in Your Hole!

In Washington, clammers are required by law to fill in their holes after clamming; in Oregon, it's strongly suggested on the regulations page. But for some inexplicable reason, California clammers don't have to do this. The theory behind the rule in Washington is that horsenecks and many associated species need tightly packed mud to travel, feed, and conduct the normal business of mudflat invertebrates. Fail to fill in your holes and they will be filled very loosely by the advancing tide. Loosely packed mudflats will, over time, become clamless ones. In addition, the Washington DFW website says this: "Before leaving the beach, refill the holes you've dug. Failure to fill holes is extremely damaging to many species of clams. Small seed clams are smothered and killed by high earth piles left after digging, while other clams are killed by the higher temperature of water that collects in unfilled holes. Harvesting regulations require that all holes created while digging clams must be refilled. Failure to do so may result in fines of up to seventy-five dollars per hole."

So, regardless of whether or not it is required by law in California, be a good citizen of the intertidal zone and fill in your hole!

Another thing: ask yourself if it's really necessary to dig ten gapers every time you go out. As we have established, these clams are big—sometimes *very* big. Honestly, how many do you need? I have noticed a tendency among many California fishers and clammers to feel as though the day was unsuccessful if they did not "get limits" of clams, rockfish, whatever. Six months later, when these folks are throwing out all the freezer-burned fillets or clam steaks, I wonder if they stop to consider how wasteful it was to take so many?

Keep in mind that although horseneck populations are susceptible to over-harvesting by humans, they are often plentiful in subtidal waters (down to fifty feet) and in rocky outcroppings where no human mortal could possibly hope to dig them up. So even in heavily clammed areas there are usually pockets of abundance that will keep the clams from being completely fished out.

THE HUNT

Most people, especially transplanted East Coasters, associate clam gathering with rolled-up trousers, pitchforks, and wholesome picnics on the beach. This type of happy clamming is possible in California, but for horsenecks we will forgo the picnic basket and the quaint accouterments of Atlantic-style clamming for a forty-inch piece of PVC tubing, a shovel, and a trip to some reeking back bay or inner harbor.

Here's the list of tools you'll need to forage horsenecks:

> Waders (or clothes you don't mind getting muddy)
>
> Clam tube[8]
>
> Shovel (not a post-hole digger and not a regularly angled shovel)

---

8 See Swim Bladder 5 for an illustration. I should point out that it is not always necessary to use a clam tube. In very densely packed mud, horsenecks may not be as deep as they tend to be in looser, more watery mud. Recently, I was able to get five lunker clams without ever breaking out the ol' tube. In fact, due to the density of the mud, all of these recent clams were easily caught within a foot and a half of the surface—would that all clamming trips were so easy! In more northerly areas of the state, where *T. capax* abounds, you may not have to dig quite so deep as those of us to the south. Also, the method of grabbing the clam by its siphon and digging it out with a hand trowel will only work if the body of the clam is not particularly deep. More often than not, attempting to do so will result in you breaking the tip of the siphon and killing the clam.

Rubber gloves

A small but sturdy hand trowel, scooper, or hand-sized bowl … as you dig closer to the clam you will find this useful

Several small-diameter sticks or ½-inch dowels, tipped with some kind of distinctive marker or flag. These sticks should be about three feet in length.

Okay, now that we've covered the basics, we can proceed.

THE WHERE, WHEN, AND HOW

During a very low minus tide (-0.4 and lower), walk along your preferred mud-flat at water's edge, looking for quarter-sized holes. Any tiny holes (smaller than a dime in circumference) are most likely ghost shrimp holes—ignore them unless you're going sturgeon or perch fishing sometime soon.

If you can't find quarter-sized holes, then get really mad, have a temper tantrum, and start stomping around. Seriously. The vibrations from this will alarm any nearby horseneck clams, and as they pull their necks back down into the depths, they will shoot a spout of water or reveal their gaping holes to you—hence their other common name, gaper clam.[9] (This is actually the official name of the species in the California DFG regulations booklet.)

Lombard's Two-Finger Rule and Flag Ceremony

If the hole is wide enough for two fingers, you're golden. A one-finger hole may hold a clam but that clam will not be big enough to justify the ridiculous expenditure of energy involved in bringing it to the surface.

At this point you will grab one of your half-inch dowels and place it in the two-finger hole. I usually bring five of these little sticks to the mudflats—all of them tipped with proud little red flags bearing my clan's distinctive coat of arms. It's a cold, hard world out there and it gets quite competitive in the good clam beds. Marking the holes you intend to dig may seem obsessively terri-torial, but trust me on this; it's preferable to having eighteen wild-eyed clam aficionados descend on your area and dig out all your clams before you've even gotten your waders on. Also, if you push the stick into the hole until it stops, you will have a good idea of how far down the clam is.

9 Experienced clammers immediately know a horseneck hole when they see one, but novices often mistake a random bubble, a divot, or a distorted ghost shrimp hole for a clam hole. Since it may take as long as twenty minutes to dig out a single clam, and you do not have an unlimited amount of time before the tide turns, make sure you feel the tip of the siphon with your fingers, see a squirt of water shoot from the hole when you stomp the mud near it, or visibly notice the widening of the hole as clam siphon descends before you start digging. Read that sentence again, it's important.

Okay, once you've marked your clam holes (anything more than five sticks is downright anti-social), place your tube around the dowel/flag so that the dowel, and hence the hole, is dead center. Shove the clam tube straight down into the mud (around the flag). Luckily, horseneck clams dig perfectly vertical holes. This is the only reason they are catchable. Natural selection will eventually favor clams with diagonal holes, so you definitely want to get your gapers sometime in the next two to three million years.

Shove your tube as deep as you can. You will probably have to stand (jump, wiggle, and dance) on it to get it to go all the way down. Once you've got the top of the tube almost flush to the mud, start digging out the sand from inside the tube. The further importance of the dowel will now reveal itself to you: it will keep you on target as you dig. And digging is what this is all about.

Down, Down, Down ...

Down into the fetid muck you go. When your back is sore, your face smeared with mud, your leaking boots awash with sulfurous spume, know this: you are getting close. As you dig, be gentle—don't just thrust your shovel blindly! Occa-

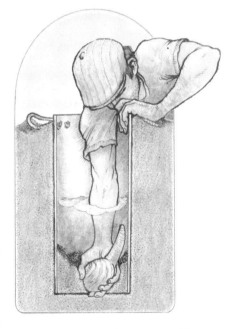

sionally the clams are quite close to the surface. When you think you're near the clam (usually two to three feet down) put the shovel aside and commence digging with your hands, a trowel, or a bowl. Lying on your side in the mud, extend your arm downward inside the tube and grope for the "nose" of the clam—the tip of the siphon. But be forewarned that you can't catch a horseneck clam by pulling on the siphon! The difficulty lies in getting your hand underneath or around the clam. Only when you've come to understand how tightly packed the mud is, how big the clams are, and how deep you have to dig will you fully appreciate how difficult this is to do.

It is here that the true aesthete can be separated from the untutored boor. Many are the clammers who, lacking skill and resolve, simply pull on the siphon (where most of the meat is), sever it, and leave the body of the clam to die and rot in the depths. A true artiste of the mudflats (i.e., a person of valor and worth) would never do this (although this is the way leopard sharks and bat rays go about things). First, it's wasteful. Second, a real clammer takes great pride in removing the whole beast, unbroken from the mud.

Now that you've got your clam, rinse it off so you can behold it in all its phallic glory. If you followed Lombard's Two-Finger Rule, you've unearthed a four-pound behemoth, a mollusk to be proud of! But don't get too full of yourself. There is more mucking to do and there are bigger clams to conquer!

Eat Them Up, Yum

Next to the gooey-duck, this is the largest clam in California. And certainly one of the meatiest. But you can't just cook these guys whole.

A Clammer Prepares

When you've finally finished with the digging and mucking about, take your clams to a place with running water and begin cleaning. Insert the tip of a fillet knife between the two shells and slice along the front edge to the adductor muscles at the back.

This will cause the clam to open. Now look inside. All the white parts are generally edible. Most of the meat will be in the siphon (which, when skinned, will be white or nearly white) and the whitish parts connected to it. The strip of meat along the rim of the inside of the shell is good. Throw away the dark, goopy parts—these are the guts and skin of the clam. One of the choicest tidbits is the foot: the fatty, off-white or beige lobe in the center of the guts. You can't miss it. Pull it out, slice it lengthwise, and clean it thoroughly.

Now take the siphon and slit it lengthwise, just as you would gut an eel (in other words, don't cut it in half—splay it). Rinse out all the sand and mud from the two parallel narrow tubes that run lengthwise inside the siphon. Cut off and discard the hard, purplish-black tip or "nose." Place the slit (one might even say circumcised) siphons in warm fresh water for ten minutes. Remove them and peel off the goopy, brown skin (appetizing, eh?). The underlying meat should be white or whitish in color. Now, if you intend to cook your clams, get a meat-tenderizing hammer and slam the hell out of the prepped tubes—but not so much that you break through them or splatter your kitchen walls. An old-fashioned meat grinder also works great for this. Once they have been reasonably pulverized, slice them into strips and add them to chowder, or batter and fry—being careful in both cases not to overcook.

In my own humble opinion, horseneck clam siphons are best eaten raw. They are sweet, tender, and utterly delicious this way—the poor man's gooey-duck. But here's the thing: gapers do not always hang out in the cleanest spots. So if you are planning to eat them raw, avoid digging them from areas adjacent to coastal creeks, sewer outflow tubes, busy launch ramps, and highly urbanized shorelines.

The Fishwife's Crockpot Manhattan Chowder

Camilla says, "Just put it in the crockpot! Let the slow cooker get the base going while you go forage clams (or a livelihood), and come home in time to toss in the clams and enjoy your bounty." This is great for cockles, butter clams, horsenecks, or piddocks.

> 2 strips bacon, chopped (always a good place to start)
> 1 Tbsp corn flour
> 1 can of diced tomatoes (or if you're feeling inspired, make your own tomato sauce)
> 3 potatoes, peeled and diced
> 1 large onion, chopped
> 3 stalks of celery, chopped
> 3 carrots, chopped
> Chunks of rockfish fillet (optional)
> 15+ cockles or small butter clams if you have 'em, or just add chopped up and tenderized gaper or piddock siphons
> Fresh Italian parsley
> Fresh loaf of sourdough for dipping

Fry the chopped bacon in a skillet. When it has browned, remove it from the skillet, mix the corn flour with the grease, and cook briefly to make a simple roux.

Then drop the bacon, roux, vegetables, and rockfish (if using) into the crockpot, set it on medium or low, and come back in 6–8 hours to some awesome chowder.

Obviously you don't want to cook your clams for 6 hours. So drop them in (uncooked) sometime in the last 15 minutes, depending on how hot the crockpot is cooking (you want it to be boiling at this point). Once the clams open, they are done. If you're using basket cockles (especially the big baseball-sized ones), you'll want to remove them from the shell once they open, chop them up, and return them to the chowder as they are a large mouthful. Likewise, if you're using gaper siphons, slam them for a few seconds with a tenderizing hammer, and then cut them into small pieces before adding to the pot.

Put into bowls, top with the chopped parsley and enjoy with some fresh sourdough.

GOOEY-DUCK

Panopea generosa

I for one am completely done with this whole "*geo*duck" business. I guess the original spelling *g'weduc,* with its strange apostrophe and linguistically advanced Nisqually *g-w* combo, was too mind bending for modern American public consumption. Okay, I get it. But I'd really like to know who the genius was who stuck "geo" on there as the alternative. A pox on this miscreant! In any case, I'm going with the transliteration here: gooey-duck. From the Nisqually *g'weduc,* meaning "dig deep."

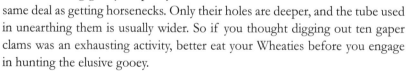

THE WHEN, WHERE, AND HOW

The gooey is the king of all the West Coast clams and is only rarely caught below the extreme northern reaches of the California coast.[10] Getting gooeys is pretty much the same deal as getting horsenecks. Only their holes are deeper, and the tube used in unearthing them is usually wider. So if you thought digging out ten gaper clams was an exhausting activity, better eat your Wheaties before you engage in hunting the elusive gooey.

EAT THEM UP, YUM

This clam is best eaten raw. Cut the clam open, remove the dark, goopy guts, soak the neck in warm water to remove the skin, and then cut it into small pieces. Eat as raw slabs or as nigiri, with some soy sauce, wasabi, and ginger over a small bed of rice.

Shellfish

---

10   The largest gooey ever caught weighed in at an almost obscene twelve pounds.

WASHINGTON CLAM
Saxidomus nuttalli (aka Martha Washington clam)
Saxidomus giganteus (aka butter clam)

Washington clams are typically found in muddy sand or sandy mud inside bays and harbors. Happily for us they require much less elbow grease than their more labor-intensive cousins: gooey-ducks and gapers—so leave the clam tube at home. Washington clams are seldom found more than eighteen inches deep and can be dug out by shovel, trowel, or hand. It should be noted that they retain PSP toxins for a long time, and that these toxins are stored in the dark tips of their siphons (so cut these off before eating them). This is evidently an evolutionary adaptation designed to impress upon bat rays and leopard sharks that biting off their siphons is a bad idea.

The picture below represents the ideal Washington clam show. But often all you will find is a vague cup-shaped dimpling of the muddy surface. The bag limit as of this writing is ten per day and there is no minimum size for either species of Washington clam.

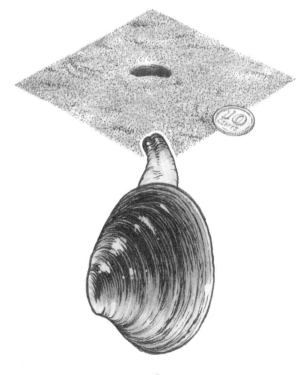

LITTLENECKS, MANILAS, AND COCKLES (OH MY)

The Where, When, and How

Now that we're finished with the dark and dirty business of horseneck and gooey-duck clam digging, let's discuss that type of "happy clamming" referred to earlier. No tubes, sticks, waders, or special shovels required. All you will need to get these clams is a four-pronged potato cultivator, a clam gauge (to make sure they're legal), and a bucket to put them in.[11]

All three of these species prefer pebbly, coarse-grained stretches of shoreline (though littlenecks will also burrow into soft rock and mud), typically inside coastal bays.[12] Once you've arrived at a prospective location, walk along the shoreline and look for empty clamshells. This is literally a dead giveaway that there are live clams nearby.[13] Having located an area with lots of empty shells, start raking.[14] If you are digging down more than eight inches, you're going too deep. Be advised that these clams blend in with rubble and small rocks very well. So focus your eyes and occasionally pick up any suspicious-looking clumps of mud or gravel to make sure they aren't well-camouflaged clams. All three species, but especially littlenecks and Manilas, tend to be found in veins. So, if you find a couple of nice ones, keep digging nearby and you will likely find more.

Once you've caught your limit,[15] rinse them thoroughly in the cleanest ocean water you can find. Then fill up your bucket with that same clean ocean water and let the clams soak in it for one to three days. This will allow them to spit out any sand or mud that may be in their digestive tracts. Some clammers insist that sprinkling cornmeal into their buckets (yes, right into the water on top of the clams) will induce them to void their bowels more quickly. I'm not really sure if this is true or not but I do it anyway since it sounds good. If you are planning on soaking your clams for more than a day, get one of those

11 Minimum size as of this writing: 1.5 inches. Bag limit: fifty, in combination, per day.

12 In areas where littlenecks burrow into soft rock, it can be a real drag getting them out—and is potentially harmful to coastal habitat, since the only way to unearth them is by prying or breaking the rocks apart. They can also be found in gravelly, rocky sections of the outer coast, but they are more difficult to find in these areas, and seldom reach the population densities that they do in protected bays and harbors.

13 In fact, this is one of the essential truths of clam digging: *when you find the shells of dead clams, the live ones are nearby.*

14 "An area with lots of empty shells" may seem a tad unspecific, but I have caught all three types of clams everywhere from a few feet from the top of the high tideline to a few feet from the bottom. The main thing is to locate pockets of empty shells and dig down beneath them, whether they are low or high in the tideline.

15 If this takes more than thirty minutes, find a different spot.

battery-powered air pumps that clip onto the side of your bucket. That way you don't have to worry about any clams dying on you.[16] And before you throw your clams into the steamer, rinse them again thoroughly in cold tap water, as they will have been spitting up the contents of their stomachs all over one another for several days.

Not everyone subscribes to the bucket model. Local West Coast seafood gourmand and crown prince of all coastal hobos, John Foss, recommends placing clams on a bed of damp paper towels and leaving them in the vegetable crisper for a day before eating them. "If you leave them in a bucket of water to void their bowels you're just creating a bacteria soup," says John.

Note: littlenecks and Manilas are very common in inner-city waters. Everyone knows that these areas are problematic from a pollution standpoint. It often strikes me as deeply ironic that I drive so far to get clams that I could very easily rake from SF Bay ten minutes from my front door. But even though they aren't very high on the food chain, clams don't move around a whole lot, so any toxins or contaminants that settle in the mud where they live could potentially end up inside them. You might want to keep this in mind before you go raking up any of the millions of clams in the Brisbane Lagoon, the Oakland Estuary, or Richmond Inner Harbor.

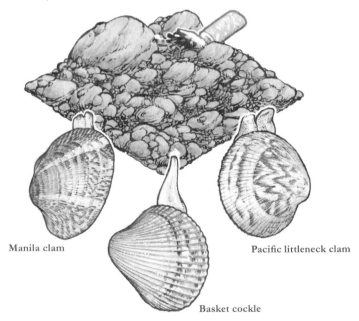

Manila clam   Pacific littleneck clam

Basket cockle

16 When bivalves die, their adductor muscles relax and the shells separate. So always make sure to tap them. If they close tight, they're good to go. If they remain open, don't eat them!

LITTLENECK CLAM
Protothaca staminea

CONFUSION

Unfortunately, in California, the colloquial name for the littleneck clam happens to be cockle.[17] To make matters more confusing, imported Atlantic littlenecks *(Mercenaria mercenaria)* are probably the most common steamer clams in local restaurants—so when the citizenry thinks littleneck, they tend to think Atlantic littleneck.[18] And when they hear "cockle" they think of local littlenecks. As of this writing there are no commercially harvested Pacific littleneck clams currently being sold in California, so if you want to eat them, you only have one option: catch them yourself.

EAT THEM UP, YUM

Littlenecks gathered higher up the tideline tend to be prettier and more appetizing in appearance than the low down ones. If you find yourself digging in black soupy mud, you are either digging too deep or too low in the intertidal zone.

Not for Chowdah

I'd like to state for the record that anyone who uses Pacific littlenecks for chowder should be tarred, feathered, and run out of town.[19] In short: clams this small and flavorful should not be smothered in heavy cream and drowned in tomato sauce. They should be steamed (using this method: sauté 1 chopped onion and 2 cloves of garlic in ¼ stick of butter, then add 1 cup wine and 1½ cups water, and simmer your clams—lid on—in this loveliness until they open, then top with a bit of chopped parsley and enjoy) and eaten one at a time (with a little sourdough to dunk in the broth), so that their delicate oceanic flavors can be appreciated in full.

Ahem, that said, littleneck vongole is really, really hard to argue with. Here's one from wonder-chef Terry Paetzold:

17 For our purposes, a littleneck is a Pacific littleneck *(Protothaca staminea),* a Manila is a Manila *(Venerupis phillippinarum),* and a cockle is a basket cockle *(Clinocardium nuttallii).*

18 *M. mercenaria* goes by four different names, according to size: tiny ones are called countnecks, small ones are called littlenecks, medium ones are cherrystones, and big ones are called quahogs.

19 I'm just kidding. Really. I swear it. Lots of clam diggers use Pacific littlenecks for chowder.

Littleneck Vongole

2 Tbsp extra virgin olive oil
2/3 of a link of Calabrese sausage, sliced (about 1/3 cup)
1 large head of garlic (about 15 cloves), finely chopped
12–15 fresh clams
½ cup white wine
1/3 cup plus 2 Tbsp chicken broth (unsalted, preferably)
2 tsp unsalted butter, broken into small bits
Freshly ground pepper
1 cup croutons (heated in a low oven)
4 sprigs fresh flatleaf parsley, finely chopped

Heat the extra virgin olive oil in a 12-inch cast iron fry pan (or heavy-duty stainless sauté pan) over medium heat and add the sliced sausage. Sauté slowly until the sausage begins to brown and caramelize slightly on the surface. Add the chopped garlic to the pan, stir, and cook for a few minutes, allowing the garlic to soften without browning.

Turn the heat up to medium-high and immediately add the clams and white wine to the garlic-sausage mixture, allowing the wine to simmer and deglaze the pan. Add the chicken broth, stir slightly, and place a lid over the clams, bringing the mixture up to a steady simmer until all of the clamshells have opened (about 3–5 minutes). Remove the lid, turn the heat to medium-low, and discard any clams that have not opened (indicates the clam is dead and not suitable for consumption). Add the bits of unsalted butter to the pan and stir well. Taste and correct seasoning with freshly ground pepper. Leave the clams in the pan or transfer the mixture to a large heated platter. Toss warm croutons over the top and garnish with freshly chopped parsley. Serve immediately.

Note: Occasionally this recipe may be saltier than preferred due to the salt content of the clams. When adjusting the seasoning, do not hesitate to add more wine or unsalted chicken broth by the quarter cup to dilute the sodium content. Stir the additional liquid into the mixture and bring to a quick simmer, then continue with instructions to garnish and serve.

BASKET COCKLE
Clinocardium nuttallii

Of the three (littleneck, cockle, and Manila), cockles are the lunkers. I've unearthed cockles the size of baseballs. Do not be intimidated by their strange appearance when cooked—the foot shoots out kind of like the tongue in the Rolling Stones emblem.

As much as I like steaming these guys (or eating them raw if I'm in a clean area and it hasn't been raining a lot), they can be sort of massive and a bit tough when cooked, so they tend to wind up in my chowder pot. In fact, because they're big and bold in flavor, cockles are the perfect centerpiece for your seafood marinaras, chowders, paellas, or cioppinos. Your enjoyment of cockles will increase drastically if you take the time to chop them up (after they're cooked), then return them to whatever dish you're making.[20]

The abundance of cockles increases as you go north. Humboldt Bay has a few. Some of the bays in Oregon—like Coos, Tillamook, and Netarts, for instance—are simply loaded with them.

Did I mention that cockles have a really gorgeous shell? Well, they do. It can be used to great effect when serving them on the half shell.

MANILA CLAM
Venerupis philippinarum

Manila clams, as the name suggests, are a non-native species that seems to be growing in abundance every year. It's hard to say if this is having a negative impact on native clams, but anecdotally speaking, in several of the author's favorite clamming locations, they have virtually taken over whole swathes of shoreline that used to hold nothing but native Pacific littlenecks. Manilas are generally the smaller and more elongate of the two and, happily, every bit as delicious. So if you're looking for an invasive clam to target, eat, and thereby help to keep in check, this is the one. If you have any doubt about what a Manila clam looks like, just go to your local Asian market. Most of these places have live tanks loaded with Manilas. This is by far the most popularly farmed clam on the West Coast of North America.

Shellfish

20 Yes, this sounds messy and annoying but hear me out. I served diver-caught Oregon basket cockles to my seafood subscribers and a lot of them were freaked out by the strange tongue-like stomach shooting out of the steamed clams. Those who attempted to chew them up whole described the experience as "kind of strange." Those who diced them and returned them to the pot raved on and on.

RAZOR CLAM
Siliqua patula

THE WHERE, WHEN, AND HOW

Speaking of deliciousness, the Pacific razor clam is considered by many to be the best eating of all the California clams. Unlike the majority of the clams listed here, razors are not typically caught inside bays but on coastal beaches. The best beaches for these clams tend to be those with fine-grained sand and a very gradual slope. Check your tide book for low minus tides. Choose your weapon: clam gun, clam shovel, standard shovel, or broomstick. Then walk down to the shoreline and start looking for holes, or "shows."

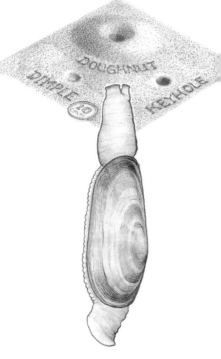

Razor clam shows come in three famous varieties: the "dimple," the "donut," and the "keyhole." Of the three, the donut is the prototypical or ideal show—the poster child of razor clam shows. The dimple is the most subtle and difficult to spot, and the keyhole is the one that tends to form after the sand has been disturbed.

If you're on a confirmed razor beach and you can't find any of these shows, it's time to play the fool. Start jumping up and down, dancing about, hopping, doing jumping jacks, whatever it takes. The vibrations you cause in the sand will alert any nearby razors, and as they withdraw their siphons and plunge deep into the sand, their holes will be revealed to you.[21] Another method is to wade just above your ankles into the swash, tap the sand with a broomstick, and look for underwater puffs. When you find them, drop down and dig like crazy!

---

21 Anecdotally speaking, the least inhibited people catch the most clams.

This is a clam of the windswept north country—but pockets of them can be found on extreme minus tides further south. Unlike horsenecks, razor clams can move through the sand at ridiculous speeds. So dig fast! As far as shovels go, the traditional razor clam shovel is the curved-blade job. Many folks swear by these, but frankly I prefer the standard clam gun (see Swim Bladder 5). A clam gun, if you are unfamiliar with the concept, is sort of like a large straw. If you take a straw, place it in a cup of water, then put your finger over the top and pull it out, what happens? That's right, you get a little column of water trapped inside the straw—same thing with a clam gun. Place it over the clam's "show," a bit off center, so there's a little more space on the ocean side. Shove it down into the moist sand, then put your finger over the little hole in the handle and pull it out. What do you get? A small column of sand. If you're lucky, that column of sand will have a razor clam in it. If not, carefully dig around in the hole with your hand or shove the clam gun in again and you'll likely find your quarry.

Other Options

Some folks find that they break more clams with a gun than a shovel. If you are going to use a curved-blade clam shovel, make sure you dig about six to eight inches to the seaward side of the show, pulling the sand toward you.

Razor clams—imagine this—are sharp. So go easy when grabbing them. And remember: the bladed front edge usually faces the waves, and the hole tends to angle that way.

EAT THEM UP, YUM

Razor clams are delicious and I'm sure there are a hundred really complicated recipes for them out there, but honestly there is no better way to eat razors than breaded and fried. My buddy in razor clamming, Walter "Waltopedia" Jorgensen, has this down to a fine art, so I include his recipe here. Bon appetit.

Fried Razor Clams

> Razor clams
> All-purpose flour
> Panko breadcrumbs
> Eggs
> Beer
> Oil for frying

Like gooey-ducks and gapers, razors need to be cleaned and trimmed. The first step in this process is to blanch the clams quickly in hot water. Some

Shellfish

folks go as far as dipping them in boiling water for 10–15 seconds. The danger here is that you might inadvertently (and prematurely) cook them. I have an extremely hot (scalding) tap in my kitchen sink and running it over a colander with 6–7 clams for a few seconds effectively causes them to pop open. It also firms them up a tiny bit, and loosens them from the shell—facilitating the cleaning process immensely.

In cleaning, basically you want to remove all the dark goopy stuff (by cutting it out with a pair of snips) and retain the firm, beige or whitish sections of meat. As I say in the section on casting nets (see Swim Bladder 1), there is no competing with moving images on some things, and this is one of them—check out YouTube for instructions on how to clean razor clams. Be advised: the foot of the clam (that beige lobe-like section) is the tastiest part. Cut it out, butterfly it, remove the dark goopy stuff from inside, and put it aside for breading and frying with the other pieces.

After blanching, cleaning, snipping, and rinsing all your clams, pat the meat dry with a paper towel. Now pull out three plates or bowls. Into the first pour some flour. Into the second, panko. Crack a couple of eggs into the third bowl and stir. Dip the clam meat into the flour first, then into the egg, then into the panko, and then put all the breaded clams onto a plate in the fridge and go drink a beer. The little extra wait allows the panko to adhere to the clams. Finish that beer (or have another one) and then pour enough of your preferred cooking oil into the bottom of a fry pan so that it's about 1/8 inch deep. Then drop those clams into the pan of sizzling oil. Cook till brown, squeeze a lemon on 'em, and dunk each clammy morsel into your favorite dipping sauce en route to your mouth.

White Sand Macoma | Bent-Nose Macoma
Macoma secta   Macoma nasuta

There are several other species of clams seldom harvested in California but nevertheless worth mentioning. Of these, the most notable are the two species of mudclams: the bent-nose clam (or bent-nose sand macoma) and the white sand macoma. In all my years hanging out in mudflats and stalking the reeking backwaters of inner bays, I've only met one clammer who specifically targets macoma clams: Brian "Macoma" Lynch. I asked Brian to comment on this strange predilection of his. Here's his reply:

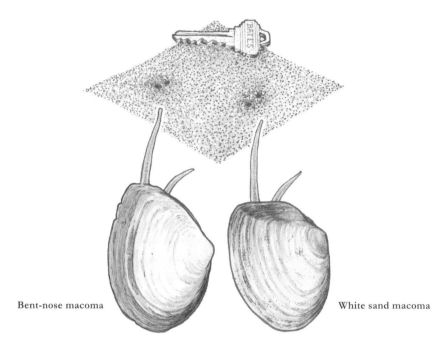

Bent-nose macoma   White sand macoma

Macomas don't dig as deep as gapers. They're rarely over a foot and a half deep. Way easier than digging out gaper clams, or gooeys. Once you learn to recognize their holes, it's easy to get them. They like the sandy mud or muddy sand inside bays. Their necks are really skinny so they leave two tiny holes, not much bigger than a pinprick. Sometimes the white macomas are surprisingly big. As big as the palm of your hand. One thing to keep in mind is that they lie horizontal in the mud. And they're similar to littlenecks in that, when you get one, you'll find others nearby. I think they taste as good as littlenecks, and way better than gapers. But one thing is for sure, they are muddy. So you have to soak them in an aerated bucket of clean ocean water for one to three days—changing the water once per day.

Right now, Brian "Macoma" Lynch has this entire fishery (clammery?) to himself, but bent-nose and white sand macomas show up in coastal shell mounds, so we know that sometime in the last five hundred years they were popular. Commercially, bent-nose clams were gathered in large numbers by Chinese clammers at least until 1876, when they were replaced (in the water and in the market) by the invasive softshell clam from the Atlantic coast. In John E. Skinner's epic 1965 tome, *The Natural Resources of the San Francisco Bay Area,* we find the following:

> The shore line of this tidal flat [the site of the present-day Islais Creek] was inhabited by a large number of Chinese engaged in the occupation of shrimp fishing and clam digging and it is with the clams dug by these Chinese that the writer would deal at this time … Up to 1876 but one species of clam was found in any quantity by these diggers and that was a white-shelled variety (*Macoma nasuta*), about two and one-half inches in greatest length. Provided with a board 18 inches wide and four feet long with a strip one inch thick nailed across each end, the digger waded out on the mud flat at low tide, pushing a basket on this sled board ahead of him. On arriving at a suitable place, he pushed his hands and arms, held vertically in front of him, elbow deep into the soft mud and then turned up the mud toward himself; by straining this mud through his fingers he found the clams, which were placed in the basket. This was continued until the basket was full or the flood tide prevented further digging.

Regarding the soaking of clams:

> Upon arriving at the camp with their catch of clams the diggers at once placed their catch in shallow water-tight boxes about 18 inches wide, 10 inches deep and 8 feet long, in one end of the bottom of which a hole was bored for draining purposes. A layer of clams 3 or 4 inches deep was placed in each box. The box was then partially filled with clean water from the bay and after 36 or 48 hours the clams were marketed, the water being changed each high tide. This clean water bath was intended to allow the clams to void all mud and sand contained in the stomach and render the clams edible.

I'm wondering at what point I will be desperate enough to build myself a mud clam sled and go finger-straining macomas in that unnameable sludge now surrounding Islais Creek. Given my obsessions with monkeyface eels, longjaw mudsuckers, clam worms, and horsenecks, I imagine it will happen sooner rather than later. Seriously though, as horrifying as this activity would be in 2016, I imagine that area was even worse in the 1870s, as it was then the center of all the animal-processing industries on that side of San Francisco: glue and tallow factories, tanneries, canneries, and the like.

Macomas are common inside bays and are found relatively high up the tideline, so you don't necessarily need a very low minus tide to get them. Their "show" (see picture above) is a distinctive double pinprick, with the two holes approximately one-half to one inch apart. Macomas are delicious steamed or breaded and fried (see *Razor Clam* section above).[22] Just remember to soak them for at least forty-eight hours first or you will find yourself with a bowl (or a mouth) full of mud.

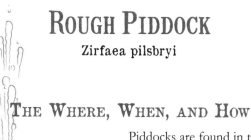

ROUGH PIDDOCK
Zirfaea pilsbryi

THE WHERE, WHEN, AND HOW

Piddocks are found in thick, seemingly impenetrable mud and clay (and sometimes in solid rock!). As you may have suspected, it's kind of difficult to dig in this stuff, but I find that a standard shovel cuts through clay fairly well—at least when you're jumping on it. Drain spades will get you down deeper but I've actually broken rusty old drain spades while trying to get at piddocks, so I don't recommend them. Like macomas and littlenecks, piddocks can be surprisingly high up the tideline and can be caught on any minus tide lower than +0.2. Also, unlike most

22 They're only worth frying if you get the big ones.

other clams, piddocks tend to have horizontal burrows, and they move quickly through them. Dig fast. You will often break off their siphons when pushing the shovel through the clay, but since most of the meat is in the siphon, that isn't the worst thing that can happen.

The shells of these clams are really cool, and if you are lucky enough to get one out of its hole without breaking it, you will have quite a souvenir. Note the spiraling, serrated teeth on the posterior end of the shell. The piddock uses these to drill or saw its way through soft rock and clay.

EAT THEM UP, YUM

I should point out that these clams have very thick siphons and must be pounded mercilessly in order to achieve a state approaching palatability. That said, piddocks make for a good chowder clam. Don't eat the guts.

CALIFORNIA JACKKNIFE CLAM
Tagelus californianus, Solens sicarius

THE WHERE, WHEN, AND HOW

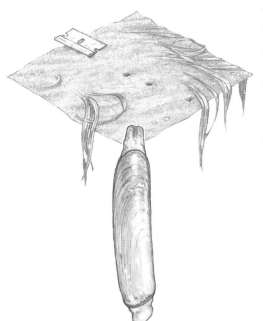

The jackknife clam is primarily used for bait in California and is often erroneously referred to as a razor clam. Although similar in appearance to the razor and equally capable of digging at Olympic speeds, the jackknife prefers muddy back bays and harbors to the open coast of the razor clam. It's also considerably smaller and narrower. The meat of the jackknife is surprisingly good, given the fact that no one eats it. In fact, in the more southern portions of our range, the jackknife is a reasonable stand-in for the razor.

My only reservation (razorvation?) about this clam is the strange Day-Glo pink stuff that tends to ooze out of the stomach. I have absolutely no idea what this substance is—but it just doesn't look right. So I invariably end up cutting out the stomach and the other questionable-looking portions of this clam—which, given its small size, leaves me with scant quantities of meat.

It took a while but I finally figured out that the best way to capture jack-knife clams is with a drain spade. The long blade of the drain spade, if shoved aggressively into soft mud, will get below the jackknife before it can scoot to the bottom of its burrow.

Jackknifes like muddy sand or sandy mud inside bays, sloughs, and harbors. As far as their "shows" are concerned, each clam leaves two small holes roughly a half inch apart, each of these similar in size to the two pinprick holes left by sand macomas. In our area they can best be found at extremely low minus tides, right at the water's edge. I have found that they like a decent flow of water, near the mouth of a bay or lagoon, and are less abundant where the flow is diminished.

This clam makes an excellent bait for surfperch, rockfish, cabezon, monkeyface eel, kingfish, leopard shark, and just about any other fish willing to bite dead mollusks, or pieces of them, on a hook.

PISMO CLAM
Tivela stultorum

It may seem odd that I've saved California's most famous clam for the tail end of the bivalve chapter. But Pismos have become exceedingly rare in this area and are so seldom encountered here, I was originally planning on leaving them out entirely. In the last three decades of foraging the northern and central California shores, I've encountered a whopping total of ten Pismo clams and in each case I found them incidentally.

It wasn't always this way. Although our area of California represents the northern extreme of this clam's natural range, fair numbers of Pismo clams were formerly targeted and caught in the Santa Cruz and Half Moon Bay areas at least until the mid-1970s. The decline of these populations in the intervening forty years probably has to do with three factors: (1) overfishing, (2) increased sea otter abundance, and (3) changing sand regimes. As fond as I may be of otters (trying to buck the trend established by Izaak Walton in

1653[23]), there can be little doubt they like Pismo clams very much and will, if other food is unavailable, consume large numbers of them. Sea otters are infamously ravenous little eaters of seafood, consuming 25 percent of their body weight per day. A single sea otter was once observed devouring twenty-five clams in 2½ hours. But lest this should tempt us to blame the decline of Pismo clams on sea otters, there is another species of mammal that should at least share part of the blame. Quoth the California DFG in its 2006 *Status of the Fisheries Report*: "Records of the commercial harvest of Pismo clams began in 1916, and continued through 1947 when the fishery was prohibited. During these 29 years, it is estimated that commercial diggers harvested 6.25 million pounds (2,834 metric tons) of Pismo clams."

And the sport harvest? "In 1949, an estimated 5,000 diggers per day harvested more than 2 million clams over a period of 2.5 months on a stretch of beach that had just been reopened to digging after being closed for 20 years. During that time, an additional estimated 1 million undersized clams were left stranded on the surface and wasted on that same stretch of beach."

In Half Moon Bay, where sea otter presence is minimal or non-existent, the decline of Pismo clams seems to have coincided with the building of the two breakwaters in Princeton Harbor in 1959. I have nothing but anecdotal information to back me up on this. But several long-time resident clammers are convinced that the shifting of sands caused by the south jetty spelled the end of harvestable Pismo clam populations in that area.[24]

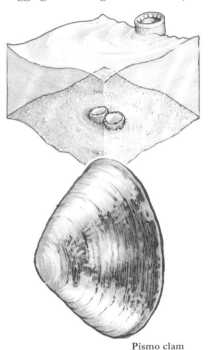

Pismo clam

23 From *The Compleat Angler*, Izaak Walton, 1653: "I am sir a brother of the angle and therefore an enemy of the otter: for you will note that we Anglers all love eachother, and therefore do we hate the otter..."
24 I say "the end" but should add that I have found several undersized Pismos inside the harbor, and occasionally one finds a shell washed up on Surfer Beach.

The Where, When, and How

In the glory days of Pismo gathering, the clammer went down to known clam beaches during minus tides, waded shin-deep, and probed the sand in the swash zone with a four- to six-tined potato fork. It was that easy. My grandfather, who caught clams in the nineteen-teens and early twenties near Santa Cruz, claimed that he occasionally left the potato fork at home and caught his clams by wading into the surf and wiggling his feet down into the sand.

In more southerly areas of the state (and in Mexico), this manner of clamming is still quite popular. However, in the last decade, diving for Pismos has become the preferred method as intertidal abundance has declined. Divers swim out just past the breakers and look for conspicuous bulges, clam siphons (or more specifically, the feathery commensal hydroids attached to the tips of clam siphons), and shells. Having located these, they use a dive knife, a trowel, or their hands to dig the clams out.

The key here is learning to recognize the clammy bulges. And although pictures can help, you will have to get in the water and start looking in order to really understand the nuances of Pismo spotting.

Rock Scallop
Crassadoma gigantea

The Where, When, and How

Although you will occasionally find rock scallops while poke poling or shore picking abalones on the lowest tides of the year, if you want to catch them consistently you will have to embrace the snorkel and the fins.

Several things to remember before diving for rock scallops.

1. They are extremely well camouflaged.

2. Legally, you may only use an abalone iron or dive knife to pry them off the rocks.

3. Any time you enter the water, you are entering the food chain … and rest assured that underwater on the California coast, your species does not represent the top of it.

4. The reward is worth the risk—these are one of California's most delicious creatures!

Shellfish

As mentioned above, rock scallops are seriously good at blending in with a background of crusty, algae-covered, subtidal rocks. But they do have one weakness: the brightly colored mantle just visible inside the shell while they're feeding. So if you haven't hunted them before, be on the lookout for a small grey, pink, purple, or orange seam, wedged in a crack or just under the over-hang of a rock. Once you've found this, it's just a matter of elbow grease (and leverage) to get them out.

The bag limit on rock scallops is ten in possession per day. There is no size limit. But don't take dinks.[25] We want to make sure that each scallop has had a chance to reproduce a couple of times in order to ensure the survival of harvestable numbers. Also, like many other mollusks, this species is a broad-cast spawner and needs fairly dense populations in order to reproduce. So as much as possible, avoid denuding the rocks, or picking scallops in areas where they've been thinned out.

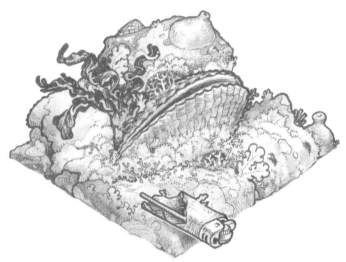

Eat Them Up, Yum

Rock scallops usually have a sort of nutty taste, but every now and then you'll get one that has the curious flavor of fresh pineapple. Everyone I've told this to thinks I'm insane. A quick Internet search proves that none of the fourteen-odd billion people sharing the world wide web have mentioned this strange phenomenon. To a person accustomed to catching the cucumber-scented members of the smelt family, a pineapple-flavored mollusk isn't such

25 Since there is no size limit on rock scallops, most accomplished scallop divers go with the "palm of your hand" measurement. This is fine unless you have really tiny hands, in which case, maybe a "whole hand" measurement would be more appropriate.

a stretch, but to everyone else I suppose it is. In any case, you will now have to go out there and prove or disprove my pineapple claims yourself.

The only challenging part to cleaning a scallop is getting it open. Or rather, finding an opening into which you can slide your dive knife, in order to cut it open. If you can't find an opening, chip the top edge of the shell with the back side of your knife till there's enough of an opening to slide the blade in. Follow the edge of the shell till the valves unhinge and then pry it open the rest of the way. The edible portion of the scallop is the circular disk (or adductor muscle). It's great breaded and fried (see *Razor Clam* instructions). But in my opinion the best way to eat a rock scallop is to slice it into thin discs and scarf it raw.

As of this writing, the last person to die from paralytic shellfish poisoning in California supposedly died from eating a rock scallop. Not to harsh your mellow, but keep this in mind.

| UNIVALVES |

OWL LIMPET
Lottia gigantea

There are many species of limpets on the California coast. All of them are more or less edible. But mere edibility is not really what we're going for here. I mean, for instance, my shoes are *edible* but you'll notice I'm not eating them for breakfast. Last year I popped a few giant keyhole limpets off a rock in Santa Cruz. After de-shelling and then smashing these puppies for about ten minutes with a tenderizing hammer and slicing them into paper-thin slivers, I found that even raw, they still had the consistency of a really tough piece of leather. And then, of course, sautéing them for thirty seconds sealed the deal and turned them into a small pile of Goodyear tire shavings. In short: I'm sure there are huaraches out there that would have been more palatable than these giant keyhole limpets.

I have now given up on all species of limpets other than owl limpets. If you want to seek out the giant keyhole limpet, the gumboot chiton, or any other related species and write me an outraged email about how great they are and how I don't know what I'm talking about, be my guest. You either have a better hammer or a stronger set of jaws than I do.

THE WHERE, WHEN, AND HOW

But owl limpets … owl limpets really are tasty little creatures. Here's the deal with owl limpets: it's hard to find the big ones. *Really hard.* The problem is that limpets are:

1. Delicious (if you can get over that weird cartilaginous quality)

2. Long lived

3. Limited to living intertidally

4. Because of 1, 2, and, 3, highly susceptible to overharvest

Owl limpet

And this is a major point. Just because you can legally take thirty-five owl limpets per day does not mean you should. Put it this way: say you're out poke poling and you come across a nice little patch of lunker owl limpets. The next day you round up a couple of like-minded coastal foragers and together the three of you descend on this patch of limpets with wild looks on your faces and sharpened hooks (and lines) in your hands. Following the rules and regulations to a tee, you leave the area with a legal catch of 105 large limpets.

Good work. You just ruined that spot for twenty years. That's how long it's likely to take for the limpets to come back to that patch of rock. Whereas, had you each selected ten to twelve of the largest limpets and satisfied yourselves with that number, you could come back the next year, and the year after that, and so on . . .

That's my take on it, anyway. If you were thinking of serving limpets as a main course for ten people, you were thinking about the resource the wrong way. Limpets are a perfect little oceanic appetizer for two to three people and, as such, ten to twelve of them is a perfect amount. Let the main course be gaper clam chowder, rockfish tacos, salmon steaks, cioppino, or literally anything else in this book. If you want a more plentiful appetizer, go with steamed Pacific littlenecks or mussels. Save the limpets for a very special meal, once or twice per year.

Eat Them Up, Yum

Cleaning owl limpets is similar to cleaning abalones but without all the thick black stuff. Take a tablespoon and scoop the creature out of its shell (my limpet spoon is sharpened at its forward edge). Then remove the wiggly blob of brown-green guts from the top, and rinse the limpet thoroughly. The best way—really the *only* way—to eat limpets is, you guessed it, raw. Take the sharpest knife in the cupboard and shave the limpets into razor-thin slices. Squeeze a lemon on 'em and scarf. The taste is very similar to abalone, the texture is unique—almost crunchy. In fact, the texture is not universally appreciated and freaks some people out. Good! More for me!

Red Abalone
Haliotis rufescens

I won't lie, I've been dreading writing this section for a long time. I mean, with all the endless verbiage about abalone out there, does the world really

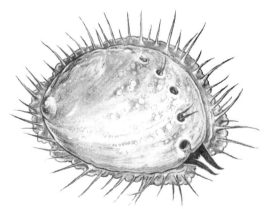

need my input? No. And yet there's no writing a California coastal foraging book without a chapter on abalone, right? So here we go.

Red abalones are only legal north of the Golden Gate Bridge—and only as long as you are in season and following all the rules.[26] If you are not

26 Black, green, pink, and white abalone are rarely encountered anymore, and cannot be legally harvested in California.

inclined to follow rules, if you are sloppy about filling out forms and following protocol, I highly suggest you find another creature to hunt. The minimum fine for an abalone violation as of this writing is something insane like 1,200 bucks, and be forewarned, if you are hunting abs anywhere in California there is very likely a guy with a crewcut, a forty-caliber sidearm, and a beige shirt with a silver badge on it watching you with high-powered binoculars from the cliffs. I will go over a few of the basics here, but do not go abalone diving or shore picking before you have studied the DFW regulations book in detail.

The Where, When, and How

Abalone can be legally picked from shore (north of the Golden Gate Bridge only!) but you will only find them on the lowest minus tides of the year. The intertidal population of abs has been hit pretty hard by shore pickers, which is why abalone are so much more plentiful in subtidal (harder to reach) waters. So, given all the effort it takes to get to the ab grounds, you really ought to consider diving for them. For this you will need a thick wet suit, snorkel, mask, weighted dive belt, and flippers. Scuba gear is prohibited, so leave the oxygen tanks home. A very cursory overview of the regulations follows.

To take abs legally you must:

1. Hunt them only in the allowable areas, times, and months.

2. Use a regulation ab iron and gauge.

3. Return small abs to the *exact* location from which they were plucked (exact means exact).

4. Not exceed the bag limit.

5. Not assist anyone else in finding them (e.g., it is illegal to point to an abalone that your friend does not see, or hand one off underwater).

6. Immediately tag your abalone after picking it, and log it on your report card.

7. Take only red abalone.

8. Make sure your abalone are at least seven inches across the widest section of the shell.

9. Free dive with snorkel or shore pick only (no scuba diving).

10. Read the abalone regulations in the DFW regulation booklet very carefully and understand all the nuances before you go ab picking/diving. I am only covering a few of the details here.

In Conclusion

When one considers the long drive (for most of us), the risk to life and limb (you know, sharks, freezing water, drowning, etc.), the possibility of having an honest mistake turn into a 1,200-dollar violation, and the fact that the daily bag limit is only three abalone, one wonders if it's really worth it. Okay, maybe *one* doesn't wonder ... but I sure do.

Yeah, the red abalone is a delicious creature, no doubt, but so are a lot of other things that are easier to get and not so rife with potential hazards. Nevertheless, every year I join the horde and make at least one pilgrimage to the ab grounds on that -1.8 tide in the spring. But I find the trip goes a lot better if I combine it with something else—a poke poling expedition, a razor clam sojourn, a hunt for the elusive basket cockle, et cetera. That's just me.

And Furthermore ...

All legal commercial take of abalone has ceased since 1979.[27] But the recreational fishery has recently become problematically popular. I've seen areas that once seemed busy when three people were out there shore picking, that are now completely overrun with folks from points south. I'm talking about seventy-five cars parked in remote areas along the highway at 4:30 in the morning, with an average of four people per car. Gone are the quiet mornings where one could shore pick abs in relative solitude. If you aren't diving, but hoping to pick your abs intertidally, be prepared for some serious early morning competition. Frankly, I'm not much of a combat fisherman ... and if you aren't either I highly suggest you take up diving, or clamming, or, I dunno ... golf.

When one talks to many of the locals in the small Northern California towns adjacent to the ab grounds, one will occasionally (not always) detect a certain amount of bitterness towards the abalone "invaders" from points south. After interviewing several of the more disgruntled of these folks on this subject, it became evident to me that the bitterness is not just about their feelings of possessiveness over what they perceive as their own dwindling resources, but about the behavior of many (not all) abalone hunters. The prevailing opinion is that many (not all) of the hundreds (thousands?) of people who throng to the ab grounds every year contribute almost nothing to the local economy; they don't stop and order lunch, they don't buy souvenirs, they don't pay for hotel rooms, they don't even stay for a beer or a cup of coffee. They show up in cars and minivans at 3 A.M., invade the ab grounds, get their limits, and head back home. In other words, they're seen as *takers*. Given this,

Shellfish

---

27   The illegal take of abalone in California is estimated to equal the legal recreational catch.

if you are of the "get your abs and hit the road" tribe, perhaps you might consider stopping for breakfast on your way home.

Mother-of-Pearl

Here in California we tend to see a lot of mother-of-pearl. But lest we should become hardened, jaded people, let's really take a minute to consider how deeply beautiful this stuff is, and how lucky we are to have a local species that produces it. And it has serious significance to many California Indian cultures. If you aren't paving your driveway with your abalone shells, or hanging them on your fence, or making beautiful oceanic jewelry out of them, or utilizing them in some other creative or significant way, send them to a Native artisan who will. Don't know your Native neighbors? The folks at *News from Native California* do and will pass abalone shells on to artists who make regalia and other ceremonial objects. Mail them to:

News from Native California
1633 University Avenue
Berkeley, CA 94703

The gift will be appreciated, and likely turned into something really, really cool.

Eat Them Up, Yum

Fried Abs

Prepping your abalones is about popping them out of the shells (use your ab iron for this) and cutting off all the guts and black stuff. Once they're prepped, grab a tenderizing hammer and take out all (or at least some) of your aggression on your abalone meat. Next, slice the meat into ½- or ¼-inch steaks—depending on your preference (it actually requires far less violence to tenderize the meat *after* you've got it sliced, but where's the fun in that?).

The next step is exactly the same as in the fried razor clam recipe, except that instead of panko (which you can also use), you will want to adhere to the ancient culture and wisdom of California by foraging some Ritz crackers from the local supermarket. Throw these into a blender and grind them up with a touch of black pepper. Although it probably isn't the hippest thing here in Foodie Nation to suggest Ritz crackers in a recipe, it's hard to argue with the end product. Honestly, there's something about a Ritz cracker crust on a fried abalone that's just ridiculously delicious.

Follow the breading (or crackering) and frying instructions in the razor clam recipe, and enjoy.

THE LANDLORD

This story, written in a previous decade, details the problematic circumstances of my first-ever abalone dive. Take heed, all you would-be "snail" hunters: there are a few crucial lessons to be garnered from this tale of near self-annihilation.

Forebodings

I dripped some crab juice on my front steps the other day and my landlord called to tell me how he felt about it. I have to say, although I love my new apartment, it kind of sucks having the landlord living upstairs. Thanks to creaky old floors and thin walls, there is never a single moment in this apartment when he doesn't know where I am. It's his building, after all, and it's not likely that anything we do here is going to go unnoticed . . . which was exactly my feeling last week, when I ran into an even more problematic landlord, one who patrols our shorelines in a dark grey suit.

I had forebodings from the outset. Last week I ran into Brian, a fellow fisheries department employee and native of Tomales Bay. When I told Brian that my buddy JB was taking me to Tomales Point for my first abalone diving adventure, he raised his eyebrows and said, "You know ... that might be a tough area for your first dive, man."

Suffice it to say I did not heed this warning.

My buddy JB (also a fellow fisheries observer) showed up at my door bright and early the next morning, and whisked me off to the abalone grounds near Tomales Point. JB has been ab diving for twenty-plus years and was confident we could pick up a few "snails" just around the corner from Bird Rock. I had been hinting to JB for a long time that I wanted to try ab diving, and with yesterday's placid conditions it seemed like a no-brainer. JB is a surfer and—as I said—ab diving veteran of twenty some-odd years. I am neither of these. My relationship with the ocean is (and always has been) from the vantage point of sitting on top of it, casting into it, or poking its intertidal regions with a wire hanger lashed to a bamboo stick. Somehow, in all the preparations for this expedition, the exact level of my inexpertise was not adequately addressed.

In short, I went into the field with borrowed equipment and a predictable combination of abalone lust and zero experience.

Despite being of an athletic disposition (baseball, football, rugby, kayaking, racquetball, et cetera), I am, sadly, not much of an underwater kind of guy. This may seem incongruous with my occupation and marine passions … but there it is, on the table. Anyway, I'd rather be an open and honest idiot than a closeted and dishonest one.

Again, to be clear: all of my former snorkeling experience was in the crystalline waters of Costa Rica and the bathtub-like coves of Hawaii. And I will now state from experience: all the tropical snorkeling in the world cannot prepare a person for the brutal waters of Northern California!

Early Omens Ignored

We arrived at Miller Ramp. The borrowed wet suit was too tight, the weight belt too heavy. (Incredibly, in my excitement and confidence, I had not thought to try them out first.) We chugged to the spot in a twelve-foot Zodiac. JB dove in and began plucking abs. He had his first one in five minutes. I jumped in the water, and, not having dealt with a weight belt this heavy before, sank like a stone. Getting back to the surface was more cardiovascular work than I'd done in fifteen years. I immediately inhaled about a pint of water. Washed that down with another quart … great start! I looked around … sea lions everywhere. I tried descending again. Wow. Much harder than it looked when JB did it. My ears exploded. Couldn't seem to pop them like I used to in Hawaii. Then, I got wrapped in kelp. This happens sometimes when poke poling. No biggie. You relax, you work your way out. "No problem," I thought, "I've freed myself from kelp dozens of times."

But then, in an instant, I was completely out of breath. My leg started to cramp, and the kelp filaments tore the mask off my face. I had been in the water for three minutes and I found myself, well, for lack of a better term … drowning.

But the indignity of dying in this trite and stupid manner, wrapped in kelp (like every weekend-warrior, abalone-diving fatality on record) while my friend JB leisurely gathered his limit of abs thirty feet away from me was not something I could live—or I should say die—with.

So with nothing left in my lungs and my head spinning, blacking out (actually it was more like little black spots and stars dancing across my eyeballs), I forced myself to relax, go limp, and in that manner barely rolled out of the kelp and made it to the surface.

My first breath was about 38 percent water. I choked, gagged, coughed, and spat. My leg tightened into a rock-hard, baseball-sized knot of sheer pain.

My flippers started falling off. I was like Charlie Chaplin out there. Only I was moments away from death. I swam back to the Zodiac, climbed aboard, and stared down at the sea lions—who were all looking at me like, *Who's this lunatic trying to kill himself out here?* JB waved at me but I really didn't want him to see how inept I was so I just waved back, as in, *Everything's cool, I'm just readjusting my flippers, bro*, and tried to get my breath. Meanwhile JB swam over and dropped his second ab in the boat. Clunk! He dove down again.

"Damn it!" thought I, "I've gotta get at least one!"

If You Don't Drown at First, Try, Try Again

So despite the obvious signs that I had no business being in the water, I tightened the mask and the flippers, massaged my leg, and dove back in. Lunatic.

JB says I looked uncomfortable out there. (Ya think?) But why, I wonder, didn't he suggest I call it quits? The thought has occurred to me that maybe he was trying to kill me … he stands to pick up quite a few shifts at work if I kick the bucket! (Just kidding, JB.)

After about five minutes (I'm a slow learner), I realized I would never see an ab. Why? Because I am nearsighted. I wear glasses. I've worn glasses every day of my life for the last thirty years. But somehow, in preparing for this trip I forgot that I wear glasses. So, the rocky, kelpy bottom looked kind of like a Seurat painting … you know, dots. No abs. No crevices. Just dots. I fluttered around and around on the surface for a while and then, beneath me, I saw someone's ab iron, like fourteen feet down. Guess what? It had an orange handle, just like mine! Hey, and a familiar gauge lying next to it. What a coincidence!

Yes, they were mine. I was so confused and disoriented I didn't even notice I had dropped them. And then there was a surge of water, and I was carried off the spot. I spent the next half hour trying to find my dropped gauge and ab iron, all the while working myself into a slight panic fighting kelp and a slight roll (to a real diver this roll would have been nothing … to a novice in those waters it was Mavericks). Luckily JB was able to dive down and get the ab iron, as I had inexplicably lost the ability to hold my breath for more than ten seconds (despite the fact that as a tuba player I can usually hold my breath for an astonishingly long time).

On and on it went: one near disaster and humiliation after another. Quarts of salt water swallowed. Finally, I swam off a distance from the boat and tried working the shallows near Bird

Rock. I had just located a decent ab—my first unaided find of the day—and was gathering myself for another short dive when I noticed that all but one of the sea lions were suddenly out of the water. I also noticed that they were almost all pups—at least the ones in my vicinity. I looked around. Everything seemed wrong to me—or maybe not wrong so much as *angry*. I don't know how else to explain it. The sea, the sky, the sun, even the rocks, suddenly seemed imbued with a sort of malevolence. Everything was too quiet. My ears were ringing. I felt heavy. I thought to myself, *This is the kind of fear and panic that all novice divers and surfers probably feel.*

The Pencil Popper

But then I grabbed onto a rock and I took a long breath. And I began to list in my mind all the ridiculous decisions I had made this day:

1. Diving in despite lack of experience in this kind of water

2. Borrowing untested equipment

3. Letting my slightly competitive nature sway my judgment

4. Ignoring obvious danger signs: leg cramps, coughing, suspicious disappearance of seal lions

Suddenly, clear as day, it dawned on me what I really was at this moment, what I had been for the last hour: I was a giant, 189-pound pencil popper lure, doing my best imitation of a wounded sea lion—gasping, thrashing, treading water spastically. And to top it off, what was the shiny ab iron I was flailing around if it wasn't a flasher?

Sensing that I was having some kind of emotional crisis, JB looked over at me from the Zodiac and waved. (Hey, JB, next time, if you want to kill me so badly, why not save the gas and slip something in my beer?)

Shellfish

At this point I put my head down and did my best Michael Phelps back to the Zodiac. Setting a new world record for the weight belt–encumbered crawl.

After flopping on board, I caught my breath, kicked off my flippers, and confessed to JB this was not a sport for me—at least not here, on my first day. Really, an afternoon snorkeling around a tide pool was about the level I was at. For the immediate future, I would stick to my kayak, my poke pole, my throw-net, my A-frame, and my beloved hair-raiser on Ocean Beach. I then suggested we go catch a few rockfish—something I'm actually good at. We drove the boat about a hundred yards—maybe less—to the other side of Bird Rock. Flat calm. Forty to fifty feet. I dropped a hex bar down to the bottom and began jigging. JB joined in.

Within five minutes I felt a nice tug. Fish on. I started reeling. I looked down: the water was crystal blue. I could see the shaker lingcod maybe twenty feet down, coming up with each crank of my reel. Then JB had a fish on. Same thing: small ling. I landed mine, shook it off. JB was still reeling his. We looked down at it.

From beneath JB's undersized ling, a blob began to materialize. *Hitchhiker,* I thought at first—a big hitchhiker chasing JB's ling! But the water was so clear and the image of the fish so distorted and nebulous it was hard to tell if it was a small fish relatively close to the boat or a huge fish thirty feet down. Then everything got weird. I heard myself say: "What the hell is that?"

The shape gained form as it ascended. And then there was a face. An eye. A large black eye, unmistakable jack-o'-lantern teeth, and a black-hole mouth that can only be described, when seen at that proximity, as the gaping portal of hell itself.

Two seconds later we were looking directly into the open mouth of a fourteen- to sixteen-foot great white shark. It was aiming for the undersized ling that JB had at the surface alongside the Zodiac—the twelve-foot *inflatable* Zodiac. But it was moving slowly, leisurely, with its mouth wide open. After a stunned pause, JB quickly ripped the short lingcod out of the water, as the shark—which had ascended in a more or less vertical manner, like the famous *Jaws* poster, turned horizontal, its dorsal fin breaking the surface, and brushed up against the boat as it passed along our port side. We were at that moment 150 yards due west of where, for the better part of the morning, I had been impersonating a pencil popper. Both JB and I measure fish for a living, so I think we got the length pretty close. For the record I'm going to say the shark was fourteen feet long. I also think, though JB disagrees, that this shark was aware of me earlier—as I was, subconsciously, of it. I realize that virtually all underwater neophytes will inevitably experience shark panic, but I had felt in my soul that a super predator was nearby when I swam back to the boat. And with the flashing ab iron, the splashing, the coughing, my spastic kicking and treading water, not to mention the insane endorphins I was releasing … it would've had to have been deaf and blind not to have known I was there.

Postscript

Seven days later, JB sent me a link to an article that confirms there have been several brutal shark attacks inside Bird Rock, only thirty yards from shore. (Which only reconfirms my earlier suspicions that he was trying to kill me so he could get more hours.)

Right, they don't like shallow water, they don't like kelp, they never come that close to shore. Uh huh. It's kind of hard for me to believe the landlord doesn't know his tenants. The way I see it, he just wasn't collecting rent last week.

Shellfish

LEWIS'S MOONSNAIL
Neverita lewisii

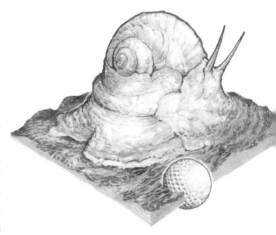

Being an inveterate baseball fan, I'll usually give something three tries before calling it quits. My third disastrous attempt at producing something halfway palatable out of moonsnail meat occurred in 2009. So I have long since given up on moonsnails. Nevertheless, I see quite a few people taking them while clamming. These people obviously have the mandibular strength of our Neanderthal forbears—or better tenderizing skills than I do.

THE WHERE, WHEN, AND HOW

I have never met anyone who targets moonsnails specifically, but if you are thinking of putting your teeth to the test, look for them on minus tides, -0.3 and lower. Moonsnails prefer mud or muddy sand. Look for slight swelling, cracks, or upheavals in the surface of the mudflat. And prepare yourself for a miniature version of the 1958 classic horror film *The Blob*.

THE LION OF THE MUDFLATS

One other thing: although moonsnails are not filter-feeding bivalves, they do like to eat filter-feeding bivalves. (No question at all that if sand macomas dream, they see moonsnails in their nightmares.[28]) Because they feed on bivalves, moonsnails are prone to pick up biotoxins, so you should consider avoiding them during warm-water months and other mussel closures.

---

28 After enveloping the clam in its blob-like mantle, the moonsnail uses its drill-shaped radula (tongue) to bore a perfectly round hole in the shell of the clam. It then essentially slurps the clam to death through this tiny hole. So, you see, sand macomas have ample reason to lose sleep over moonsnails.

TURBAN SNAILS (TEGULAS OR TOP SHELLS)

BLACK TURBAN | BROWN TURBAN | RED TURBAN
Tegula funebralis   **Tegula brunnea**   **Pomaulax gibberosus**

Red turbans are the hawgs of the turban family. (Okay, maybe "hawg" is a bit misleading: two or three inches is a big red.) They are most commonly found clinging to kelp in tide pools at the southern edge of our range. Black and brown turban snails are undoubtedly two of the most common intertidal snails found in the area described in this book—if not in California in general.

THE WHERE, WHEN, AND HOW

You will find turbans during any low tide, on any stretch of rocky shoreline, pretty much statewide. Despite their abundance, two factors may prevent you from foraging them. They're small, and the bag limit is only thirty-five per day—which, to quote one of the great recreational fishermen of our area, Ron Garcia, "ain't even enough to feed the cat."

That said, they really are quite tasty, fun for kids to harvest, and will complement a Caesar salad like nothing else (except maybe anchovies à la boquerones).

To remove these tiny snails from their shells, steam them for five minutes and then break out the tweezers. Once you've pulled 'em out, remove "the door" (the hard protective flap that keeps the snail locked up in its portable house) with a sharp paring knife and drop the turban whole into the waiting bed of lettuce.

Most species of snail in California are not legal to take. So if you're a big snail fan, you've got turban snails and moonsnails (and garden snails—the best of the lot) and that's about it.[29] Down in Southern California, a new fishery for the Kellet's whelk opened in 2013. But that species is seldom found north of Santa Barbara.

| CEPHALOPODS |

PACIFIC RED | GIANT PACIFIC
OCTOPUS | OCTOPUS
Octopus rubescens | Enteroctopus dofleini

Occasionally while stalking the intertidal zone in our area, one will encounter an octopus—or, more often than not, the inky cloud left in its wake.[30] The two species, red and giant, look remarkably similar as juveniles. The main difference between them is the papillae (bumps), or eyelashes, found underneath the red octopus's eyes—the giant has no such bumps.

There has been quite a furor over these creatures of late, as we are given to understand that their intelligence level is around that of the average American teenager. Tales of octopi unlocking doors, twisting the lids off bottles, sneaking in and out of their rooms at local aquariums (as teenagers are wont to do) abound. I am a bit of a hypocrite on this subject. When I'm dining at my favorite Italian restaurant in SF, the octopus puttanesca is the first thing I order. But when I encounter them on the coast, I can never quite bring myself to kill them. There are several species in this book about which I feel the same way. Creatures that, no matter how plentiful they may be or delicious they may taste, I don't eat for dinner. If spot prawn fishermen and rock crabbers are to be believed, however, there are many, many millions of these creatures crawling around the depths of the Pacific Ocean, and their life cycle (high numbers of offspring plus a short life span) would seem to indicate that their populations are reasonably resistant to predation.[31]

29 Though, technically speaking, limpets and abalones are snails too.

30 The intertidal red octopus is apparently more common south of Point Conception.

31 According to the Monterey Bay Aquarium, a recent remotely operated vessel survey of the Monterey Canyon revealed that the red octopus is "the most common animal found along the continental shelf at depths of 600 feet."

The Where, When, and How

Should you be interested in catching your own octopi, be forewarned that they aren't easy to target in our area. The most effective method is diving and searching for them in cracks and holes under and between rocks. Only thing is: leave the spear gun at home. Octopi can only be caught by hook and line or by hand—or so the regulations stipulate at this writing. In the old days, octopi were commonly caught by turning over stones in the rocky intertidal during minus tides. But several octopus aficionados tell me they very seldom catch them this way anymore. Also take into account that by turning over rocks you are destroying the homes and the eggs of several other species of fish and invertebrates.

Octopi move inshore to spawn in the late spring and early summer, so you'll do best to look for them on the large minus tides between May and September.

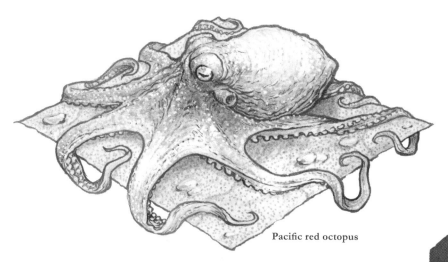

Pacific red octopus

And be forewarned, as tempting as it is to let them crawl all over your hands and arms, they bite, and may even deposit a bit of venom into the wound. So mind that beak!

One of the more unfortunate and unsustainable methods formerly used to catch octopi in Southern California is detailed in *Between Pacific Tides*.[32] It involved pouring chloride of lime into a suspected octopus lair (thereby poisoning the tide pool) and gaffing the panicked creatures as they attempted to

---

32 "Two men, armed with gaff hooks and carrying gunny sacks, station themselves quietly by a large isolated rock in a pool. Finding a hollow that indicates the possible entrance to an octopus's under-rock lair, one of the men pours into the water what he calls "lye" solution, probably chloride of lime. Usually within a minute the mollusk is forced to come out and seek less irritating water, whereupon he is hooked and deposited in the gunny sack." (Ricketts and Calvin, *Between Pacific Tides*, 95)

swim to happier waters. Fortunately there are now specific regulations against poisoning cephalopods.

Interesting Factoids

1. Octopi are by far the intellectual giants of the mollusk family. Their brains are evidently quite complicated. They are not only capable of solving problems but show a tendency to get better at simple tasks through repetition. In other words, they are capable of *learning*.

2. As brainy as they may be, they also have plenty of heart—three of them, to be exact. One is located centrally and two others next to the gills.

3. Octopi, like salmon, are terminal spawners. The males lose their virginity and die in one fell swoop, while the females linger on for a short while after giving birth, to help get the kids headed in the right direction.

4. The procreative organ of the male octopus is actually one of its legs. For those who want to impress their friends, this specially adapted leg is called the *hectocotylus*. The tip of the hectocotylus is called the *ligula*. With the chromatophores in his ligula, the male attempts to seduce the female. The ideal male being one with a large and expressive ligula. The ideal female being a full-figured, heavyweight sort of gal.

SQUID

The Where, When, and How

Two types of squid are typically caught by anglers in our area: the voracious and powerful Humboldt squid and the small and almost surreally abundant market squid. Both of these will require boats. In the case of Humboldt squid, you may have to drop your line down to insane depths (three hundred to five hundred feet). So you'll need a heavy enough jig to get it down that far (one to two pounds). In the case of market squid, you can sometimes luck into them while on a kayak and they're commonly found at more gentlemanly depths than their larger, more aggressive counterparts. Squid jigs are the way to go for both. Obviously, you need a larger squid jig for Humboldts than you do for common market squid. Humboldt squid populations in our area are migratory and given to fluctuation. Some years it's hard to find any, some years they're everywhere. El Niño events seem to trigger massive migrations of these giant mollusks. Look for them normally in the fall. And that is all I have to say about Humboldt squid.

Humboldt Squid
Dosidicus gigas

Too Much of a Good Thing

Okay, I lied, there's a bit more to say. Listen, I've fished for these guys exactly once in my life, went out with a couple of total strangers who contacted me and asked if I'd be interested in tagging along on a squid trip. As far as fishing goes, I'll do anything once. And that is exactly how many times in my life I need to fish for Humboldt squid. We followed half a dozen squid-crazed boat owners twenty-five miles offshore (three-plus hours out, in high swell) and dropped in on these wretched creatures with two-pound homemade squid jigs—the ugliest fishing rigs I've ever seen—six diamond jigs end-to-end on an improvised wire leader. When I got mine down about three hundred feet, the first one hit. It was like hooking into a Jet Ski pointed straight down. Yes, this was thrilling. For about five minutes. But then, it sort of petered out. And there was the task of reeling this fifty-pound behemoth up from 350-odd feet—as Herculean an undertaking as one can entertain in the realm of sport fishing. And periodically the massive dead weight on the line would come to life, fire up the turbo jets, and launch itself straight down again.

When I finally landed this ... *thing* ... I was ready to go home. This was nothing like the joy of landing a sixty-pound sturgeon or seabass—equally large, hard-fighting local species. A sixty-pound seabass or sturgeon promises several months of five-star dinners. Conversely, a sixty-pound squid represents a half decade's worth of inch-thick calamari steaks— way too much of a good (read: *decent*) thing. As the day progressed, a truly massive pile of cephalopods littered our decks. I caught one more and quit for the day. What on earth were these weekend warriors intending to do with the massive pile of dead and dying mollusks? You could have fed the U.S. Marine Corps for a year on what we caught that day. And cleaning the boat afterwards, a task that I somehow unbelievably *volunteered* for, again, could only be likened to one of the twelve labors of Hercules.[33]

And *that* is all I have to say on the matter.

Squid jig

---

33 Augeas's stables had nothing on this boat.

MARKET SQUID
Doryteuthis opalescens

It is my own humble opinion that, as far as squid are concerned, less is more. The common market squid, when caught and eaten fresh, is one of the great joys of the seven seas. If this strikes you as an overly hyperbolic statement then you either have something wrong with your taste buds or haven't eaten a fresh, *just-pulled-from-the-water* market squid.

As far as finding the squid when they're reasonably close to shore, your best bets are Half Moon Bay and anywhere in Monterey Bay. Look for large commercial squid seiners lighting up the horizon (they use powerful lights to attract the squid) at night. The best months for squid in our area tend to be midsummer to early fall. Over-the-counter squid jigs are the best for these mollusks, but they will also hit shrimp flies and diamond jigs. If they are close to the surface, a long-handled fine-mesh dip net, like the one you use for sand crabs, will work like a charm. The most common way to find them is to look for huge swarms of diving birds and pelicans. Be aware, though, that these may also indicate small fish like anchovies, sardines, or mackerel.

SUSTAINABILITY

Despite the thousands of tons of squid caught by California's commercial squid fleet, our local squid are thought to represent one of the most sustainable fisheries on the planet. This is because squid populations have evolved to deal with massive amounts of predation—and are therefore resilient to high fishing pressure. Like anchovies, sardines, mackerel, and herring, most squid will end up (one way or another) in the belly of an animal. They breed in huge numbers and live a short, fast life. If we as a species are going to harvest any other species in large quantities, it should probably be something that reproduces like a squid. But still … sometimes when I see the hundreds of tons coming back to the wharf every day in the summer, I wonder if we're really thinking of all the creatures that are depending on them.

Eat Them Up, Yum

Cleaning a squid involves removing the skin, the guts, the "ears," the eyes, and the beak. Start by running it under a tap in your kitchen and gently scraping off the outer skin.[34] Then remove the barbs (or "ears") at the top of its body. Remove the head by pulling it out (some of the guts will conveniently come with it), and, in one straight slice, cut the eyes away from the tentacles. Looking at the spot where all the tentacles are joined, locate the beak of the squid and push it out with your fingers and/or cut it out. Now remove and discard the "pen" from inside the white tube. (The pen is the hard, plastic-like structure that stabilizes the squid while it is swimming.) If you are keeping the tubes whole for stuffing purposes, dig out the guts (the creamy-goopy white stuff) with your finger or a butter knife and rinse out the tube thoroughly. When you finish all this, you should have one cleaned-out white tube and eight tentacles (without eyes and beak). Cut the tubes into rings if you don't plan to stuff them, spritz them with olive oil, sprinkle with salt and pepper, and throw directly onto a hot grill. The tentacles are the best part!

SEA URCHINS

PURPLE SEA URCHIN | RED SEA URCHIN
Strongylocentrotus purpuratus   Mesocentrotus franciscanus

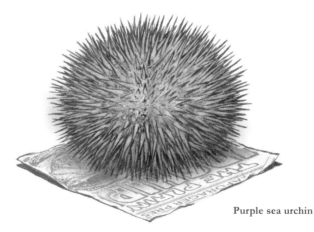

Purple sea urchin

---

34 Some squid aficionados dip their squid in boiling water for a few seconds to firm up the meat and facilitate the cleaning process.

THE WHERE, WHEN, AND HOW

The two types of sea urchins in our area are the purple and the red. The red urchin is the more common commercial variety and is typically caught by commercial divers in subtidal waters.[35] The purple urchin is common in the intertidal zone and can be easily harvested by shore pickers, but it is much smaller than the subtidal red and contains just a fraction of its highly coveted *uni*.

Because sea urchins are echinoderms, not mollusks, you can use a tool (usually a screwdriver or dive knife) to pry them out of their rocky divots.

For intertidal purple urchins, go out to the rocky shorelines on low minus tides (-0.8 and lower). This species prefers soft rock and can actually burrow several inches into it. So if you're staring into the bottom of a tide pool, way out at the furthest edge of the tideline, and don't see any purple urchins, stare a little harder.

Red urchins are occasionally just visible underwater on the lowest tides of the year, but you will likely kill yourself trying to reach them and it will be far safer and more productive if you take up diving.

EAT THEM UP, YUM

It's All about the Gonads

There are several approaches to cleaning a sea urchin. The main thing is to effectively remove the gonads, that is, the uni. The two things getting between you and your urchin gonads are the shell (more correctly called the *test*) and the guts. There are various approaches to getting past these barriers. Some folks simply tap the bottom of the shell (where the mouth is), crack it open like an egg, and remove the uni from the little side compartments, picking off or rinsing away any dark goopy parts.

The method preferred by those interested in preserving the test is to shave off the spines with a pair of scissors, then to remove the urchin's mouth structure—otherwise known as its "Aristotle's lantern"—and, finally, through a process of gently rinsing and shaking, to extract the roe through the hole made by the vacated "lantern."[36] The empty, de-spined shell is then boiled and

---

35   Sea urchins, cancer crabs, and rock scallops are the only invertebrates that can legally be taken while using scuba gear in California.

36   There is some confusion about what Aristotle meant when he wrote in his *History of Animals:* "In respect of its beginning and end, the mouth of the urchin is continuous, though in respect of its superficial appearance it is not continuous, but similar to a lantern not having a surrounding skin" (IV, v). So the sixty-thousand-dollar question is, was the father of modern science referring to the test or the jaw? I say the test. You say the jaw (let's call the whole thing off). Seriously, though. If we comb the archeological record for what a classical Greek lantern looked like, it looks surprisingly similar to a sea urchin test—not to its jaw.

bleached, producing a whitish/purple globe with a mathematically appealing arrangements of bumps and spots. It seems to me these beautiful urchin shells should inspire something more interesting than the table lamps people invariably make out of them. But I am at a loss for what that would be. And actually, urchin lamps are pretty cool.

CRUSTACEANS

DUNGENESS CRAB
Cancer magister

The region covered in this book coincides conveniently with the California range of the Dungeness crab. The "dungy" is one of the most important species caught on the coast of California, both recreationally and commercially. One might make the case that squid generate as much money, and that salmon is king of the sport fisheries, but the economic value of the Dungeness crab is spread out over a lot more commercial licenses and benefits a larger swathe of the seafood-catching and seafood-eating public than any other species. And one other thing, thanks to the invention of the crab snare, that effective and aesthetically appealing device, Dungeness crabs are accessible to shore fishing (in season) throughout their entire range.

There's no doubt: if you have a kayak or boat, you will catch more crabs than the person slinging snares from shore. Nevertheless, there are snare slingers out there who feast on crabs from November to July, and, as one of them adds: *I didn't have to paddle around freezing my butt off for any of 'em.*

It really just depends on what your idea of a good time happens to be. Ten years ago, the thought of launching my kayak on my local beach and smashing my way through a big, nasty shore pound, then disentangling my crab pots and ropes and buoys, then rigging the traps, dropping them in the water, and paddling around all day thinking about what it would feel like to be bitten in half by the great whites that are known to cruise our local beaches, only to start pulling up the pots, reentangling the ropes and buoys, making a mad dash through the surf, missing the timing slightly, and winding up providing a free acrobatic performance and subsequent garage sale of knotted lines, broken poles, oars, net bags, buckets, and crab buoys for the enjoyment of everyone on the beach seemed like a great idea.

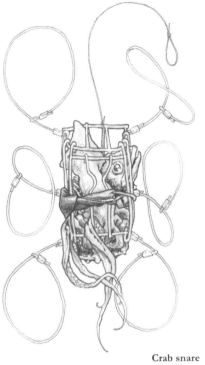

Crab snare

Now, not so much.

Which is to say, my best kayak crabbing days are behind me. And many dry, painless days of crab snaring lie ahead … albeit with a lower overall total of crabs.

THE WHERE, WHEN, AND HOW

First thing: you will do a lot better soaking pots or using snares for crabs in the early days of the season. Typically in California, the sport season begins a few weeks before the commercial season. This is your best window to bang out some high numbers. You can snare crabs at any time of the tidal cycle but the best time is the flood tide, within two hours of the top or bottom. Remember to open up all the loops of your snare before you cast. As far as bait goes,

Dungeness crabs like squid. But really they like any meat.[37] This is a creature of the sandy bottom, so keep that in mind when choosing your spot. If you are snaring from a beach, just make sure you can get the snare out past the first line of breakers—or, if possible, further.

For gear, go with a big spinning reel (as big as you can comfortably handle), loaded with fifteen- to twenty-pound mono and a big eight- to fourteen-foot surf rod. You want to cast your snare far, but you don't want to worry about breaking your line, either from pulling hard or from abrasion.

As with all fishing, crab snaring is about tight lines. Cast your snare past the breakers, put it in a sand spike, make sure the line is tight, and wait anywhere from five to twenty minutes. In most cases you will not see or feel a nibble. This type of fishing is largely a matter of guesswork. When you become familiar with certain beaches, you will start to figure out what the best wait time is. Once you are ready to reel your snare back in, remember that it's the force of the snare being pulled through the water that keeps the loops tight around the crab's limbs. A strong pull (to set the loops) and a fast, steady retrieve are what you are going for here. People with herky-jerky or slow retrieves lose a lot of crabs.[38]

Another thing: choose your days wisely! It can be very challenging (read: nearly impossible) to catch crabs in the middle of a wild Pacific gale, with brutal shore pound and stiff onshore winds. The conditions don't need to be perfect, but if they're terrible, stay home!

As far as kayak or surfboard crabbing goes, tide and time don't really matter as much as they do for snare casters. However, huge tides (low minus tides followed by king tides) may submerge your buoys or move your traps, so keep that in mind before heading out. I find that pool noodles make for excellent and easily stowed crab buoys; see Swim Bladder 1.

37 At the beginning of crab season there's a growing contingent of crabbers who spend their off-hours scraping roadkill raccoons and possums off the side of the road to use as an alleged sort of super-duper crab bait. If this kind of activity is appealing to you, go for it. If not, old freezer-burned chicken, squid, sardines, mackerel, et cetera will work just as well—in fact, better.

38 Herky-jerky retrieves tend to happen when the rod is too big for the angler.

ROCK CRABS

BROWN ROCK CRAB | RED ROCK CRAB | YELLOW ROCK CRAB

Cancer antennarius | Cancer productus | Metacarcinus anthonyi

THE WHERE, WHEN, AND HOW

All the details pertaining to catching Dungeness crabs apply to rock crabs, with one obvious difference: rock crabs prefer rocky shoreline or rocky bottom structure (or gravel or mud), and Dungeness crabs prefer sand.

Let's face it. The rock crab is the ugly red-headed stepchild of the California crustaceans—sort of a Rodney Dangerfield type.

I recently provided all the rock crabs for a local "pop-up" dinner in SF. It was a rare chance to see local seafood eaters compare and contrast the two types of crabs. The two commercial Dungeness crab fishermen in the room claimed that the rock crabs tasted like mud, and showed no interest in eating more than a claw or two. Every other person at the event raved about the rock crabs, and thought they seemed sweeter, if somewhat smaller and harder to deal with (on account of their thicker shells) than the dungies.

And this is pretty much the way it plays out everywhere. People who own expensive licenses and boats tend to disparage rock crabs and everyone else thinks they're great. Again, I can't back this up with pie charts and graphs but it seems to be a fair assessment of the thing.

Inside San Francisco Bay, where it is illegal to take Dungeness crabs, the rock crab is king. Rocks can be caught from most (if not all) of the public piers inside the bay. And if you are worried about eating crustaceans caught from our highly urbanized shorelines, the California Health Department tells us that even pregnant women or children under the age of sixteen can safely consume two servings of SF Bay–caught rock crabs per week.[39]

THE RED, THE BROWN, AND THE YELLOW

Reds and browns are caught inside bays or offshore around rocks and other structures. Yellows are caught at the southern end of our range, typically over

39 Everyone else can eat them four times per week.

rocks in sixty to two hundred feet of water. Browns have longer antennae (hence, *antennarius*) and tend to be smaller but may have gigantic claws in proportion to their bodies. They also tend to be found in shallower water, and may have a slightly bitter taste. Reds and yellows can reach epic sizes, and because of this, tend to be the more sought after of the three.

DON'T DO THIS

Snaring, trapping, and hoop netting are the most common methods of catching rock crabs (see *Dungeness Crab* above for details). But last year, while poke poling on a medium minus tide, I saw a guy lying flat in a tide pool with his hand wedged under a rock. I went over to see what he was doing and saw two buckets filled to the brim with rock crabs. When I expressed astonishment, he looked up at me and frowned: "This is the *only* way to catch crabs," he said. "By hand." I figured the guy was either extremely brave or … extremely something else. I told him I was going to write about his secret method of catching rock crabs someday because: (1) it was so effective, and (2) I doubted anyone would ever deign to copy him. He went on to say that he had learned this insane technique from his father ("bravery" evidently being an inherited trait). The secret, he explained, is to find little surge channels and cracks between rocks and to wriggle your fingers into them and feel around for "sleeping" crabs.

Brown rock crab

I asked him how often the crabs woke up while being fondled thusly. He held his bloody hands aloft. "Occasionally," he said. "But you get used to it. Most of them are sound asleep."

I want to state for the record that this is problematic on several levels. I mean, a Dungeness crab pinch can *really* hurt—in fact, it can ruin your day. But when a rock crab gets your finger, it's a life-altering kind of pain. This is a creature that evolved to crush clamshells. I have no doubt that a big rock crab could break a human finger with little difficulty. So when the crab grabber said "occasionally," it was kind of like saying that he *occasionally* likes to smash his fingers with a hammer. In any case ... he had a lot of rock crabs (mostly browns) to show for his (ahem) bravery and so I am mentioning this method here for the few masochists out there who won't be satisfied with a snare, hoop, or trap.

EAT THEM UP, YUM

Boiled Crabs

Cooking Dungeness crabs and rock crabs is a very simple matter of dropping them into a pot of boiling water. There must be enough water in the pot to cover them completely. I always pour a beer into the water—but that's just me. Once the water comes back to a boil (dropping the crabs in lowers the temperature), give it 15 minutes and pull them out. If you aren't eating them right away, plunk them into an ice bath for 5 minutes so that they don't continue to cook inside their shells, and get them into the fridge.

For steaming, everything above applies, except that you will want to steam your crabs for about 20 minutes.

Cleaning Crab

Some folks insist on cleaning their crabs before cooking them. The people who do this generally do it for one of three reasons: (1) They are traveling far enough that they won't be able to keep their crabs alive. (2) They live in a small apartment and don't like the crabby smell that lingers on a few days after a big crab boil. (3) They get squirmy about dropping a living creature into a pot of boiling water.

To clean a crab, place it belly down on a chopping block (some folks do it back down, belly up, but it's easier for them to pinch you when they're on their backs). Position the knife blade in the center of the back (imagine a dotted line going across the back, from between the eyes to a spot between the two hind legs) and chop it in half. It's easier than it sounds. Tear the shell off both halved sides. Grab one half, remove the gills, get a good grip on the legs (all five of them), and with one or two quick motions shake the guts out (best to do this outside). Then pack in ice and go home. Cook them within twenty-four hours of cleaning. You won't have any of that highly coveted crab butter but at least you won't stink up your kitchen. As to whether this is a less painful demise than death by boiling is anybody's guess … though it is definitely a quicker way to go.

SEAWEED

Seaweeds are marine algae. Like terrestrial plants, they photosynthesize sunlight, but unlike plants, they lack complex systems for the transport of nutrients.

Marine algae are divided into three basic groups: green, red, and brown. The most commonly foraged of these are as follows:

Green

Sea lettuce, *Ulva lactuca*

Red

Nori, *Pyropia* spp.

Turkish towel, *Chondracanthus exasperatus*

Turkish washcloth, *Mastocarpus papillatus*

Brown

Rockweed (aka fucus), *Fucus distichus*

Bullwhip kelp, *Nereocystis leutkeana*

Native wakame (aka winged kelp), *Alaria marginata*

Invasive wakame, *Undaria pinnatifida*

Kombu, *Laminaria setchellii*

Giant kelp, *Macrocystis integrifolia*

The following is a very cursory overview of the salient classifications and anatomical features of these seaweeds. I'm only putting this here so that when I say, "Don't pull native wakame up by its *holdfast*, but rather snip the *blades* so the *thallus* can grow back next season," you will know what I'm talking about.

Seaweed

Holdfast: the anchor by which seaweeds attach themselves to a surface. It can be relatively large and disc-shaped, root-like, or barely noticeable.

Stipe: the "stalk" or "stem" of the plant. It might be stiff, soft, hollow, or almost nonexistent. Its main function is to orient the blades. Kombu has a very dominant stipe, while nori seems to lack one altogether.

Blades: leaf-like structures. Sea lettuce, for instance, seems to be made up almost entirely of blades, while *Laminaria saccharina* (a species of kelp rare in California) consists largely of a single, well-defined blade.

Thallus: the whole body of a single "plant."

INTERTIDAL CITIZENSHIP

Here are the essential laws (written and unwritten) that all mindful seaweed harvesters should probably follow:

1. Where possible, don't pull kelp up by their holdfasts, but rather snip the blades at least twelve inches from the stipe, so they can grow back next season. Nori (*Pyropia* spp.), a red algae, does not need to be snipped and can be taken whole. In fact it's been plucked on the California coast for thousands of years and seems to be doing just fine. It's also okay to pluck sea lettuce, Turkish towel, and Turkish washcloth.

2. The daily bag limit for seaweeds is ten pounds as of this writing.

3. Surprise, surprise: all seaweed foragers sixteen and over are required to have a current California sport fishing license.

4. Sea palm, surf grass, and eelgrass cannot be harvested legally in California.[1]

A NOTE ON DRYING

All of the seaweeds listed here (with the exception of the bullwhip kelp stipes used for pickles) can be eaten raw as fresh snacks, or dried and later rehydrated. The main challenges to drying seaweeds are humidity and wind. If you don't have a backyard, it is possible to dry out your seaweeds in an oven, as long as the temperature is *extremely* low. A clothes drier can also work in a pinch. But be forewarned: seaweeds like nori and sea lettuce are very thin and are therefore prone to burning. The simplest way to dry your seaweed is by hanging it on a clothesline. This is particularly true in the case of the longer seaweeds.

Dried seaweeds left exposed to damp, moist, or foggy air will rehydrate and become potentially vulnerable to mold, but if you see a dry white powder on your seaweed, don't freak out: it may just be surface sugars and salts. The easiest way to tell? Taste it.

---

1 Take of sea palm is allowed for licensed commercial seaweed harvesters, but not recreational foragers.

HEALTH BENEFITS

Seaweeds are universally lauded for their health benefits. They are a good source of potassium, iodine, protein, and iron and are thought to be 10 to 20 percent higher in healthy minerals than most terrestrial plants. Additionally, the alginic acid found in brown seaweeds (kelps) is thought to remove heavy metals and radioactive elements from our bones and digestive tracts.[2]

Without getting too deep into the chemistry of it, seaweeds are susceptible to soaking up radioactive isotopes—whether they are found in your body or in the ocean. In the aftermath of the Fukushima debacle in 2011, many seaweed fans have expressed concerns about whether their favorite food is still safe to eat. A cursory search of the Internet will bring up hundreds of articles and chat board discussions, and an equal number of opinions on the subject. So it really depends on who you're going to trust. Thus far, from what I've read on the subject, local seaweeds have shown no more radioactivity than terrestrial plants and animals, but don't take my word for it: do your own research and see what you can find out.

WAKAME | WAKAME
Alaria marginata   Undaria pinnatifida

To be clear, there are two different seaweeds that go by "wakame" in this area: native North American wakame, or winged kelp *(Alaria marginata)*, and invasive wakame *(Undaria pinnatifida)*.

Alaria wakame is distinguishable by its smallish hold-fast, spore fronds, and lengthy blade. Both species are easily identified by a conspicuous midrib (see illustration). *A. marginata* seems to favor areas with moderate to heavy surf, which is why it is typically foraged on low minus tides in the summer. On higher low tides you may need a kayak to get to it. There's a lot of it in Mendocino and Humboldt counties and some epically large plants, over nine feet in length. Like other kelps, *Alaria* will die if pulled up or cut too close to its holdfast. So make sure to leave at least twelve inches of blade beyond the stipe when cutting, so the seaweed can reproduce.

2 The Sea Forager Center for Improved Vocabulary suggests you look up this word: *chelate.*

Undaria pinnatifida

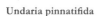

As far as the invasive *Undaria* wakame is concerned, show it no mercy. Grab it by its holdfast and rip it out. This invasive species can grow at the astonishing rate of six feet per month and is now found in marinas from Los Angeles to San Francisco. In addition to fouling nets, ropes, hulls, and aquaculture facilities, it out-competes native species for habitat and light. Just remember that the legal limit for seaweeds is ten pounds (wet) per person, even for invasive, potentially destructive species like *Undaria*.

After thinking about this I've decided to go ahead and burn a spot. I don't do this very often but what the hell. Let's try to get rid of this seaweed before it colonizes our coast. (*Ha!* cries the wakame spirit. *You're too late, pal.*) Drop everything, go to Pier 1.5 in San Francisco (located along the Embarcadero behind an overpriced seafood restaurant, between Piers 1 and 3). The thick forest of seaweed growing under that dock is invasive wakame. It can also be found in the SF Marina, and at South Beach Harbor near the Giants ballpark. It's sort of a roll of the dice as to whether this inner-city wakame is healthy to eat. The Sea Forager Center for Gallows Humor is on the fence. When you think of all the hazards of modern life, a bit of *Undaria* wakame from the shores of San Francisco doesn't seem all that bad—and really, in the end, *something's* gonna kill ya.

BULLWHIP KELP (BULL KELP)
Nereocystis luetkeana

This kelp is probably the easiest to identify of all the seaweeds in this chapter. It's the long whip-like kelp commonly found washed up on local beaches. Often, when fishing in small skiffs or kayaks, one finds dense forests of bull kelp that extend from depths of more than sixty feet to the surface. The top end, when mature, consists of a softball-sized float, attached to which are two sections of flattened, leaf-like blades.[3] These blades are extremely delicious (if salty) when raw, but can also be steamed or dried. In mid- to late summer, you may encounter strange dark-green patches on the blades. These "spore patches" are surprisingly sweet—especially given how salty the rest of the plant can be.[4]

Remember, if you clip the blades off a few inches above the float, the plant will live. Cut the float or the stipe and it dies. Bullwhip kelp blades are a nice

---

3 If you are only harvesting enough bullwhip kelp for yourself, why not just snip off part of one of the two sections (leaving one intact and at least twelve inches of the other)?

4 Spore patches fall out of the blades (leaving conspicuous holes) not long after their initial appearance. They then sink to the bottom and initiate bull kelp reproduction.

alternative to nori, and can be used as an ingredient in Japanese sesame goma-sio. If, however, you are in it for the pickles, and not the blades, go to any beach in our area the day following a storm. You will likely find all the bullwhip kelp stipes your heart desires, readily hewn from the floor of the ocean and lying on the beach for you to forage. Do it this way and you won't be responsible for having killed the plant and adversely affected some coastal creature's food or habitat.

As far as gathering bullwhip kelp stipes from the beach, you want to make sure your piece hasn't been lying there rotting for a week. White splotches will often indicate that it's past its prime. Pick it up. Look at it. Is the "skin" leath-ery and shriveled, or tight and brownish green? If you bend it, does it snap? Or does it just bend like rubber? To quote Peter Howorth from his seminal 1970s classic *Foraging along the California Coast:* "If it bends like a rubber hose, it will probably taste like one."

If the stipe seems fresh, take a knife and cut off however much you need (a foot or so is plenty for most) of the top end, near the float. Then cut that into as many half-inch circles as you can eat. Some folks like to skin the outside with a carrot peeler, but if you have a fresh piece, it isn't necessary. Having cut your bullwhip circles, go home and get your pickling solution ready. (You can use the one in the herring section of chapter 1, minus the brining stage.) Bring your pickling solution to a boil, and place the raw kelp slices (as many as you can fit or eat) in glass jars along with sliced onion circles and a clove of chopped garlic. Then pour the hot pickling solution on them. Let them cool and then put the lids on and place jars in the refrigerator for 24–48 hours.

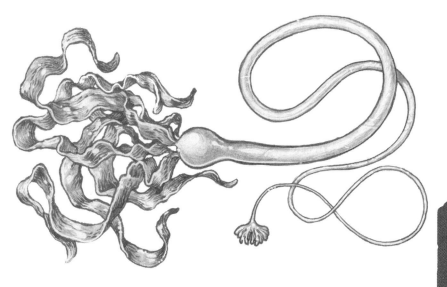

KOMBU
Laminaria setchellii

The Pacific coast of North America is home to numerous species (and genera) of brown algae (kelp) and it can be a bit of a challenge to tell them apart. The type of kombu featured here is *Laminaria setchellii.*

You will find these kombu at the farthest (seaward) reaches of the intertidal zone during minus tides. On its own, kombu can be eaten raw as a fresh (salty, chewy) snack, but normally it is dried and added to soup stocks or miso. You can also use it as a wrapper for steamed "seafood tamales," and it goes especially well with monkeyface eel fillets.

If you look at the shape of *L. setchellii,* you will see that it's sort of challenging to follow the proper citizenship guideline about only snipping the tips of the blades: if you snip the tips there isn't much left to hang on a drying rack or clothesline, so cut along the dotted line as pictured.

That weirdly slimy or slippery quality of kombu is sodium alginate, the principal chemical that causes kombu to chelate toxins. So if you're drinking kombu broth and it seems a tad goopy or snot-like, just think how good it is for you, and you'll have no trouble chugging it down. Add a four-inch strip of kombu to a pot of cooking beans for a rich, nutritious, and more digestible dish.

GIANT KELP
Macrocystis pyrifera

This kelp grows in great profusion from Monterey Bay south. It forms the base of the marine foodweb in much of its range and is one of the largest (as its name suggests) and fastest-growing kelps on the Pacific Coast. Vast forests of it occur in waters from thirty to one hundred feet deep. Most of the harvesting of this species is done by mechanical mowing machines that snip off the top three feet and leave the rest to grow back. Giant kelp is an important

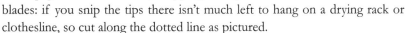

source for the alginates used in the industrial production of everything from paint to salad dressing. For the coastal forager, the leaves of giant kelp can be snipped and eaten raw, dried and later rehydrated, or used as a "baking wrapper" for various seafood dishes.

Macrocystis is the seaweed used in the HEOK (herring eggs on kelp) fishery inside San Francisco Bay. Rafts with kelp hanging under them are placed in areas where herring are likely to spawn. The resulting herring eggs on kelp are harvested, packaged, shipped to Japan, and sold as a coveted New Year's treat, *kazunoko kombu.*[5]

ROCKWEED (FUCUS)
Fucus distichus

Evidently this algae is very good for your thyroid. But *thyroid* is not really the most delicious of words. And *fucus* rhymes with mucus.[6] So of the naming choices, rockweed is probably the best if you're bringing it home for dinner, or serving it to someone who's never had it before.

Pretty much everything you read about this seaweed begins by telling you how good it is for you. As if, to choke it down, you'll need an incentive beyond its flavor and appearance. As to the latter, rockweed is a brown seaweed (usually dark green in color) that literally covers the intermediate rocky intertidal zone in our area. Eels slither in it. Herring spawn on it. Its salient anatomical feature is the small (and fun to pop) gas-filled bulb at the end of each branching blade. As to its culinary properties: raw or steamed rockweed has a slimy, okra-like quality. (Okra of the seven seas, it might be called.) In fact, steaming turns it into a sort of ocean-flavored, snot-like goop. Dried, it has the consistency of a

5 There was a brief window in the 1990s when the price for herring tipped the scales at three thousand dollars a ton. An old-time herring fisherman told me he caught well over a hundred tons in three days during this period and paid off his house, his boat, and his son's last two years of college. In 2014, with the Japanese economy in the dumps, the price for herring roe bottomed out at two hundred dollars a ton and nobody made any house payments. As of this writing, the future of the SF commercial herring fishery looks glum.

6 Though it's sometimes also known as *bladderwrack,* that name more properly refers to the related Atlantic species *Fucus vesiculosus,* which grows abundantly in the British Isles.

really tough piece of jerky. So the best way to eat rockweed is raw. Pop a fucus bladder to access the slippery fucoidan. I realize that "pop a fucus bladder" isn't making this sound any more appetizing, but seriously, fucoidan is another polysaccharide found in seaweeds that is being studied for potential health benefits. The tender young shoots make for an excellent snack (and iodine infusion) while poke poling. In fact, a common nickname for fucus is "Indian popcorn," due to its popularity with Native American foragers. If you have a thyroid condition or iodine deficiency, this is the stuff for you (just be sure to eat a little at a time to see how you feel, as iodine affects everyone differently). Likewise, if you're allergic to these things, go chew on something else.

Turkish Towel | Turkish Washcloth
Chondracanthus exasperatus   Mastocarpus papillatus

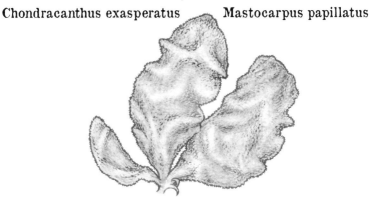

Turkish towel, *Chondracanthus exasperatus*, has a bigger and more pronounced blade than the similar Turkish washcloth, or cat's tongue (*Mastocarpus papillatus*). In fact, *M. papillatus* has a very poorly defined blade structure, with the outer blades curling a bit at their edges. The blade of *C. exasperatus*, on the other hand, could almost be described as looking like a proper leaf. The defining feature of both algae is their papillate (bumpy) surface—which really does evoke a towel, washcloth, or the tongue of a cat.

Eat It Up, Yum

Like other red seaweeds, these two contain high quantities of the polysaccharide carrageenan—a well-known thickening agent in industrial food production. For foraging purposes, these seaweeds work well as nutritious thickeners for homemade ice creams or puddings. Seaweed gatherer extraordinaire Kacie "She Sells Seaweed" Loparto adds this recipe for:

Turkish Washcloth Pudding

To make a pudding with Turkish washcloth, simmer a heaping handful of dried seaweed in a few cups of milk for about 15 minutes, or until you notice the seaweed beginning to break down. Then gently strain the milk through a cheesecloth bag or a fine-mesh strainer, removing all the seaweed. Now add semisweet chocolate chips and a small amount of sweetener to taste and stir until melted on low heat if necessary. At this point you can get creative and stir in frozen berries or spices. Pour into a glass bowl and place in the refrigerator. When chilled, the pudding will thicken to a consistency that's reminiscent of the chewiness of a pudding pop.

NORI (LAVER)
Pyropia spp.

There are about a dozen different species of *Pyropia* on the California coast and it isn't particularly easy to tell them apart. Some are yellowish, some are purplish, some are dark green or brown. Most are good eating. The *Pyropia,* or nori, that is commonly gathered in our area grows on rocks in the high intertidal zone. Nori is probably the most famous of all seaweeds, the stuff of California rolls and crispy seaweed snacks. It is also the favorite seaweed of many Native American communities in California.

Nori is at its most harvestable in the summer, though small, tender tufts can be found growing on rocks at low tide in the late winter and spring. As far as identifying it goes, nori is remarkable only by how *un*remarkable it looks. Despite belonging to the red algae group, it's a sort of dullish brown-green and dries to almost blackish brown. If, after looking at the drawing here, you still can't quite get a handle on identifying it, remember this: the blade of nori is usually only one or two cell membranes thick, and has a slightly elastic quality.[7] Nori can be eaten as a fresh snack,[8] but it is more commonly dried and then toasted, fried, or added to soups and stews.

7   Due, evidently, to its high protein content.
8   If you enjoy chewing on paper.

How to dry it? You can use a clothesline, a tarp, or a stiff piece of screen. My preferred method is to sandwich it between two old screen doors laid flat on the ground in the sunniest part of my backyard (the top door keeps it from blowing away in the breeze). Those who live in apartments and have no access to a backyard don't need to fret. You can effectively dry your nori in the oven set at low heat, or in a clothes dryer—but keep an eye on it, as it is thin and apt to burn. On hot days nori dries quickly on the dashboard of a car.

Eat It Up, Yum

Here's a recipe from Heyday editor Lindsie Bear for a Native Californian comfort food, a kind of deep-fried nori sandwich.

Nori Tacos

Dry nori on rocks, on a sheet protected from the wind, or in a food dehydrator. Fry a handful of the dry strips in ½ inch of oil on medium heat until they are crisp, slightly translucent, and green. This takes just a few minutes: they cook quickly and burn easily. Drain the crispy strips on paper towels and pop straight into your mouth. Or, try the California Indian method: wrap the fried nori up in a freshly grilled tortilla for a starchy, salty, crunchy snack.

Sea Lettuce (Green Laver)
Ulva spp.

The ubiquitous sea lettuce is one of the most abundant intertidal seaweeds. It's the bright green (almost chartreuse) leafy stuff draped over rocks and in mudflats throughout California's intertidal zone.[9] Unfortunately, it often seems happiest in polluted, oxygen-deprived areas in back bays and muddy harbors. In these locations you can sometimes see many tons of it washed up in the mud. Considering it from a health standpoint, I quote my friend Kacie Loparto, professional seaweed harvester and goddess of the intertidal zone: "It's probably a better idea to gather sea lettuce from reasonably clean intertidal areas of the open coast than from the mouths of sewage outflow tubes and harbors." Novel idea, Kacie!

EAT IT UP, YUM

Sea lettuce is normally used as a sort of salty, oceanic condiment. To use it as such, dry it out or toast it lightly, then grind it into a powder, and sprinkle liberally on soups and salads. Blend with nori to increase nutrients and protein.

---

9 Bright green and leafy, not bright green and fuzzy or stringy.

SWIM BLADDER I : GEAR

WHERE AND HOW

On the Beach: Surf Casting

Most surf casters prefer rods at least 8.5 feet in length, medium-sized spinning reels or bait casters, and 10- to 20-pound test line (see illustrations).[1] After all, striped bass can be quite large, and you will need a reasonably strong line not to break them off in the swash. Likewise, crab snaring requires a fairly big rod, reel, and line combo (see illustration).[2] For one thing, snares are clunky to cast with a light setup. And it's nice to be able to tug away with reckless abandon and not worry about snapping anything off. Rods for surfperch may be lightweight, but should still be big enough to handle a striper if it happens to scarf that pile worm.

The following is a guideline for people just getting started surf fishing in our area. There are, of course, other options, but these are the basics.

> **Crab**: For crab snaring, go with at least a 10-foot rod, 15- to 20-pound test, and a medium-to-large spinning reel. 20-pound test (minimum) is a must when targeting rock crabs, since (as you may have guessed) they live near craggy rocks where snags are likely. A good crab-snaring rod need not be fancy—just long enough to get you out past the breakers and stout enough to hurl and retrieve a baited and weighted (and crab-laden) snare.

> **Striped Bass**: For top water poppers and plugs, use a 9- to 12-foot rod and a medium-sized spinning reel with 12- to 17-pound test mono or 20- to 40-pound braided line. For casting hair-raisers, spoons, swim baits, and SP Minnows, try a stiff 9- to 11-foot medium-action rod with a bait-caster or spinning reel.[3] For bait-soaking stripers use a medium-sized

1 Anglers using braided line will typically go with 20- to 40-pound test since it has the same diameter as lighter mono—but where's the fun in that? On a sandy beach, line strength depends on skill level.

2 Kids, and anyone under 5'3", should by all means go with a shorter rod. Better to fish with what's comfortable than force yourself to comply with these suggestions.

3 Bait-casting reels are extremely popular with the hair-raiser set. They also seem to work a lot better with braided line than spinners. I personally like using bait-casters from the beach but I find that even now, after five hundred thousand–some casts, I'm just way better with a spinning reel. I grew up with spinners and they're second nature to me. It really comes down to a matter of aesthetics. However, as simple and streamlined and aesthetically appealing as bait-casters may be, they are a bit more prone to tangling and backlash—at least the ones I can afford are. Though how much of this is due to the reel and how much to the braided line (and how much to the dummy holding them), I'm not sure.

spinning reel and at least a 9-foot rod. Fish live anchovies, smelt, herring, sardine, perch, or any other small fish. If you can't get live ones, go with fresh dead ones. If you can't get fresh dead ones, go with frozen. Yes, stripers will slam a pile worm. And they love sand crabs. Hi-Los or slider rigs (with the customary beach chair, sand spike, and rod bell) are the tools of the bait soaker's trade.

Surfperch: Your choice of rod and reel size will depend on whether you want to use a big surf rod and sand spike to soak bait on a Hi-Lo with a big 3-ounce pyramid sinker (for meat hunting) or use a lightweight setup to cast grubs, sand crabs, and gulp worms on a Carolina rig (for sport fishing).[4]

Other Surf Fish: In our area most people fishing in the surf are targeting striped bass, surfperch, or Dungeness crab. However, some folks are in it for the sharks and rays, or for the odd halibut that happens to swim into the surf zone. In this case the slider rig with a whole squid or sardine is probably the best bet, though larger Hi-Los baited with chunks of fish or squid are also quite effective.

Fly Fishing on the Beach: Again, this is all about the perch and stripers. The Internet offers a veritable encyclopedia of information about fly fishing the surf but here are the basics. You'll need a stripping basket to keep your line untangled and a big enough rod to get that shooting head out to where the fish are. Go with a 6-weight to 9-weight rod, a sinking line, 20-pound leader,  and any flashy fly that the fish can see in turbid water. The famous Crazy Charlie/Zorro Loco pattern works great for perch and stripers. Clouser minnows and deceivers (or variations on these) will also work well.

On the Rocks: Fishing from Rocky Shores

Lingcod, rockfish, cabezon, greenling, surfperch, monkeyface eels, and rock crabs are the usual quarry of the rocky shore angler. The setups for all these, with the exception of monkeyface eels, are pretty much the same as in surf fishing and crab snaring, with a few minor adjustments especially as regards the type of sinker and rod. As far as lines go, generally speaking, when fishing rocky shoreline you will want to use heavier line to deal with snags and abrasion.

---

4 See chapter 2 for best perch baits. The Carolina rig (or some variation of it) is preferred by grubbers and bait fishermen who are concerned with ephemeral concepts like *sportsmanship* and *playing the fish*. The Hi-Lo, unless used with a light sinker, not so much.

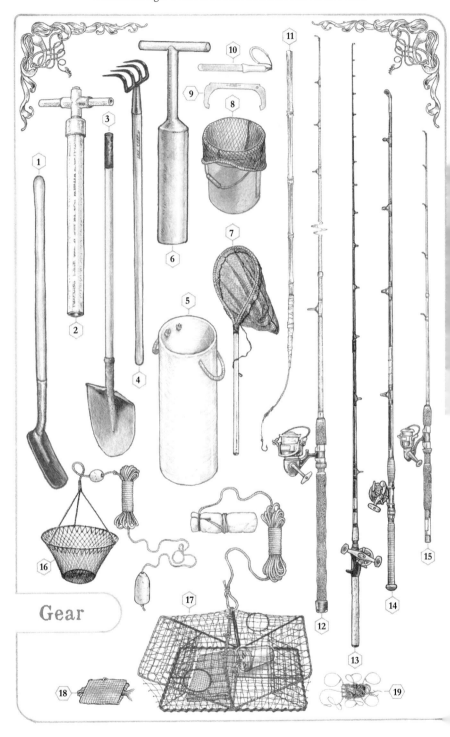

Gear

1.) Razor clam shovel, 2.) Ghost shrimp pump, 3.) Shovel for digging out inside of clam tube, 4.) Cockle/littleneck/Manila rake, 5.) Gaper/gooeyduck tube, 6.) Clam gun, 7.) Sand crab net, 8.) Five-gallon bucket with mesh abalone bag (imperative for rinsing smelt), 9.) Abalone gauge 10.) Abalone iron, 11.) Poke pole (4 to 12 feet) consisting of bamboo, wire hanger, 60-pound test mono, 1/0 octopus hook, and duct tape, 12.) Large surf rod/spinning reel combo (9 to 12 feet), for casting crab snares, large top-water lures, and heavy bait rigs, 13.) Baitcaster (for beach, bank, pier, or boat), 14.) Classic boat rod/reel, 15.) Light spinning setup (6 to 9 feet), 16.) Crab hoop net (for pier or kayak), also doubles as landing net when fishing on piers. Buoy is not necessary when pier fishing; just tie the rope to a rail. 17.) Fold-up Promar-style crab trap with bait cage, bait cup, carabiner, rope, and pool noodle buoy, 18.) Bait cage. A good strong bait cage (preferably of thick steel mesh) is important if you want to catch crabs and not spend the day feeding sea lions. Zip-tie your bait cage to the bottom of your hoop net or Promar trap. 19.) Crab snare, for catching crabs from shore/pier (also see image in *Dungeness Crab* section).

Artificials: For fishing from rocky shores for rockfish, cabezon, or lingcod, it's hard to argue with swimbaits (see illustration). The most effective methods are to jig them up off the bottom or to cast and retrieve just above the rocks. I find that when bait fishing or jigging swim baits on rocky shorelines or jetties, it's nice to have a long, medium-weight rod (10+ feet) so you can extend it out from the rock or boulder you're standing on and jig your bait from directly above, as opposed to casting into the rocks and reeling in at an angle—an approach that is more prone to snagging. You'd be surprised how many fish are swimming around the base of that boulder you're standing on.[5] Your line should be strong enough that it won't break every time you get snagged (and rest assured, you will get snagged). If you are using braided line, tie the lure to a shock leader (see illustration), in case a bad snag forces you to break it off.[6]

Bait: Bait fishing from shore in rocky areas is usually done with a Hi-Lo rig (see illustration) baited with pieces of squid, grass shrimp, pile worms, or whole anchovies. The best sinkers to use in these areas are river sinkers, torpedoes, and tear-away tobacco bags. If you are in it exclusively for the lings and want to fish a whole squid, herring, jacksmelt, or other small whole fish, go with a slider rig, with a double hook leader (see illustration) and a river or torpedo sinker—both are a bit more forgiving than a pyramid sinker in the rocks (see illustration).

Surfperch: Follow the guidelines for surf casting for surfperch above, but swap the pyramid sinker for something less apt to snag. Fishing a Carolina rig on rocky bottom is (for me) the very definition of a futile enterprise, but some folks insist on it. To each their own. One option in very shallow water is to put a float above the sinker, so that the bait passes a few inches from the bottom. This will also work with a Hi-Lo.

---

5 Of course poke polers are not at all surprised by this.

6 Shock leaders are especially important when plugging for striped bass: there isn't much give in braided line but a mono shock leader will stretch a bit when a big fish hits it. Also monofilament is harder for a fish to see.

Poke Poling: When I first came to California, I operated under the mis-guided assumption that the secret to catching fish lay in casting the bait as far from shore as was humanly possible. Little did I realize, as I stood on my favorite spot atop a gigantic boulder at the south end of Muir Beach (aptly named "Squack Rock" by Sea Forager lexicographer, the broad-chested J. Paczkowski), that the fish were hiding in tide pools in the shadow of my empty bucket. Now, after many years of trial and error, I can confidently state that poke poling is by far the most effective method of fishing rocky shoreline. This is especially true if you are (a) in it for your dinner and (b) not really excited by the prospect of losing a lot of gear. Poke poling, or "sniggling" as it was called in medieval England, is the act of catching (or more accurately, *attempting* to catch) eels with a baited stick. The technique is a simple matter of tying a hook to a piece of stiff wire attached to a piece of bamboo, baiting it with strips of squid, and probing it in, under, and around large rocks at low tide. This is the primary method of catching the not-so-elusive monkeyface eel, and is also an effective means of catching rock eels, cabezon, greenling (should you want them), and rockfish—especially grass

rockfish and browns. Optimal length for a poke pole is 7–9 feet. Some folks like shorter ones and some longer. A single piece of bamboo is hard to beat, but poke polers will use anything from old beater surf rods, to tomato stakes, to the flagsticks from golf course greens. The wire hanger lashed, glued, or taped to the tip is essential. Three inches of 60-pound test tied directly to the loop in the hanger is how I go about it, but other folks will put a swivel directly onto the hanger (see illustration). The swivel prevents big eels from spinning off the hook (as they are wont to do), but keep in mind that occasionally a large eel won't fit back through the hole you found it in. And in these cases, if you have a swivel on there, you won't be able to break off the fish, but will be forced to tear the hook free, gravely wounding the eel.

On the Pier: Pier Fishing in California

If you haven't already, Google the second part of that subheading and become familiar with one of the most exhaustive (and exhausting!) fishing websites on the planet, pierfishing.com. I'm obviously not going to add more to the subject than pier guru Ken Jones already has, but here are a few of the basics:

No License Necessary: For fishing on a public pier (or jetty) in the state of California, no fishing license is required. You can also fish two lines—just make sure it's actually a *public* pier before you drop them in.

Hoop Nets: Since public piers sit rather high up above the water, what exactly is your plan to land a big fish should you hook into one? Hopefully you thought ahead and brought a crab hoop net (see illustration) with

enough line to reach the surface. And hopefully you, or someone nearby, is adept at getting the fish to swim into it. Nothing brings out the camaraderie and joie de vivre of neighboring fishermen like a successfully netted trophy-sized fish hauled hand over hand to the pier via crab net. And nothing brings out the raging demons like the idiot who tangles the line, bonks the fish with the net, and blows the big moment. Oh yeah ... while you're out there on the pier, you can also use that crab hoop net to great effect for (get this) *crabs*. In fact, since the only way to dunk and retrieve a hoop net is from a position directly above it (unlike crab snares, which can be cast and retrieved on a more horizontal plane) and since most people do not own boats, the best chance the majority of Californians have to catch a crab is the *hoop net from a pier* option. But be advised, it is absolutely imperative to invest some time in creating a robust and foolproof bait cage. Heavy-gauge diamond industrial mesh sandwiched around three pounds of squid and zip-tied to the bottom of the net is the way to go. Unless of course you are more inclined to feed pinnipeds all day than to catch crabs.

Mooching: To be clear, mooching from shore and mooching from a boat are two different animals. For the shore-based angler, mooching means fishing the top or middle of the water column by means of a leader attached to a float. Shore mooching works best when you're high above the water on a pier, jetty, boulder, or cliff. To start you'll need a large pyramid or grappling claw sinker. Cast that out and let it sink; when it stops, crank or pull it forward till it grabs the bottom and holds. When all is snug, clip your float to the taut line and slide it down to the surface. The egg sinker near the bottom of this leader will keep it vertical in the water column (see From Shore illustration). But be forewarned: before you can reel in a fish, the claw sinker must be dislodged from the bottom and reeled up until it hits the swivel on the float—not until this happens will you actually be able to fight the fish. Just when I thought the shore-mooching rig had fallen out of favor, I started noticing an increasing number of anglers mooching for stripers off Bay Area piers. Mooching rigs are also sometimes used for small schooling fish like sardines, mackerel, and jacksmelt in heavy currents—but a Sabiki (or standard floating setup) is a lot less of a hassle, and works just as well ... better, in fact.

Baitfish Rigs: On piers, Sabiki rigs are usually either baited and fished near the surface underneath a big ol' bobber (for jacksmelt) or jigged (either baited or unbaited) parallel to barnacle-encrusted pier pilings. The most common species caught this way are jacksmelt, shiner perch, anchovies, and sardines. Of the lot, shiner perch are the least likely to bite an unbaited Sabiki.

On the Boat: Fishing from Boat or Kayak

Conventional reels or bait-casters are the reels commonly associated with boat and kayak fishing. The "thumb on free spool" option on a conventional reel allows you to play out your line on a moving boat a lot more effectively than you can with a spinning setup. Plus, there isn't much need for casting on a boat (until there is), and in any case many fishermen become adept at casting with conventional boat reels—so they aren't really missing anything by not having a spinner on board.[7]

As far as rods go, there are hundreds of varieties to choose from. But if you're new to this, when fishing from a boat or kayak, you want a rod that allows you to bring a big fish close to the boat so it can be netted or gaffed easily. So, in other words, any rod over 7 feet is cumbersome on a boat.

Mooching: Mooching from a boat or kayak is simply a matter of idling the engine or putting the paddle aside and allowing the vessel to drift with the tide. This is a common way to catch lingcod, halibut, rockfish, and white seabass in our area. It's strange that, even with the high prices of gas in the last few decades, halibut and salmon anglers seem to prefer trolling to mooching. The advantage of covering more ground evidently outweighs the gas expenditure in the minds of these people. Pictured here are some common setups for mooching from a boat or kayak. Note the use of the banana weight and circle hook for salmon mooching.

Trolling: Trolling is fishing with a line that is pulled by boat power through the water. There are so many nuances to this that it would be absurd to include them all here. The most commonly trolled-for coastal species in our area is Chinook salmon. If you've already got the boat you're probably far enough along that you understand what a watermelon apex is. If you don't, look at the illustrations provided and they will hopefully give you a clue. Other equally famous salmon trolling rigs are the various "crash helmet" options (used with whole herring, sardine, or anchovy): RSK (Rotary Salmon Killer), FBR (Franko Bullet Rotator), and Crippled Herring. Hoochie rigs trolled behind flashers are equally if

---

7 If you are hoping to learn how to become an expert caster of conventional reels, be advised, a sensitive thumb is key.

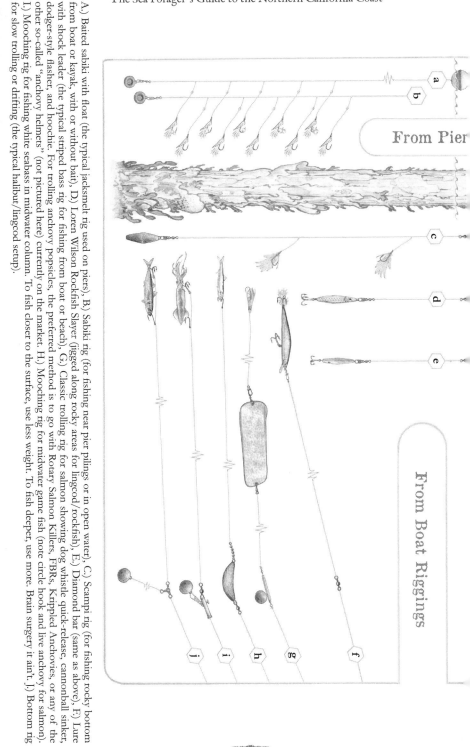

A.) Baited sabiki with float (the typical jacksmelt rig used on piers), B.) Sabiki rig (for fishing near pier pilings or in open water), C.) Scampi rig (for fishing rocky bottom from boat or kayak, with or without bait), D.) Loren Wilson Rockfish Slayer (jigged along rocky areas for lingcod/rockfish), E.) Diamond bar (same as above), F.) Lure with shock leader (the typical striped bass rig for fishing from boat or beach), G.) Classic trolling rig for salmon showing dog whistle quick-release, cannonball sinker, dodger-style flasher, and hoochie. For trolling anchovy popsicles, the preferred method is to go with Rotary Salmon Killers, FBRs, Krippled Anchovies, or any of the other so-called "anchovy helmets" (not pictured here) currently on the market. H.) Mooching rig for midwater game fish (note circle hook and live anchovy for salmon). I.) Mooching rig for fishing white seabass in midwater column. To fish closer to the surface, use less weight. To fish deeper, use more. Brain surgery it ain't. J.) Bottom rig for slow trolling or drifting (the typical halibut/lingcod setup).

From Shore

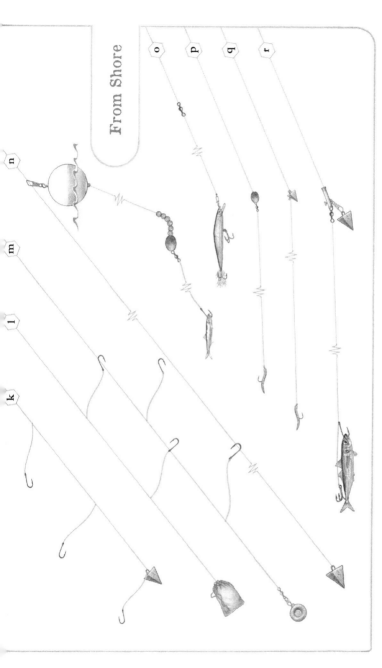

K.) Hi-Lo surfperch rig with pyramid weight (note tail hook attached to sinker), L.) Hi-Lo rig with tear-away tobacco bag for fishing rocky areas, M.) Standard Hi-Lo with river sinker for beach or rocks, N.) Mooching rig for shore/pier fishing (grappling sinker works better than pyramid weight), O.) Standard shore rig for striped bass, showing shock leader and Rapala-style lure, P.) Standard Carolina rig with egg sinker and Gulp worm, Q.) Improved Carolina rig with small pyramid sinker for holding bottom in stronger current, R.) Standard slider set up for live or dead bait not more popular (see illustrations). The ideal trolling speed for salmon appears to be around 2.7 knots. As slow as that seems, you'll want to slow it down a little more for the second most trolled-for species of game fish in our coastal waters, California halibut. Troll for halibut with the same basic rig used in drifting the bottom (see illustration), though you might want to add a small flasher midway between the three-way swivel and the hook.

Anchoring Up: Really the only time you are likely to anchor up while fishing in a boat or kayak is when sturgeon fishing, or tying off to a piling inside a local bay to fish for surfperch. I know of at least one rockfish aficionado who anchors up near promising pinnacles and rocks so he can stay on a hot rockfish bite, but he is a rare eccentric in this.

More on Rigs, Sinkers, and Lines

Carolina Rig

It is harder to master the use of the Carolina rig than the Hi-Lo, especially when the former is employed with an egg sinker in the surf, where wave or tidal action push the bait north, south, or toward shore. In this case the angler must follow the movement of her rig, either reeling it slowly toward shore (to match the drift), or following it parallel to the beach. "Tight lines," that most pervasive of fishing axioms, is ever true to the fisher using the Carolina rig. The moment the line goes slack, all is lost. Where fishing from a boat or kayak is concerned, the Carolina rig becomes tangled or otherwise ineffective when the boat stops drifting or trolling.

One option for using Carolina rigs in the surf is to replace the egg sinker with a small ½- to 1-ounce pyramid weight, essentially a small slider setup. Since pyramid weights are designed to grab hold of sandy bottom, this option allows the fisher to stay in one spot (more or less) and not have to jog along the beach while the egg sinker rolls in the surf.

Slider Rig

The slider rig is similar in design to the Carolina rig but is generally bigger. The idea with a slider is to keep the sinker anchored in a fixed position while the bait dances about enticingly in the water. This setup is commonly used on beaches and piers and is generally the way to go when using live baits from shore. Slider rigs are also used by kayak and boat anglers anchored up and fishing for sturgeon (using a pyramid weight) or drifting in the middle of the water column for seabass (using a cannonball weight).

Hi-Lo Rig

This is the rig associated with surf leaders and scampi rigs (see illustration). The exact sizes and shapes of this rig's sinkers and hooks are (obviously) determined by the depth, the type of bottom being fished, and the species being targeted. Remember there are hook restrictions on several species commonly caught from shore: rockfish, cabezon, greenling, and lingcod.

As most snagging and gear loss are the sinker's fault, one strategy you might want to employ is the use of the tear-away cotton bag as a sinker (see illustration). Alternatively, you can attach your regular sinker using a piece of 8- or 10-pound test line so that it will break away when stuck. Not ideal, but at least in this case you won't be adding a leader, swivels, and two or three hooks to the mess every time you break off a rig. You can experiment with different types of sinkers to see which ones work best on the rocks, but getting snagged and breaking off rigs is sort of unavoidable when fishing these areas. If you aren't getting hung up occasionally, you're probably doing something wrong (like not putting your bait where the fish are).

The main advantage of two-way rigs like Hi-Los is that you have multiple baited hooks in the water and, because of this, a higher likelihood that something's going to bite one of them. If you're surf casting with a big pyramid weight and that something is a perch, there will be little nuance to bringing it in beyond reeling fast and beaching it. But if a larger fish (e.g., a striper, lingcod, shark, halibut, or bat ray) gulps your bait, you'll be in for a pleasant and exhilarating ride. Another thing: heavier line tends to be stiffer than light line. If your surf leader and hook leaders are made of stiff line, they will stick out horizontally and offer a better presentation to a passing fish than they will if they are loose and wrapped up around the main leader. That is why, if you're using a store-bought surf leader, you may want to go with a thick one (30-pound test is perfect), regardless of whether you're fishing for perch or bass.

Baitfish (Sabiki) Rigs

Popularly known as "Sabikis" for one of the companies that manufactures them, bait rigs come in many sizes and colors but they are all used the same way. Tie the top of the rig to your line and clip a small (½- to 1-ounce) sinker to the bottom. Drop it off a pier near the pilings or cast it out from shore—and begin jigging. For sand dabs and shiner perch, you will need to take the additional step of baiting the Sabiki with tiny pieces of squid or shrimp, but most small, schooling fish species will bite at the flashing hooks without the added enticement of bait. Jacksmelt fishermen seem to like baiting the hooks

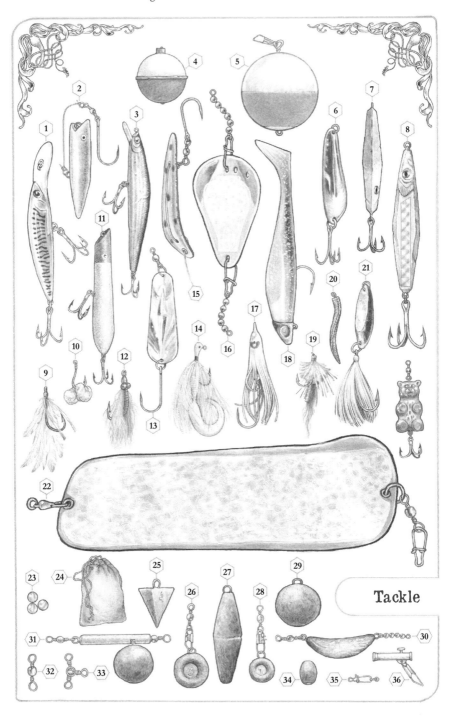

Tackle

) Deep-diving mackerel imitation trolling lure, 2.) Salmon plug (for trolling), 3.) Rapala-type lure (for asting and/or trolling), 4.) Standard plastic bobber, 5.) Pier mooching bobber (leader clips to bottom f float), 6.) Krocodile lure (mostly used for striped bass), 7.) Diamond jig (for bottom fish, e.g., ling-od and rockfish), 8.) Loren Wilson Rockfish Slayer (for bottom fish, e.g., lingcod and rockfish), 9.) hrimp fly (see scampi rig on "From Boat" page), 10.) Standard octopus hook (with pieces of shrimp or bait), 11.) Pencil popper (for striped bass), 12.) Crazy Charlie fly pattern (for perch), 13.) Trolling poon for salmon, 14.) Hair-raiser (mainly for shore-fishing striped bass and halibut), 15.) Watermelon pex (for salmon trolling), 16.) In-line flasher (for trolling bait), 17.) Hoochie (for salmon trolling), 18.) vimbait and jig head (for halibut, striped bass, bottom fish), 19.) Zorro Loco fly pattern (for surfperch nd, occasionally, striped bass), 20.) Gulp worm (for surfperch), 21.) Kastmaster (big ones for striped ass, small ones with treble hook sans tail for structure surfperches), 22.) Large dodger-style flasher or trolling hoochies), 23.) Beads (for mooching rigs), 24.) Tear-away tobacco pouch sinker (for fishing ocky shoreline), 25.) Pyramid sinker (for fishing sandy beaches), 26.) 3-ounce river sinker (can be a t more forgiving than pyramids or torpedoes when shore-fishing from shore in rocky areas), 27.) Torpedo nker (for boat fishing over rocky areas), 28.) Small river sinker (ideal for sabiki), 29.) Canonball sinker,).) Banana sinker (for mooching from a kayak or boat), 31.) Dog-whistle quick release (for polluting e ocean with lead), 32.) Barrel swivel, 33.) Three-way swivel (important for bottom troll/drift rigs), .) Egg sinker (see Carolina Rig), 35.) Clip, 36.) Standard slider

and sticking a big old bobber on top of the whole thing. But this strikes me as a poor use of time and effort.

As far as storing your baitfish rigs after using them, let it be known that this is a royal pain in the arse for *everyone*—many fishermen simply throw away their Sabikis after use. The combination of thin line and multiple tiny hooks often leads to bloody fingers and prolonged untangling of snags. Rest assured, if you are wearing a sweater while handling a Sabiki, you will hook yourself at least six times per hour. A happy solution to this dilemma is the pool noodle. Pool noodles, which also double as awesome kayak crab buoys, are perfect for wrapping and storing used Sabiki rigs.

On Not Losing Your Gear

There are several strategies one can employ to minimize the loss of gear. When on a boat you can keep your bait one or two cranks off the bottom and not miss anything. The folks who think they need to drag bottom in order to catch fish tend to lose a lot of gear and although they may catch a few extra fish this way, how much bait-in-the-water time do they lose rerigging every twenty minutes?[8] Most boat fishermen going for bottom fish with Hi-Lo rigs use torpedos or cannonball sinkers. The size of these sinkers can vary from 2 to 8 ounces depending on the depth and the speed of the drift.

What's My Line?

As far as line goes, it really depends on your skill level, how far you like casting, and how much of a sporting chance you want to give the fish. When fishing

8 If you absolutely have to ride the bottom, *bounce*, don't drag.

from a boat for rockfish, lings, and halibut, I use 20-pound test mono. When surf casting, I notice that my line strength tends to increase when I'm on a losing streak—as the *next* fish becomes an obsession and the thought of snapping off a rare lunker becomes unthinkably painful. For surf fishing, the problem with heavier line is that it doesn't cast as far.

When choosing between braided line or monofilament, know this: braided line is magically strong. You get twice the strength with half the diameter. But as a renowned tackle shop owner once told me: "You're taking away the one chance the fish has to get away"—or its best chance, in any case. It's up to you how you feel about that. Another thing: braided line, when repetitively cast from shore by anyone other than an expert, is prone to "wind knots." Given how expensive the stuff is you might want to consider your skill level before buying a pricey spool of it.

Lures and Flies

Leighton's chart shows some of the most popular lures and flies used in our area of California. Under each illustration you will see a list of the species that are most likely to be caught on that particular lure—or on ones like it. All of these are either cast out and retrieved, jigged in the middle of the water column, bounced off the bottom, "popped" on the surface, trolled, or some combination of these.

NETS

Hawaiian Casting Nets

Casting nets are only legal from Point Conception to the Oregon border, and never in fresh water. As of this writing, the species one can take using a Hawaiian casting net in California are: smelt, herring, anchovies, Pacific staghorn sculpin, shiner perch, and squid. Anything else that happens to get caught in your net must be released immediately. In waters where casting nets are legal, there are no limits on net size or the size of the mesh.

As far as technique goes … the author would like to refer you to the world wide web, where you can pick the throw-net instructor of your personal preference: macho redneck, bikini beach beauty, tanned Floridian, dopey kid, or self-serious expert.[9] I will offer this bit of advice: if the instructor has you holding the net in your teeth, or draping it over your shoulder, at any point in the process of wrapping and throwing, find another video. Using teeth is only really necessary with huge nets (which are unnecessary and unsporting in our

9 There is simply no competing with moving images on some things.

waters) and draping the net over your shoulder is really going to harsh your mellow when you're throwing on herring in SF Bay in February and suddenly find yourself soaked to your skivvies.

Some folks operate under the misguided assumption that catching fish with a throw-net is easy. It's not. Throwing a net a thousand times off a public pier in June is not going to catch you any herring (and even if you throw in January, you have to know where they're spawning in order to catch them). Blind tossing in the waves is unlikely to catch you any surf smelt (see chapter 1 for why that's a bad idea). By which I mean to say: you need to understand some basics about the fish you are targeting (time, tide, month, moon phase) before you start chucking your net into the Pacific Ocean.

A-Frame Nets

A-frame nets are dip nets used in the surf to scoop night smelt out of the waves. One can also catch surf smelt with A-frames when they are running in high concentrations. Actually, on days when the water is turbid and visibility poor, it may be a good idea to have an A-frame handy, as it will allow you to catch dayfish without resorting to the desperate act of blind tossing. As far as technique goes, the fish are caught in the wide, front part of the net and then tipped back into the sock. The sock is then pinched off and gripped in the right hand (for righties) against the upright, as pictured. This way, the smelt jumper doesn't have to go running back to the bucket after every dip.

For directions on building your own A-frame net, see Swim Bladder 4.

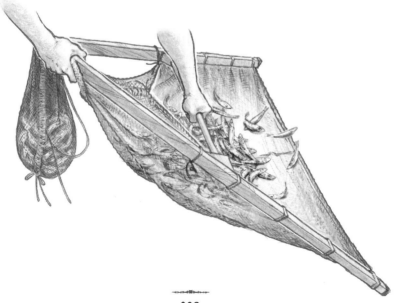

Landing Nets

Landing nets with standard-size mesh (1–3 inches) tend to split the tail fins of medium to large fish. This is only a problem if you've just caught an undersized fish and hope to catch it again someday. Fish with split caudal fins have a high mortality rate. If that bothers you (and I hope it does), then invest in one of the many small (under 1-inch) mesh net types currently on the market, which are designed to make the release of undersized fish a more sustainable enterprise. These nets can also double as go-to sand crab catchers, and work perfectly for landing monkeyface eels, which, with their penchant for squirming and wriggling, can foul (and escape from) a standard landing net like nothing else. See Swim Bladder 2 for proper catch and release techniques.

SOME NOTES ON KAYAK FISHING

In the last decade or so, kayak fishing has become quite the rage in California. All of the most popularly pursued coastal species of fish can be reached and caught on kayak. Hooking and landing a salmon, white seabass, or large halibut on kayak is really one of the great experiences available to a sport fisherman. For those who do not wish to take on the pounding surf, there are many sheltered bays and lagoons in our area with easy-to-access shorelines that will get you on the fish in a matter of minutes.

Crabbing from kayak or paddleboard is another way to go about getting a five-star dinner from our local shores. The best crab traps for this are the lightweight fold-up jobs sold by Promar or the hoop nets used by pier crabbers.[10] For buoys, a cheap and convenient option is the pool noodle. Not only are the bright pink ones easy to see out there, but you can wrap your rope around them and store them inside the flattened traps on the way out. When you reach your spot, clip the bottom end of the rope onto the top of the crab trap with a carabiner, chuck the whole mess into the water, and watch the pool noodle slowly spin as the crab pot and the line descend. Crabbing on a kayak (or paddleboard) is all about economy of space. And with pool noodles— and fold-up lightweight traps or hoop nets—you can get the most out of a little room.

Keep in mind that the cheap plastic cord used by many sport fishermen tends to float to the surface and become a nuisance to anything passing by that happens to have a propeller. So either weight your line appropriately or go with a rope that sinks.[11]

---

10 Hoop nets, being unenclosed, will need to be checked more frequently than box traps or Promars.

11 Some of the cheap cotton ropes commonly used for clotheslines, for example, will sink after soaking a few minutes.

Swim Bladder 2 : On Keeping and Releasing

Catch and Release

If you catch an undersized fish or a fish that you don't want to keep, touch it sparingly and pamper it obsessively (see "TLC" below). Avoid using a landing net or get a small-mesh one, if possible: landing nets may split the fish's tail fins or scrape the protective slime off its skin (see "Landing Nets" in Swim Bladder 1). Also, if you are boat fishing, try not to let an undersized fish flap around on the deck too much. Where possible, grab the hook with pliers, hold the fish over the side of the boat, measure it if you're not sure if it's legal, and, if it isn't, shake it back into the water. This can be difficult with lings and halibut that are close to legal (and more than happy to smash things and/or bite your fingers while you're trying to measure them), but in the case of obvious dinks, this is the way to go. They don't call small fish "shakers" for nothing.

Many species of rockfish will embolize on their way up from the bottom. In other words, they get "the bends." But just because your fish's stomach is shooting out of its mouth doesn't necessarily mean it's dead. Fishermen have invented various ways to return these baro-trauma sufferers back to the depths so that they have a fighting chance at survival. One method is to pop the stomach with a needle, but this can lead to infection and a high mortality rate (just ask yourself how long you'd last if someone jabbed a dirty needle through your stomach). Another method is to place a weighted milk crate over your fish and drop it overboard—when it hits bottom, you pull the crate up with a rope and the fish (theoretically) swims free. The problem here is that the fish may get banged up in the crate, or may actually be too big for it. By far the best method of sending a fish back down to the rock pile from whence it came is the "fish descender" now available in most tackle stores.

The advantage here is that you can actually fish with the descending pin attached above your leader. This way you don't have to set up a separate rod, but can merely pin the fish to the descender and send it back down the next time you drop your bait to the bottom.

TLC

The gentle rocking back and forth of a tired fish to get the water circulating through its gills, commonplace among trout anglers in sparkling mountain streams, can also work wonders for a saltwater fish's recovery. I've done this with eels (yes, eels!), rockfish, and perch and seen them swim off in much better condition than they had been in only a few moments earlier.[12] The idea that anyone might do such a thing with some rugged creature of the intertidal zone might seem excessive, but I guarantee that Poseidon will take note—and, in the end, why not take a little extra time to ensure the survival of a fish? Aren't they *all* important to you?

RELEASING CRABS AND SHELLFISH

Just because a crab has a hard exoskeleton does not mean it's going to survive being chucked off a high pier or thrown from a jetty. Where possible, get as close to the water as you can before placing, dropping, or gently lobbing your crab back in the water. In short, fading back and chucking it Hail Mary style (like Tom Brady with a deflated ball) isn't the best way to go about releasing a crab.

Some species of clams can survive being taken out and returned to the sand or mud. Some cannot. The ones that cannot are gapers, gooey-ducks, and piddocks. The ones that can are cockles, Pacific littlenecks, and razors.

BONKING AND BLEEDING

As far as putting your fish "out of its misery" goes, I hope I won't be hunted down by PETA activists for saying this, but I tend to prolong the misery of my fish by keeping them alive (i.e., fresh) as long as possible in an abalone bag, a live well, a bucket with a pump on the side, or a stringer. When I'm done for the day, or they start to show signs of languishing, I take a knife and quickly slit their gills. A fish cut in the water will bleed out a lot more quickly and effectively than one bled "dry." Honestly, if I were a fish, I think this is the way I'd want to go out—no bonking, no pithing, just slit my gills and let me drift off to fish heaven. Bonking can be kind of sloppy and ... I dunno ... sort of ... disrespectful.[13] And there are certain fish that, no matter how hard you bonk

12 Yes, in the back streets of San Francisco, in the shadow of the Bay Bridge, while hardened hoodlums mocked me, I have gently rocked polluted pogies back and forth, back and forth, back and forth ... till I was sufficiently convinced they would recover. I am proud to say I've even done this with shiners and bullheads.
13 I've seen fishermen whacking their halibut half a dozen times and I often wonder how many of those blows end up hitting edible portions of the fish's body. Especially in a moving boat.

them, just ain't gonna go along with the program—like, for instance, cabezon, halibut, and the diehard of the lot, the monkeyface prickleback.[14]

While I was working on this section, someone sent me a link to a website about *ikejime*, the Japanese method of instantly killing a fish by inserting a sharp object directly into its hind brain.[15] All I can say is, if you have a steady hand, good aim, and a firm grasp of fish anatomy, go for it. But the average Joe (of whom I am evidently one) has no idea how to do this. I've been on tuna boats where weekend warriors repeatedly jabbed awls and knives into the heads of their fish—everyone *ooh*-ing and *aww*-ing about traditional Japanese fish-killing techniques while the poor creatures had their heads perforated with holes. And frankly, I detected no difference in taste between these "awled" fish and their bonked counterparts. I suppose there's an outraged sushi chef reading this right now, but he can go ahead and write his own book. In any case, if you're bonking your fish, just make sure your aim is true. Bonk the fish on its head and/or bleed it out.

And Furthermore …

As far as bleeding goes, general consensus among fish nerds is that the meat will taste better, look better, and last longer if the fish are properly bled out. Regardless of whether you agree with this or not, the important thing is to keep any recently deceased fish reasonably cold (and, if possible, *unreasonably* cold). For boat or pier fishers, this is simply a matter of bringing along a cooler with ice (and maybe some rock salt for a slurry).[16] But for a kayaker, poke poler, or surf caster, bringing ice along for the day is obviously more problematic. Sometimes you just have to improvise: surf casters and smelt jumpers often bury their fish a foot or two down in cool sand. Poke polers use stringers, net bags, or burlap sacks to hold their fish in tide pools; kayakers hang fish on stringers over the side of the boat.[17]

Since the rise of so called foodie-ism in California, fishermen have become increasingly obsessive about all this stuff. By and large that's a good thing. It shows reverence for meat and respect for the resource. But remember, that

---

14 Colin Turnbull, in his epic tome *The Forest People*, tells us that the Mbuti pygmies of the Ituri forest recognize multiple levels of death or death-like states: sort of dead, kind of dead, dead, definitely dead, absolutely dead, and so on. If monkeyface eels could speak or write, "death" would no doubt encompass a similarly wide range of definitions.

15 Aka "pithing." Yes, like with frogs in high school biology.

16 For a 100-quart cooler, two 5-gallon buckets of crushed ice, plus two buckets of ocean water, plus half a handful of salt makes for a very cold slurry. Don't go crazy with the salt, lest you should inadvertently freeze your fish!

17 A practice that always makes me nervous while paddling on the Landlord's coastline.

striped bass that's been dead and un-iced for two hours, that rockfish that died in the net bag earlier in the day: both are fresher than 99 percent of the dead fish for sale in the state of California. So don't freak out if you forgot to bleed them or didn't get them on ice immediately.

Commercial salmon fishermen in our waters set the standard for how a fish should be treated. First they gut and gill every fish that comes on board. Then they take the spoon side of the gutting knife and scrape out the bloodline (the dark blood along the spine) and with the back of the spoon push any remaining blood up out of the veins. The fish are then immediately put into a slurry, refrigerated, or packed in crushed ice. As you can guess, when these salmon arrive at dockside they're stunningly gorgeous. The question is, how much of this is about aesthetics (and getting a higher price for the fish) and how much is about actual taste? Personal experience tells me that food that looks better often tastes better, but I can't actually say that the salmon I ate twenty years ago, before we all started immediately princess-cutting our fish, tasted any better or worse than they do today. Is it a good idea to treat each fish with the type of veneration that a commercial salmon fisherman lavishes on his? Sure. Why not. It's easy enough. But are your fish going to be ruined if you just drop them in an icy cooler and don't go through the whole process of bleeding them and extracting their gills? Not at all.

STORING YOUR FISH

The thing that makes fish smell and taste bad is supposedly called trimethylamine oxide. When exposed to air, this chemical breaks down into something similar to ammonia. How quickly this happens depends on how well you've iced your fish. Personally, I tend to go with the old American adage attributed to Ben Franklin: "Fish and house guests start to smell after three days." If you consider that few people in Ben's time had access to ice, you will understand that with modern refrigeration you can extend that three days a bit. But what's the point of fishing if you're going to leave your catch in the refrigerator for three or four days? Better to vacuum seal it and freeze it while it's fresh.

Freezing

I have worked in the seafood industry for enough years to have seen what normally passes for a "fresh" fish in the commercial marketplace.[18] The main advantage to catching or foraging your own seafood is that you know exactly when it came out of the water. But sometimes a fish is just too big, or your

---

18 Believe me, you don't want to know.

rockfish taco fest in the park gets rained out, or your eyes are bigger than your stomach—and you end up with more leftovers than you can eat in two or three days. In short, if you intend to fish on a semi-regular basis you're going to have to freeze your fish occasionally, and it's probably a good idea to invest in a decent-quality vacuum sealer.

Having dealt with a few different types of these over the years, I highly recommend that you shell out a few extra bucks for the warranty. I'm not sure what it is about these machines but they tend to lose suction after about a year (if you fish a lot), and a good vacuum sealer is all about suction. The commercial-grade models are much better (i.e., they suck harder) than the over-the-counter variety, but they can be ridiculously pricey.

As far as thawing goes, at the fish-processing warehouse where I spend much of my life, whole, blast-frozen, rock-solid albacore and salmon are typically thawed by soaking in bins of cold water inside a walk-in refrigerator. This process can take one to two days—depending on the size of the fish. Most folks reading this book don't have access to industrial-size walk-ins, but you can do the same thing at home. Just drop your wrapped, vacuum-sealed fillets into a large Tupperware container, fill with tap water, and leave until the fish no longer feels frozen.

SWIM BLADDER 3 :
HOW NOT TO KILL YOURSELF
OUT THERE

1. Follow the health department guidelines on local fish and shellfish species and don't pick mussels in the summer (see "Health Risks" in chapter 5 for biotoxin info). And be advised that some nonfilter-feeding creatures like, for instance, moonsnails and crabs, may pick up biotoxins from eating clams and other bivalves. Always call the OEHHA hotline when harvesting wild bivalves or other filter-feeding organisms on the California coast. As of this writing the number is: 800-553-4133.

2. Be able to determine these three things about the seafood you pull from the Pacific Ocean: (a) Does it live a long time? (b) Does it spend most of its life in sketchy waters? (c) Is it high or low on the food chain? (The healthiest answers are: a. No, b. No, c. Low). Ideally, what you want is something like a salmon, a squid, or a surf smelt: species that don't live long enough to bio-accumulate a lot of toxins, live most of their lives in non-yucky waters, and feed relatively low on the food chain (yes, a salmon is high on the food chain, but it lives fast, dies young, and has a varied diet—and frankly there's just a magical quality to salmon that defies explanation).

3. Do not gather shellfish or seaweeds from the butt ends of manmade inner harbors, industrial dumping grounds, launch ramps, sewage outflow tubes, or other high-use areas. One would think this was a rather obvious point, but trust me, there are people gathering clams and mussels in some deeply sketchy places even as you read this.

4. Eat the following species sparingly: sturgeon, leopard shark, striped bass ... and, strangely, kingfish (white croaker) and shiner perch (if for some strange reason you are tempted to whip up some shiner soup).

5. Always make sure to put the plug back in the kayak after draining it.

6. If you're kayaking in areas with lots of boat traffic, or heading far offshore, invest in a decent portable radio.

7. Always have at least 100 feet of rope on your anchor.

8. When poke poling, surf casting, or smelt jumping, don't turn your back on the ocean.

9. Do not wade in over your knees, in heavy surf, when wearing waders.

10. When diving for abs, keep in mind that approximately 40 percent of all recorded shark attacks in the United States have occurred within that area known as the "Red Triangle," which stretches from the Farallon Islands in the west to Bodega Bay in the north and Big Sur in the south. And remember that you can still drown in three feet of water.

11. Minimize the risk of marine worms. Most parasitic marine worms are harmless—as long as you cook your fish. If you like to eat your fish raw, however, and you feel that freezing it at impossibly low temperatures defeats the purpose of having it so fresh (which it does), then you have two choices: (a) roll the dice, take your chances, and scarf your fish with a hearty Viking-like laugh, or (b) "candle" the fillets with a flashlight or head lamp. I candle every fillet of every fish that I eat raw.[19] Many of my friends think I'm overly obsessive about it. But the idea of a pissed-off nematode waking up in my stomach, realizing it's not inside a sea lion, getting angry, and boring its way through my stomach lining strikes me as deeply unappealing. If you are interested in candling your fish, it takes about fifteen seconds to do one fillet. Just put the flashlight under it and search for little shapes that look like pieces of rice, coiled springs, or small bundles of string. If you find a few, don't throw out the fillet! Just get a pair of tweezers and pull them out. Again, if you are cooking your fish this is not an issue, as marine worms die when cooked—and, in any case, a little extra (cooked) protein won't kill ya. I should also add that the lime juice in ceviche does not reduce risk of marine worms, nor does salt brine.

Swim Bladder 3

---

19   The FDA suggests that fish served raw should be frozen at -4F for seven days, or at -31F for fifteen hours. But since most home refrigerators don't get that cold, freezing isn't really an option. See FDA, "Parasites," in *Food and Fisheries Products Hazards and Controls Guidance,* 4th ed., April 2011, www.fda.gov/downloads/Food/GuidanceRegulation/UCM252393.pdf, accessed November 2015.

Swim Bladder 4 : DIY

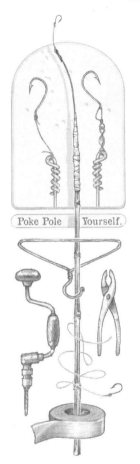

Poke Pole   Yourself.

How to Make a Poke Pole

After procuring your bamboo (and hacking off the branches), go to your closet and grab a wire hanger.[20] Unravel it, clip off the twisty parts, and bend a small loop in one end (see diagram). For added stability, drill a small hole halfway through the pole, about a foot down from the tip (or far enough down that at least 12 inches of wire will be left jutting out from the end when you're done). Bend a ½-inch L shape in the back of the wire. Put the tip of the L into the little hole and then, using only the highest-quality bargain basement duct tape, wrap the wire flush to the end of the stick. Once you've secured it firmly, tie a 1/0 or 2/0 octopus hook to the loop in the wire, using 2–4 inches of 60- to 80-pound test monofilament. Or you can put a snap swivel directly onto the wire hanger before twisting the loop, then easily clip your hook to it.[21]

How to Make an A-Frame

It would be easy to explain this A-frame business in pictures but, frankly, we're at the end of this enterprise and Leighton Kelly is already about thirty-five drawings over what he was originally contracted to do. So I'm going to give it a shot in words. Hopefully you'll get the gist of the thing.

---

20 A good piece of bamboo is hard to beat. Bamboo is strong, supple, and in many cases free—if, like me, you can find a friend with a small thicket in his back yard.

21 The problem with using a snap swivel is that the eel has no chance. I mean this. Occasionally, the entrance to the hole is smaller than the circumference of the eel. In this case, one can often reach down and snip off the line so that the eel can escape, and at least have an outside chance at survival (this scenario is why I poke pole with barbless hooks). But with a snap swivel on the wire, the only alternative is to rip the hook out, shredding the eel and leaving it to die and rot at the bottom of the hole. No doubt rock crabs will appreciate this, but it seems (to this poke poler, anyway) like a wasteful way to go about things.

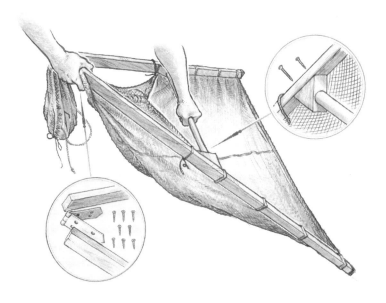

Making an A-frame net is a simple task. But it is time consuming and I suppose complicated sounding, if you ain't looking at one. The frame consists of two 1x2s. (I use hardwood but I suppose you don't have to.) The cross piece is a 1-inch dowel. Use a strap hinge at the top to hold the two 1x2s together. You can make both brackets for the cross beam out of a single 6–8 inch square piece of 2x4. Rather than me trying to describe this simple task—and thereby ensuring that it will become complicated—just look at the square and think about it for a minute... Here's a hint: drill the holes first (catty-corner to each other, 1 inch from the edge) and then cut diagonally.

Typically I stain the wood to make it aesthetically appealing (to all the smelt I'm killing in the dark), and then coat all the wooden parts with three coats of polyurethane. But I imagine you could get away with two coats and no stain. Up to you. Thus concludes the easy part.

As for the net, you'll need to find yourself some ½-inch webbing (stretched, diagonal measurement). This stuff is hard (but not impossible) to find in California.[22] It's also rather expensive. In any case, you'll need a 6x11-foot piece of netting. (Most net makers use a 6x10-foot piece but I find that 6x11- is better: the extra foot helps to create the sock at the end.)

22 Call Englund Marine Supply in Eureka and tell them you want smelt netting. In SF, ½-inch webbing can often be found at Coast Marine on Jefferson Street.

Take a long piece of thick seine twine (25–40 feet, depending on how many loops you tie in it) or some other kind of strong rope or cordage and weave it in and out of the webbing, forming three sides of a rectangle or square in a U shape roughly along the outline of the net. In other words, you are weaving the two sides and the base. At each corner of the base tie a loop in the line just big enough for the uprights to fit into them. You will need to weave some of the webbing into this loop so it holds. The base needs to be 6 feet across but you don't need to weave clear to the end of the two upright pieces; 6–7 feet of weaving on the sides should be fine. If you want, you can tie multiple loops into the line (again, weaving the loops into the webbing so they hold) or you can drill holes in the upright and just lash the main line to the frame. In either case you'll have to drill holes near the top and lash the lead line there, in order to keep the net from sliding down to the bottom. This will all be quite apparent when you have all the parts laid out before you.

Once you've got the rectangular lead line sewed into the net you can lay it on top of the frame and then figure out where the loops should go. You will notice that you are putting a rectangular net onto a triangular frame. The excess bagginess that results is what creates the all-important sock. As explained in the night smelt section, the fish are caught in the tighter portion of the net, across the base, and then tilted back and dumped into the sock. (Without the sock you'd have to run to your bucket after every dip.)

There are some nuances here you'll have to figure out as you go, but these are the basics. The main thing is to keep the rectangular shape of the net but make the edges adhere to a triangle, making room for the sock (and all those night smelt).

How to Make a Ghost Shrimp Pump

There are more ways to do this than there are to skin an eel. The easiest and most popular is the "threaded rod with washers, nuts, and rubber ball" method. The Champion de la Banana (à la Lombardian rubber disc) approach, pictured here, with its sleek and aesthetically appealing lines, is the best style of ghost shrimp pump I have found.

Here's the list of ingredients:

> One 36-inch piece of 2-inch PVC and a cap for it (this will be the main body of the pump)
>
> One 34- to 36-inch piece of 1-inch PVC, plus a cap for it, and a PVC T-joint (for the plunger of the pump)
>
> Two 5-inch pieces of 1-inch PVC (for the handle of the plunger)

One carriage bolt (¼ inch in diameter and 2 inches in length) plus four standard nuts, a lock washer (optional), and two 1-inch washers

Two 2-inch-diameter rubber discs, or one spongy rubber ball with a 2-inch diameter. (If you are going for the discs you can use the rubber sheet that usually comes in a gasket kit at the local hardware store.)

Epoxy

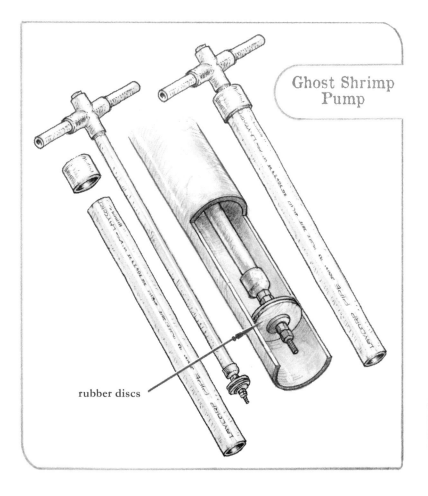

Ghost Shrimp
Pump

rubber discs

Picture this as a giant syringe with no needle. The 1-inch PVC with rubber ball (or discs) is the plunger, the 2-inch PVC is the body of the pump.

To start, drill a ¼-inch hole in the center of the 1-inch PVC cap. Push the carriage bolt through the hole from the inside of the cap and put two nuts (one on top of the other, obviously) onto the carriage bolt on the outside of the cap. Tighten them down so that the carriage bolt is firmly in place, jutting from the top of the cap. Put one of the 1-inch washers on top of the second nut, followed by the two rubber discs (or the rubber ball), followed by another washer (with a lock washer on top of that if it makes you happy), and finally two more nuts. Cinch the two nuts tight (ouch!) and you're almost there.

Now epoxy this cap to the end of the 34- to 36-inch length of 1-inch PVC. While it's drying, drill a 1-inch hole in the center of the 2-inch PVC cap and set it aside. Now take your two 5-inch pieces and glue them into the side holes of the T joint; this will be the handle of the plunger. (Writing sentences like these is enough to drive me to the brink of madness … to think that all those creative writing classes and haiku workshops in Berkeley have led me to this lonely place.) Ahem … where was I? Okay … right. Push the nonbolted end of the 1-inch PVC pipe through the inside of the big (2-inch) cap, then push the bolted side (with rubber discs) down through the length of the 2-inch PVC piece, pushing the big cap in place as you do this. Now epoxy the T-joint handle to the other end of the long 1-inch piece. If you want to drill a ¼-inch hole in the side of the pump, just below the cap, to allow water to pass out, go for it. (You can also put an extra PVC handle in that spot for better leverage.)

Congratulations! You now have yourself a Champion de la Banana (à la Lombardian rubber disc) ghost shrimp pump. Now go get 'em![23]

---

23 One last note: the carriage bolt, washers, and nuts are prone to rust rather quickly when exposed to salt water, so make sure you rinse the inside of the pump from time to time, in order to extend its life.

SWIM BLADDER 5 :
MOLLUSK GEAR

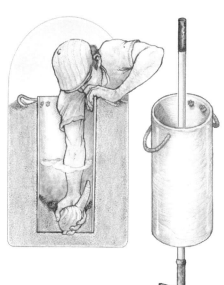

Clam tube for horsenecks and gooey-ducks

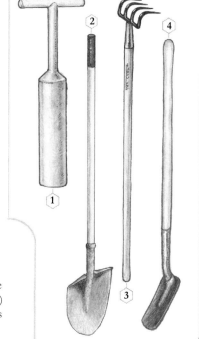

1.) Clam gun for razors and ghost shrimp
2.) Perfect shovel for clam tube (can also be used for razors, piddocks, and macomas)
3.) Rake for littlenecks, cockles, and Manilas
4.) Razor clam shovel

Squid jigs should be used like unbaited Sabikis.

Squid Jig

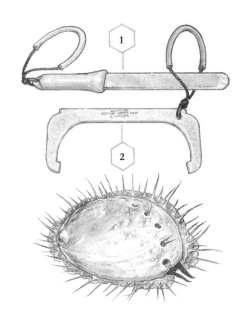

1.) Ab iron, 2.) Gauge

RESOURCES

California Department of Fish and Game, Resources Agency. *California's Living Marine Resources: A Status Report*. Davis, CA: University of California Agriculture and Natural Resources, 2001, updated 2011.

California Department of Fish and Wildlife, Marine Region, www.wildlife.ca.gov/fishing.

Fitch, John E., and Robert J. Lavenberg. *Food and Game Fishes of California*. Berkeley: University of California Press, 1971.

Guy, Adam. "A Different Kind of Fishing." Fishing Fury (blog), December 2005. www.fishing-fury.com/a-different-kind-of-fishing/. Accessed November 2015.

Howorth, Peter. *Foraging along the California Coast: The Complete Illustrated Handbook*. Santa Barbara: Capra Press, 1977.

Jones, Ken. *Pier Fishing in California: The Complete Coast and Bay Guide*, 2nd ed. Roseville, CA: Publishers Design Group, 2005.

Kramer, Donald E., William H. Barss, Brian C. Paust, and Barry E. Bracken. *Guide to North East Pacific Flatfishes: Families Bothidae, Cynoglossidae, and Pleuronectidae*. Fairbanks, AK: Sea Grant Program, University of Alaska, 1995.

Love, Milton. *Certainly More than You Want to Know about the Fishes of the Pacific Coast: A Postmodern Experience*. Santa Barbara: Really Big Press, 2011.

———. *Probably More than You Want to Know about the Fishes of the Pacific Coast*. Santa Barbara: Really Big Press, 1991.

Miller, Daniel J., and Robert N. Lea. *Guide to the Coastal Marine Fishes of California*. Fish Bulletin 157. Sacramento: California Department of Fish and Game, 1972.

Mondragon, Jennifer, and Jeff Mondragon. *Seaweeds of the Pacific Coast: Common Marine Algae from Alaska to Baja California*. Monterey, CA: Sea Challengers, 2010.

Moyle, Peter B. *Inland Fishes of California*. Berkeley: University of California Press, 2002.

Office of Environmental Health Hazard Assessment, www.oehha.ca.gov/fish.html.

Ricketts, Edward F., and Jack Calvin. *Between Pacific Tides*. Stanford, CA: Stanford University Press, 1939.

Skinner, John E. *An Historical Review of the Fish and Wildlife Resources of the San Francisco Bay Area*. Resources Agency of California, Department of Fish and Game, Water Projects Branch Report 1, June 1962. http://downloads.ice.ucdavis.edu/sfestuary/skinner/archive1000.PDF.

Tasto, Robert N. *Marine Bivalves of the California Coast*. Marine Resources Leaflet 6. Sacramento: California Department of Fish and Game, 1974.

Turner, Charles H., and Jeremy C. Sexsmith. *Marine Baits of California*. Sacramento: California Department of Fish and Game, 1967.

Waaland, J. Robert. *Common Seaweeds of the Pacific Coast*. Seattle: Pacific Search Press, 1977.

Washington Department of Fish and Wildlife, http://wdfw.wa.gov/fishing/.

ACKNOWLEDGMENTS

This book could not have happened without the patience of my dear wife, Camilla, who did a whole lot of extra baby rearing, family business running, recipe writing, and cooking while I was out in the garage railing on ad infinitum about Hi-Los and blind tossing and midshipmen and such. Thanks, babe—I am forever indebted.

Oh, and speaking of indebtedness ... most of what's in here came indirectly from conversations with hundreds of fishermen, many of whose names I don't even know. Of the fishermen, biologists, and seafoodetarians that I can actually credit here, the main ones are: Milton Watson, John "Champion de la Banana" Bebelos, Kacie "She Sells Seaweed" Loparto (you rawk, girl!), Loren Wilson, Brian "Macoma" Lynch, Mike Chin, Brian Haller, Mikey "Caveman of the High Seas" Dvorak, Nico "Sharky" Von Broembsen (the semi-Boer), Mark "Surfperch.net" Won, Walter "Waltopedia" Jorgensen, Josiah "Radagast" Clark, Jon Han, Jason Chin, Lloyd Kahn, Kenny Belov, "Pissed Off" Pete Anastole, Big Jim Russel, Chris "Clayman" Mayes, Mark S. Congdon, Terry Paetzold, Christina Piotrowski, and Allen "O to Be Pelagic" Leepin. My thanks to Ken Oda, Peter Howorth, Ken Jones, and Milton Love for all the great stuff they've written about fish. And special thanks to Lindsie Bear, who did triple duty as psychologist, life coach, and editor throughout this project. I hope I'm not forgetting anybody! Thanks, guys!

ABOUT THE AUTHOR

Kirk Lombard lives in Moss Beach, California, with his fishwife, Camilla Lombard, and their two kids, Django and Penelope. Kirk teaches, writes, fishes, sings a skull-cracking baritone, and plays tuba for the SF-based band Rube Waddell. Kirk worked for seven years as a fisheries observer for the PSMFC. He and Camilla are founders of Sea Forager, a sustainable, sub-scription-based seafood delivery service, which also offers coastal fishing and foraging classes in the San Francisco Bay Area. For more information visit www.seaforager.com.

ABOUT THE ILLUSTRATOR

Leighton Kelly is living the dream one day at a time.

NOTE FROM THE ILLUSTRATOR

My grandfather, William Alston Ritchie Lovejoy, was a newspaper reporter for the *Monterey Peninsula Herald* and an illustrator on the side, whose style his close friends described as "lifelike." Multimedia creative exploration was a common feature of the Bohemians of that time. Musicians were also painters, writers were also marine biologists, newspapermen were also illustrators, and everyone, I have been told, was an expert at drinking. That very potent era on the northern Pacific coastline became a hotbed for the poor, restless, creative souls looking for somewhere inexpensive to drink and invent new ways to live. And as luck would have it, due to myopic thinking, that led to industrial bankruptcy, a dilapidated Monterey Bay beckoned them like a great white whale ever forward toward their looming fates.

My grandparents were close friends with a handful of the uniquely significant starving artists who would later become inspiring influences to the world. Two close friends of my grandparents who later made names for themselves were John Steinbeck, the author of *Cannery Row,* and Ed "Doc" Ricketts, who was the titular character of said book. As well as being a marine biologist, Ricketts wrote *Between Pacific Tides,* along with Jack Calvin, who coincidentally was married to my great-aunt Sasha Kashevaroff, one of the five beautiful Kashevaroff sisters that Ricketts once boasted of knowing, biblically. *Between Pacific Tides* was an educational and insightful book of marine species and ecosystems of the Pacific Northwest coast that has become universally known as one of the foundational tomes of marine biology. When I informed Kirk that my grandfather had in fact illustrated *Between Pacific Tides,* I was surprised to discover that the book was already quite well known to marine biologists and to other fishy types, as well as being a key inspiration to Mr. Lombard in the spewing forth of this book, *The Sea Forager's Guide to the Northern California Coast.*

As a child, I would look through our family copy of the book and draw, redraw, and redraw again the sea creatures Grandpa Ritchie had illustrated for Ricketts so long ago. That eerie feeling one would expect from this karmic familial storyline did not escape me, as I myself drew the illustrations for this book that you are currently fingering, you animal. In addition to being widely known as one of the founding grandfathers of marine biology, Ricketts also wrote an essay on his theorem of non-teleological thought, positing that all things are intrinsically and fundamentally connected. No doubt a conclusion formed from working so closely with the thriving ecosystem of the Monterey Bay and watching it, in turn, suffer from overfishing practices of the canneries of the time. A theorem that at the time seemed far-fetched, even rejected by Stanford University, but is so blindingly obvious in this ecologically chaotic day and age, it boggles the mind.

Rickett's indefatigable postulation of non-teleological phenomena is most obviously, if only to myself, evident in this now lengthy and overwrought biopic of mine. Grandpa Ritchie, Ricketts, Lombard, myself, and now you are undeniably and incomprehensibly intertwined just like any overlooked, yet important, ecosystem on the outskirts of this vast, torrid, and brutally beautiful living dream we all infinitely commingle within, one day at a time.

— Leighton Kelly[1]

1 The southeast Asian breathing freshwater catfish (*Clarias* sp.), pictured here, shares the artist's nickname, LeLe, but does not yet inhabit the California coast.